Infant Development and Mental Health in Early Intervention

Infants &
Young
Children
Series

Edited by

James A. Blackman, MD, MPH

Professor of Pediatrics
Director of Research
Kluge Children's Rehabilitation Center and Research Institute
Department of Pediatrics
University of Virginia
Charlottesville, Virginia

AN ASPEN PUBLICATION®
Aspen Publishers, Inc.
Gaithersburg, Maryland
1995

Library of Congress Cataloging-in-Publication Data

...and Mental Health/edited by James A. Blackman.
p. cm.
Articles reprinted from Infants and young children.
Includes bibliographical references and index.
ISBN 0-8342-0647-1
1. Infants—Mental Health Services 2. Child development
deviations—Psychological aspects. 3. Infant Psychiatry.
4. Child psychopathology—Prevention.
I. Blackman, James A. II. Infants and young children.
[DNLM: 1. Child Development Disorders—psychology—collected works.
2. Child Development Disorders—collected works.
3. Child, Exceptional—psychology—collected works.
4. Mental Health—collected works.
WS 350.6 I425 1995]
RJ502.5.I47 1995
618.92'89—dc20
DNLM/DLC
for Library of Congress
94-24186
CIP

Editorial Resources: Ruth Bloom

Library of Congress Catalog Card Number: 94-24186
ISBN: 0-8342-0647-1
Series ISBN: 0-8342-0652-8

Printed in the United States of America

1 2 3 4 5

Table of Contents

Preface

Carla, seven months old, had a serious feeding problem. She was not gaining weight and refused food. A thorough medical evaluation revealed no clue of an explanation for either the poor weight gain or food refusal. Her development, except for feeding skills, was age-appropriate.

Observation of a mealtime quickly suggested that parent–child interactional difficulties likely were involved. The parents (mom feeding, dad hovering) darkened the room, insisted on absolute quiet for fear of distracting Carla, argued with each other over every bite refused, and ended the session feeling total failures. Carla's mother acknowledged anger at becoming pregnant (at her husband's insistence), having to leave her job, and experiencing a difficult pregnancy, labor, and delivery. She positioned herself to Carla's side during feeding and made no eye contact. There was little interaction except for cajoling and expressions of exasperation.

A typical, but misguided, approach to Carla's poor growth and feeding problem would have been to launch an extensive medical "work-up" including multiple, perhaps exotic, laboratory tests, x-rays of the bones, and an MRI of the brain. Therapists might have focused on Carla's tactile defensiveness (which she certainly exhibited), seeking to overcome it with gradual desensitization procedures. No one would have noticed or paid much attention to mom's depression, or dad's impatience with mom's incompetence.

If training programs are deficient in the teaching of basic child development, they are abysmal when it comes to mental health issues. Not that all of us need to be pseudo-psychologists or social workers, but we must be cognizant of psychosocial contributions to developmental or behavioral dysfunction, particularly if our disciplinary orientation is toward the physical or physiological. Also, recognition of psychosocial strengths can be a powerful asset to successful interventions of all kinds.

In this volume, authors discuss developmental variations of special populations as well as very complementary infant–caretaker mental health concepts. With a stronger understanding of these issues, which should form a core knowledge base in the early intervention field, we will be better prepared to meet the specific needs that individual disciplines are expected to address.

—James A. Blackman, MD, MPH
Editor

Concepts in infant mental health: Implications for work with developmentally disabled infants

Stephen Seligman, DMH
Assistant Clinical Professor
Staff Doctor of Mental Health
Infant–Parent Program
Department of Psychiatry
San Francisco General Hospital
University of California
San Francisco, California

THE TRADITIONAL view of infants as passive and disorganized beings has given way to a picture of competent, active persons born with significant capacities for physiologic, emotional, and cognitive organization and able to evoke social responsiveness and care. This dramatic shift has been paralleled by a renewed interest in early intervention. While some of the attention has been focused on children who are at risk for environmental or emotional problems, much of it has addressed the concerns of children with developmental disabilities. In general, the impact of intervention in the early years on future development has been emphasized; most providers agree that early intervention with constitutionally and environmentally at-risk children can be particularly effective in preventing more severe difficulties later in life. Moreover, early intervention is now considered to be worthwhile for its immediate as well as its preventive effects. There is a new recognition of infants as individuals in their own right; that is, as people who can be helped to function more effectively and with less suffering in the present, without having to justify intervention as enhancing their future development.[1]

However, these new approaches have not been consistently applied to work with developmentally disabled infants. In many programs, infants are treated within a traditional model that focuses on their medical and physical disability, rather than one that understands the disability as a critical aspect of a larger developmental process in which infants and their families are involved in a complex interplay of biologic, psychologic, and social issues. Recent clinical and theoretical research in infant mental health may contribute an essential orientation to the efforts of those working in this field. After reviewing some recent developments, this article will discuss some of their implications for the assessment of and intervention with developmental disabilities.

RECENT DEVELOPMENTS IN INFANT MENTAL HEALTH

The biobehavioral-developmental perspective

Infant development has been conceptualized in terms of a series of evolving stages that are characterized by relatively coherent and interrelated patterns of

The author acknowledges the contributions of Barbara Kalmanson, PhD, Jeree Pawl, PhD, and Judith Pekarsky, PhD, to the conceptualization of this article.

Inf Young Children, 1988; 1(1): 41–51

organization in the neurologic, cognitive, and socioemotional areas. Physiologic maturation is viewed in the context of the infant's relationship with the caregiving environment such that it can never be considered in isolation. The phases of infant development are "biobehavioral," or "biopsychosocial," in nature, simultaneously involving related biologic, psychologic, and interactional issues.[2,3]

In the first few months of life, for example, issues of the organization of the infant's basic capacities and rhythms span the physiologic, neuromuscular, cognitive, and socioemotional domains; activities such as feeding and regulating sleep/wakefulness cycles, and regulating the quantity and quality of stimulation encompass a variety of functions, ranging from organismic organization to the complexities of the infant–caregiver relationship.

In such developmental phase models, periods of relatively stable "consolidation" are interrupted by periods of "biobehavioral shift."[2] During these periods, the established organizational patterns change rapidly as emerging capacities and environmental expectations become integrated into new physiologic, behavioral, and interactive structures. During the second six months of life, for example, changes in neurologic capacity, cognitive ability, emotional organization, and motor capacity seem to converge in the emergence of a new set of more complex and refined senses of autonomy, individual effectiveness, and focalized attachment in relationships. Concomitantly, the parents' and other caregivers' expectations shift to match the infant's new abilities. The new organizational patterns in both the infant and the environment become established over the next months, to be reordered into more complex and sophisticated structures in subsequent months as new capacities emerge.

All current developmental accounts emphasize the wide variation that exists even within normal development. However, researchers have reached a general agreement that biobehavioral shifts between periods of relative stability occur at birth and at ages 2 to 3 months, 7 to 9 months, and 15 to 18 months. A more detailed account of the particular stages is outside the scope of this article but can be found elsewhere.[2,4–9]

By conceptualizing development in biobehavioral terms, the physical and socioemotional aspects of a developmental disability may be more easily integrated. Although children with disabilities will often lag behind the normal developmental schedules, they and their families will face challenges similar to those described by theories of normal development when their capacities match those of the younger "on-schedule" child. Thus, the attainment of wheelchair competence in children at any age may be linked to issues of separation from parents much like those experienced by the mobile toddler and his or her family. Similarly, blind children will experience stages of attachment and separation distress similar to those of sighted children (though often at a slightly older age) if given opportunities to use hearing and other senses to support their capacity for internal representation.[10] At the same time, these transitions can be extremely complicated because the uneven development of an infant with a disability can make it particularly difficult for parents to sort out the exceptional aspects of the new developments from those that correspond to "normal" schedules. This can lead to confusing and even contradictory patterns of expectation in both sensorimotor and socioemotional spheres.[11]

The families of children with handicaps are also particularly likely to experience grief and other distress responses when their children reach ages associated with normal developmental milestones. Although this may be particularly true with such typical infant achievements as walking and talking, such reactions continue throughout the life cycle with such issues as school transitions and adolescent social and athletic activities.

The infant as a social being

The infant is an active, social being who is innately able to evoke and use caregiving responses. Within days after birth, for example, newborns prefer human faces and high-pitched voices to other sounds and shapes, and can discriminate the smell of their mothers' milk.[9] These capacities evoke complementary responses from caregivers, such as smiles and high-pitched "baby talk," which further encourage the infant's social behaviors. Subsequent neurophysiologic development supports the emergence of new capacities, such as locomotion and speech, which are continuously reintegrated into increasingly complex and differentiated relational systems. Increased myelinization in the nervous system over the first two years of life, for example, is a biologic substrate for the evolution of disorganized babbling through longer chains of reciprocal vocalization and, finally, to language competence.

Conversely, the caregiving relationship supports the maturationally driven emergence of sensorimotor capacities. At all levels of neurophysiologic adequacy, infants need an organizing, responding environment to reinforce their new abilities and give them meaning. The interplay between maturation and the caregiving environment is ongoing; it is not possible to conceive of infant development without such an environment.

Infant development is thus conceptualized in terms of continuum in which both physiologic and environmental factors play a part. From this point of view, the impact of developmental disabilities on the infant's capacities for relatedness and socioemotional organization must be taken into account simultaneously with their immediate impact on sensorimotor functioning. Developments that may be taken for granted in the course of normal infant development, such as the fundamental sense of individual continuity, effectiveness, and relatedness, depend on sensorimotor competence, and may be impaired in developmentally disabled children. In short, deficits in the sensorimotor and cognitive spheres are likely to lead to deficits in other spheres as well.

This point can be illustrated by observing a young infant playing with a mobile that sits above the crib. Over the first months, the infant gradually learns, among other things, to associate the execution of a particular motor sequence with the production of movement and sounds from the mobile. Along with many similar associations, this experience leads to such fundamental achievements as the recognition of relationships between means and ends, the sense of individual effectiveness, and the difference between oneself and the outside world.[9] When sensorimotor deficits impede the capacity for such achievements, the infant is at both physical and socioemotional risk, for these domains cannot be separated: The relationship between socioemotional and sensorimotor development is a reciprocal one. Just as sensorimotor exploration generates an inner sense of being in the world, socioemotional developments—a sense of initiative, effectiveness, frustration, and self-esteem—affect the infant's ability to develop whatever physiologic capacities are available to him or her. Such issues might be useful in planning treatment in even relatively behaviorally oriented intervention programs, since infants are more likely to achieve behavioral goals when their socioemotional development is enhanced. Because infants organize their experience and behavior with respect to such issues within the first months of life, it is useful to consider the infant as a whole person no matter how young or how developmentally delayed.

The infant–caregiver relationship as the context for development

Such issues become even more complex when viewed in the context of the ongoing parent–infant relationship, since the caregiver's responses both determine and are determined by the infant's behavior. With disabled infants, the usual parental task of providing opportunities for competence and relatedness is rendered more difficult by limitations in the infant's ability to provide the parents with clear behavioral emotional signals. The risks of such intrinsic limitations can be intensified by the possibility that parents will withdraw, misread or ignore cues, lose patience, become discouraged, or otherwise respond so as to block whatever potential exists for successful development.

Parents' own emotional reactions to their infant's disabilities can further exacerbate such risks and impede their responsiveness. Typical of these reactions are guilt, ambivalence, loss of self-esteem, and grief over their child's suffering and their own lost ideals. Such reactions are complicated by preconceptions, personality characteristics, and behavior patterns that they bring to the caregiving transaction and that are determined by a wide variety of factors, including the parents' own temperament, family structure, and experiences of being cared for by their own parents. Such experiences can be evoked particularly vividly by the birth of a child, and their being evoked repeatedly can be particularly destructive in cases in which the parents' painful experiences of childhood remain unresolved.[11] For example, a father who hopes to repair a sense of personal failure through a son whom he expected to fulfill his unmet ideals will be particularly disillusioned by the birth of a daughter with Down's syndrome. This conflict might impede his ability to respond with encouragement to his daughter's real accomplishments, which might in turn dampen her self-esteem and struggles to achieve maximum sensorimotor and cognitive performance. In other situations, the particular fit between the parents' personality and the infant's developmental disabilities can enhance the caring situation. In one case, the mother of an infant with severe cerebral palsy abandoned his care to her own mother, who felt relatively isolated and had always occupied herself by taking care of others at her own expense. Paradoxically, this self-sacrificing style worked to the infant's advantage since the grandmother provided extraordinarily attentive care to him. Although this tendency might have been burdensome to an intact infant struggling to establish autonomy, it was particularly helpful for this intensely needy infant.

The importance of socioeconomic and sociocultural variables in determining the parents' responses to their infant's disabilities should not be underestimated. A poor family with a limited capacity to obtain high-quality services for a handicapped child, for example, may become discouraged and respond with grim hopelessness to the infant. This would impede the development of self-esteem and a sense of competence in the infant. Similar effects can be observed in cultures that stigmatize the disabled.

Individual differences between infants

Recent research on individual differences between infants suggests that the distinction between intact and disabled infants may be somewhat less clear-cut than previously thought, especially when the effect of differences in caregivers is taken into account. Infants demonstrate innate variability along such dimensions as activity level, sensory threshold and responsiveness, curiosity, irritability, and "soothability."[12-14] Each infant has a particular style of evoking and responding to caregiving behavior; each parent must adapt to the infant's individuality, and vice versa.[15] Subtle variations in the infant's signaling style (eg, intensity and duration of crying and facial expression) and sensitivity to stimuli, for example, can create problems for some parent–infant pairs but not others, even in subclinical situations. A mother with a tendency toward a very vivid, intense interactive style might overwhelm an infant with a low sensory threshold while providing, alternatively, appropriate responsiveness to a child who needs a high level of stimulation.

Such constitutional factors interact with the parents' personalities and prior experiences in cases which may be within normal dimensions, as well as those in which developmental disabilities are prominent. The effect of a subtle abnormality such as weak signaling in an otherwise physiologically intact infant will vary greatly depending on the readiness of the parent to feel rejected and uncertain of his or her capacity to provide adequate care. While an experienced parent with a reservoir of parenting success and self-esteem might patiently wait for the infant's signaling system to emerge more forcefully while taking subtle steps to enhance the infant's sense of effectiveness, a more fragile, inexperienced parent might withdraw in anger and frustration. Such a failure of responsiveness would be of particular concern in this case since an infant with a weak signaling system might be especially vulnerable to giving up almost all attempts to communicate. A mutually reinforcing system of ineffectuality might develop, which could have profoundly negative consequences for both infant and parent. These difficulties might be ameliorated relatively rapidly by an occupational therapist intervening to increase the infant's responsiveness along with specialized developmental guidance to help the parent adapt to the infant's particular style.[16]

Developmental disabilities are thus seen on a continuum with more optimal situations, with the most severe disabilities lying at one end.[17] A key issue in all cases is whether the caregiver and infant can fit together their capacities, limitations, idiosyncrasies, and interactional styles relatively harmoniously and in such a way as to maximize whatever potentials may exist, rather than reaching some objective standard. Although the possibilities for optimal development may be more severely constrained in some cases, there is always a dynamic interplay between both members of the caregiving transaction.

The transactional model of the infant–parent relationship

The caregiver–infant relationship can now be described as a "transactional system" in which each element (eg, the infant's psychophysiologic characteristics, the parent's confidence) is viewed in terms of its effect on the other elements in the system; no person or factor can be fully understood without reference to its effects on the others in the system. Furthermore, these effects have their own subsequent effects that make themselves felt continuously as transactional processes develop over time.[17] Adequate caregiving relationships are characterized here as ongoing and sufficiently flexible negotiations in which both parties work to accommodate each other well enough to keep the developmental process proceeding. Variation, accommodation, and the emergence of developmental potentials are emphasized rather than any specific factor, timetable, or set of appropriate child-rearing practices. For the most part, parents are understood to be engaged in reciprocal efforts to find a basis for adapting to their infants' evolving demands. This perspective emphasizes the potential for adaptive and progressive development inherent in caregiving systems. In cases of developmental disability, the potential generally remains available although it may emerge at an abnormally slow pace.

From this point of view, the key issue in assessing parenting behavior is whether the parents and infant are responding to each other's particular needs and capacities in such a way as to maximize the emergence of whatever potentials exist for competent development in each member of the caregiving transaction— as opposed to the parent and infant exacerbating each other's vulnerabilities. One risk in such situations is that such processes of exacerbation will amplify one another, as in the case of the mother whose withdrawing from her weak-signaling infant leads to the infant's giving up, or that of the abused child who learns to provoke violence as the only way to gain any recognition from an otherwise entirely unresponsive parent. In any case, although transactional outcomes vary in their desirability, each caregiver-infant relationship must be understood on its own terms and in the context of its own limitations and possibilities.

As was illustrated above, the effect of specific characteristics of both infant and parent will depend on how they are articulated in the caregiving transaction; particular characteristics that are liabilities in one relationship may be assets in another. One mother had particular difficulty in allowing her neurologically intact son to express normal striving toward independence in his second year of life because his behavior evoked her ongoing fear of separation that was linked to being abandoned as an infant by her own mother. Her tendency toward clinginess, however, was also beneficial in that it allowed her to be extraordinarily attentive to her severely brain-damaged daughter.

The transactional model of the caregiver–infant relationship can also be applied to the network of societal and family relationships that surround the care of the infant. Each member of a family affects and in turn is affected by the other members. A child with a developmental disability will affect his or her entire family and thus the way that the family responds to the disability as it unfolds. In one case, a 5-year-old girl began to bully her hearing-impaired younger brother. As their mother became preoccupied with the need to protect her son, she began to resent both children and became increasingly inattentive. After a psychotherapist helped the daughter understand her jealousy and anger over the added attention that her brother required, her bullying decreased, and the mother's capacity to encourage both children was restored.

Cultural attitudes and social policy toward handicaps and other at-risk conditions also have a substantial and complex impact on the individual relationships between infants and their caregivers. For example, high-quality, government-funded, low-cost services for children with special needs provide support, hope, and encouragement to parents, who communicate these attitudes in a variety of ways in their everyday interactions with their children. The presence of disabled people at all levels of business, government, and universities can also provide encouragement to parents and older children. Support groups and social activism can have similar effects. One mother reported that she was better able to sustain an energetic stance toward her daughter's cerebral palsy-based disability as she became involved with an organization that was pressuring the state legislature for increased services for the handicapped.

IMPLICATIONS FOR WORK WITH INFANTS WITH DEVELOPMENTAL DISABILITIES

Assessing developmental disabilities

The various perspectives suggested by findings in the infant mental health field call for a reorientation of those approaches that have focused entirely on behavioral objectives. From the current point of view, the assessment of a developmental disability should focus on the parents' adaptation to the disability, the infant's socioemotional development, the extent to which the parent–infant relationship maximizes the infant's potential development, as well as the particular sensorimotor handicaps and their amelioration. The development of various capacities should be considered together rather than in isolation, since progress or impairment in one area can lead to similar effects in others. Specific developmental disabilities can have an adverse effect on all lines of a child's development, including other cognitive, motor, and communicative capacities and socioemotional well-being.[18] Conversely, an overall sense of competence and self-esteem will increase the child's ability to ameliorate or find alternative pathways to the impeded sensorimotor skill.

Therefore, the capacity of the parents to protect and enhance their disabled infant's sense of competence and self-esteem should be considered. This includes the parents' general emotional response to the disability, as well as specific personality issues and conflicts that it evokes and the quality of parental interaction with the infant. Where possible, specific interactional variables such as the maintenance of behavioral interchanges and enthusiasm in the face of frustration should be assessed. Parental tendencies to withdraw from or be overprotective of their infant should be described. In addition, the general adequacy of family and community support networks and services should be evaluated.

Conceptualizing intervention

Interventions should be conceptualized in terms of their effect on the quality of the caregiver–infant relationship and in terms of the socioemotional development of the infant rather than exclusively with reference to specific behavioral goals. The effectiveness of all interventions can be enhanced by an awareness of their effect on the infant's experience of self and the relational environment. Infants may be willing to attempt new tasks or persist with difficult ones when the learning environment is pleasurable and supportive, and will be relatively inactive and unresponsive when they feel ineffectual, passive, or inappropriately challenged. This applies on both the macroscopic levels of program design, treatment planning, and outcome assessment and the microscopic level of specific behavioral interventions.

In structuring the moment-to-moment dynamics of therapeutic interaction, workers should be aware that the effectiveness of specific sensorimotor lessons will be enhanced when the infant experiences the behavioral interventions as a source of pleasure and competence. The parent who observes this will sense an alternative to the pervasive experience of ineffectuality and hopelessness that can accompany a severe disability. Taken together, the infant's pleasure and the parents' optimism can stimulate a relatively rapid process of developmental progress. Achieving such experiential shifts depends on the therapist's monitoring the infant's emotional readiness for each behavioral lesson, having a general sense of the infant's psychologic state in terms of such variables as self-esteem and frustration tolerance, and cultivating a sensitive, mutually supportive relationship with the parents.

In cases where these issues are overlooked, interventions that are otherwise technically adequate may prove to be ineffective. In one case, a 7-month-old boy with Down's syndrome had difficulty in maintaining an attentional set to novel stimuli without becoming extremely distressed. The occupational therapist did not take this fact into account as she designed an otherwise state-of-the-art behavioral training schedule, and the infant became repeatedly detached and disorganized, tensing up and crying as the therapist approached. By taking into account his need for exceptionally small increments in stimulus intensity, the therapist was able to develop a new and ultimately successful therapeutic strategy.

Maintaining provider–parent relationships

The therapist–parent relationship is of primary importance in supporting the achievement of behavioral and socioemotional objectives. Therapists must work carefully to build and maintain a working alliance with the parents, and must vigilantly monitor their working relationships for signs of dissonance, indifference, frustration, and antagonism. Providers should also observe their own responses to children and their parents. These are often useful early warning signs of problems in the therapist–parent alliance and can be discussed with supportive colleagues and supervisors.[19,20]

In the previous case of the irritable 7-month-old boy, the mother was aware of her son's hypersensitivity and felt that the therapist was devaluing her maternal competence. As the behavioral interventions went awry, her expectable tension was heightened by this feeling, which in turn added to the anxiety of both therapist and infant. In refining her approach, the therapist was careful to inform the mother of her infant, adding that she had perhaps overlooked some important information that the mother had known for some time. The mother then felt like a respected member of the intervention team, which enhanced self-esteem and readiness to repeat the behavioral lessons at home. The effectiveness of the therapist's renewed efforts was thus amplified.

Similar issues have been noted in the field of pediatrics. Pediatric intervention depends on parental compliance with medical advice and office appointments. Parents of at-risk infants may fail to maintain appointments or treatment regimens for many reasons, including the wish to deny their infant's limitations, severe emotional or cognitive disorganizations, or unspoken or unconscious negative feelings about pediatric providers. Effective treatment planning usually considers such provider–parent relationship issues.

Parents may also feel burdened or bewildered by the number and variety of professionals who are involved with their child. In such cases, providing clear and accurate information to parents and systematically dividing the labor among the professionals is essential. Professionals will also benefit from maintaining open and frequent lines of communication among themselves, particularly in dealing with parents who tend to deny or avoid the implications of worrisome findings about their child, since the parents will be unlikely to provide complete information. Parents may also express their own inner conflicts by using one provider to help solve problematic feelings about another provider. These tendencies often appear simultaneously. One mother, for example, who was dissatisfied with her speech-impaired daughter's special-needs class hired a private speech therapist without telling the teacher, since she did not want to appear to be critical and feared confrontation. The teacher became increasingly puzzled over her pupil's new response styles and sensed a growing awkwardness between herself and the mother. After consulting with her colleagues, the teacher politely but firmly asked the mother about influences on her daughter's language. This led to a meeting of all involved professionals, including the pediatrician and the mother's counselor, which resulted in the child's remaining in the class and continuing with the speech therapist and making additional progress.

This example also illustrates how parents' complex and intense feelings about their child's disabilities can combine with personal dynamics to impede the effectiveness of the intervention efforts. Providers can sometimes make significant progress in these cases if they proceed with tact, care, and reassurance that they mean to help the parent in his or her efforts to help the child, rather than criticize or reveal the parent's shortcomings. In more difficult cases, referring the parents to a counselor, psychotherapist, or support group will be most helpful. Many agencies offer ongoing support groups for parents, and some include psychologic consultation as a part of the case assessment and staff development processes.

Planning and evaluating treatment

Interventions can now be viewed as attempts to enhance and restore whatever positive potential exists in the developmental-transactional system; unproductive or counterproductive interventions are those in which dysfunctional patterns are not disrupted or are even accelerated, as in the case of the infant with Down's syndrome described above before the therapeutic strategy was revised. Cases can be conceptualized by determining which aspects of the developmental-relational system require intervention, what potential for change each aspect offers, and how particular intervention strategies affect different people in the infant's world as well as the infant's emerging developmental capacities. The socioemotional effect of physiologically oriented and behaviorally oriented intervention should be considered, as should the physiologic and behavioral effects of socioemotional intervention such as group support or psychotherapy for children and parents.

A number of specific questions can now be asked in planning treatment: What impact will any particular intervention have on the infant's and parents' sense of effectiveness, relatedness, and development progress; in other words, how do the child and family experience the intervention? To what extent are the infant and parents able to draw on their internal sense of competence and connectedness, along with their personal strengths and social support networks, to make use of the specific goal-oriented help that is offered? What kind of working relationship with the child and parents will best serve the immediate goals of the intervention, even an apparently limited one such as a sensorimotor training program. Other, similar questions can be framed and monitored as the intervention proceeds, taking into account the infant–parent and therapist–parent relationships as well as the specific technical objectives.

This perspective calls for a high degree of flexibility and comprehensiveness from service providers and family members, and often involves considerable interdisciplinary collaboration. Such flexibility and comprehensiveness are a necessary correlate of the attempt to maintain awareness of the infant as an active, integrated, socially organized person in the face of the sometimes massive impact of various difficulties that may impinge on his or her developmental progress.

Planning and evaluating programs

Recent infant mental health findings suggest that programs that have previously focused on the medical and physical aspects of a disability should also emphasize socioemotional issues, the capacities of caregivers to influence developmental outcomes, and the quality of provider–parent and provider–infant relationships. Such issues should be included in the ongoing case evaluations. Similarly, assessments of a program's effectiveness should address the infant's socioemotional development, the family's adaptation, and the parents' attitudes toward intervention programs.

•   •   •

Training programs for professionals involved with infants at risk for developmental disabilities should include perspectives such as those discussed here. Professionals who are currently practicing can obtain more information through continuing education and inservice conferences. They will also find mental health-oriented consultation on both programmatic and case-centered levels to be useful.

REFERENCES

1. Fraiberg S, ed.: *Clinical Studies in Infant Mental Health. The First Year of Life.* New York: Basic Books: 1980.

2. Emde R: Toward a psychoanalytic theory of affect. In Greenspan SI, Pollock GH, eds.: *The Course of Life. Psychoanalytic Contributions Toward Understanding Personality Development.* Adelphi, MD: National Institute of Mental Health; 1980. vol 1.

3. Engel G: Clinical application of the biopsychosocial model. *Am J Psychiatry.* 1980;137:535–544.

4. Greenspan S: *Psychopathology and Adaptation in Infancy and Early Childhood. Principles of Clinical Diagnosis and Preventive Intervention.* New York: International Universities Press; 1981.

5. Greenspan S, Lourie RS: Developmental structuralist approach to the classification of adaptive and pathologic personality organizations: Infancy and early childhood. *Am J Psychiatry.* 1981;138:725–735.

6. Mahler MS, Pine F, Bergman A: *The Psychological Birth of the Human Infant: Symbiosis and Individuation.* New York: Basic Books; 1975.

7. Sander L: Issues in early mother-child interaction. *J Am Acad Child Psychiatry* 1962;1:141–166.

8. Stern D: *The First Relationship. Infant and Mother.* Cambridge, MA: Harvard University Press; 1977.

9. Stern D: *The Interpersonal World of the Infant.* New York: Basic Books; 1985.

10. Fraiberg S: *Insights From the Blind: Comparative Studies of Blind and Sighted Infants.* New York: Basic Books; 1977.

11. Fraiberg S, Adelson E, Shapiro V: Ghosts in the nursery: A psychoanalytic approach to the problem of impaired infant-mother relationships. *J Am Acad Child Psychiatry.* 1975;14:387–422.

12. Brazelton TB: Behavioral competence of the newborn infant. *Semin Perinatol.* 1979;3:35–44.

13. Korner AF: Individual differences at birth: Implications for early experience and later development. *Am J Orthopsychiatry.* 1971;41:608–619.

14. Thomas A, Chess S, Birch HG: *Temperament and Behavior Disorders in Children.* New York: New York University Press; 1968.

15. Lewis M, Rosenbloom LA, eds.: *The Effect of the Infant on Its Caregiver.* New York: Wiley; 1974.

16. Greenspan S, Weider S, Nover RA, eds.: *Infants in Multirisk Families: Case Studies in Preventive Intervention.* Clinical Infant Reports: Series of the National Center for Clinical Infant Programs. New York: International Universities Press; 1986.

17. Sameroff AK, Chandler, MJ: Reproductive risk and the continuum of caretaking casualty, in Horowitz FD, ed.: *Review of Child Development Research.* Chicago: University of Chicago Press; 1975, vol 4.

18. Freud A: The concept of developmental lines. *Psychoanal Study Child.* 1963;18:245–265.

19. Seligman S, Pawl J: Impediments to the formation of the working alliance in infant-parent psychotherapy. In Call JD, Galenson E, Tyson R, eds.: *Frontiers of Infant Psychiatry.* New York: Basic Books; 1984, vol 2.

20. Sandler J: Countertransference and role responsiveness. *Int Rev Psychoanal.* 1976;3:34–47.

Maltreatment of young children with disabilities

James Garbarino, PhD
President
Erikson Institute for Advanced Study
    in Child Development
Chicago, Illinois

THE SERIOUS mistreatment of children by their parents and guardians arouses public indignation, motivates professional service providers, and frustrates researchers perhaps more than any other single public issue.[1] Despite the high level of public attention given to the topic of child abuse, however, major factual and ideological issues remain unresolved. For example, although there are volumes of research, theory, and speculation on the topic, there is still no altogether satisfactory definition of abuse. Broadly speaking, of course, child abuse is willful behavior by parents or guardians that harms a child in their care; however, the unresolved issue has to do with what constitutes harm. While few would doubt that savage and severe beatings, burnings, or assaults with a deadly weapon constitute abuse, it is difficult to draw a firm line between corporal punishment and abuse in cultures, such as our own, that sanction the use of physical assault as a legitimate means of discipline within the family. For this reason, we must rely jointly on community standards and scientific expertise to know which behaviors by a parent are threatening to a child.[2] Community standards tell us what is normal in a culture, such as scarification in some tribal African communities and spanking in North America. Scientific expertise gives us a basis from which to evaluate values and norms—for example, the finding that rejection is psychologically damaging no matter what its cultural standing.

In the broad perspective we see the principal social causes of child abuse and neglect as being of three types. First, there is cultural support for domestic violence and inadequate child care: Our values permit a range of behaviors by parents and guardians that set the child up for maltreatment. Second, there are the joint concepts of family autonomy and parental ownership of children. Together these deeply entrenched ideas conspire to reduce a sense of community responsibility for children, to permit and even encourage social isolation and to break the weak link in our chain of concern. They permit us to define the problem in a particular family as belonging to someone else, rather than as being a matter of collective responsibility and obligation. Third, there are the stresses of day-to-day social and economic life that exacerbate the sense of personal inadequacy and permit family vulnerability to develop into risk, which ultimately translates into abuse and neglect. These three factors together fuel a "social machine" that is apt to produce large quantities of abuse and neglect. It is this social machine that is most dangerous to infants and children in general, and to handicapped children in particular.

All of the many causes and contributing factors involved in child maltreatment combine to produce psychosocially impoverished families and physically damaged children. This process will inevitably continue in the social isolation that is

Inf Young Children, 1989; 2(2): 49–57

characteristic of our individualistic culture. Our growing knowledge base makes this quite clear.

WHAT HAVE WE LEARNED ABOUT CHILD MALTREATMENT?

Empirical and clinical studies of child maltreatment now number in excess of 1,000, and each study contains numerous findings. However, research[3,4] suggests that much of the confusion and uncertainty in studying, legislating against, treating, and preventing child maltreatment derives from inconsistency and lack of precision in the definitions used in research, policy, law, and practice. Thus, for example, estimates of the incidence of child maltreatment number in the tens of thousands if only life-threatening assault and total failure to offer care are used as criteria, but in the millions if we define maltreatment as any form of damaging treatment (ie, emotional, sexual, educational, or physical). Nonetheless, analyses based on a comparison of officially reported cases and a broader survey of cases known to any community professional dealing with families are reassuring in that we are beginning to get reliable information about incidence and prevalence. What is more, real progress has been made in differentiating among physical, sexual, and psychological maltreatment. Also, preliminary studies of adolescent victims of maltreatment, who constitute more than 25% of the total number of reported cases, suggest that the causes, correlates, and consequences of adolescent abuse are somewhat different from cases involving children, and that gender differences in victimization persist from infancy through adolescence.

Causes

Even given the problems of definition, we do know something about the factors that contribute to child maltreatment.

- It is clear that both psychological and social factors play a role in producing child maltreatment, although debate continues about which is more important. Low income and other aspects of social stress are associated with higher rates of child maltreatment, which is evident during periods of economic recession and increased unemployment. This relationship between economic deprivation and maltreatment appears to be stronger with respect to infants and young children than to adolescents.
- Some cultures, societies, and communities experience more child maltreatment than do others. Economic pressure, values concerning the role of the child in the family, attitudes about the use of physical punishment, and the degree of social support for parents seem to account for these differences. Ethnic and cultural differences appear to exist with respect to overall inci-

dence and with respect to the relative frequency of different forms of maltreatment (eg, abuse v neglect).

- Poor general coping skills and parenting skills, including those directly involved in discipline, play a significant role in child maltreatment. Social isolation is associated with a greater likelihood of child maltreatment, both because abuse-prone individuals isolate themselves and because they lack the means to participate in their communities. Personal characteristics of parents (eg, untimely childbearing, physical illness, poor ability to empathize) and of children (eg, aversive crying, unresponsiveness) can substantially increase the likelihood of child maltreatment, particularly when social stress and social isolation characterize the family. These patterns find expression in a relative lack of success at dealing nonviolently with problematic behaviors of children.

- A history of maltreatment in the parent's background (particularly if untreated or "unprocessed") increases the likelihood of child maltreatment, as does the contemporary presence of interspousal violence.

- Families involved in child maltreatment tend to exhibit a pattern of day-to-day interaction characterized by a low level of social exchange, low responsiveness to positive behavior, and high responsiveness to negative behavior. This style may extend beyond the family to the workplace and school.

- Although many abusive parents exhibit barely adequate personality characteristics, overt mental illness plays a small role overall in child maltreatment.

Community responses

Based on analyses of community responses to child maltreatment, we know that it is very difficult if not impossible to identify reliably, before the fact, families that will mistreat their children. However, predicting the degree of risk is possible, based on the known correlates of maltreatment. Thus far, most community responses to specific cases of maltreatment have been ineffective.[5]

Current knowledge may be summarized as follows:

- To reduce risks to the youngster, protective services should adopt as their foremost goal an adequate permanent family placement for the child. This means preventing removal, if possible, by offering supportive and therapeutic services to the family that are sufficient to protect the child and to improve family functioning. If removal is necessary, however, a realistic decision should be made quickly regarding permanent placement of the child. If the goal is to return the child to the family, then the family should maintain contact with the child placed in foster care, and rehabilitative services should be offered. If the child is to be permanently separated from the family, the child should be placed in a new permanent home as soon as possible.

- Conventional casework approaches typically result in a 50% success rate at best. Some intensive and resource-laden programs report very low recidivism rates with selected clientele, however.
- Interdisciplinary teams for case management and development of community services are best. Paraprofessional and volunteer staff in conjunction with mutual help groups can provide effective social support and concrete aid in meeting day-to-day problems. Comprehensive implementation of high-quality programs that require heavy involvement of professional staff exceeds both current and projected levels of fiscal resources devoted to protective services. Using paraprofessionals, volunteers, and mutual help groups is highly cost-effective under most circumstances. Teaching parents skills for successfully handling the problem behavior of children in a nonviolent manner is often useful. Most current treatment approaches address parents, although the exclusive treatment of parents does not appear to reverse the damage done to children. Children generally receive no treatment at all, and may even be harmed by outside intervention that places them in foster care or institutional care that is often traumatic in its own right. Even if the initial placement is benign, the risk of repeated placements is high and a matter of great concern. The issues involved in serving adolescent victims differ somewhat from those involved in serving the needs of children. Resolving custody issues and dealing with negative behavior appear to be greater problems when adolescents are involved.
- Prevention remains underdeveloped. However, several strategies that have generated very encouraging results include home-health visitors, family centered childbirth, and social skills training aimed at improving parental effectiveness. We are rapidly approaching a point at which it will be feasible to set specific goals for preventing child maltreatment and to have realistic expectations for meeting those goals.

Developmental effects of maltreatment

We know that child maltreatment and the family environments associated with it pose a clear and present developmental danger to the children involved.

- Specific acts of maltreatment produce acute and chronic medical problems that impair growth and development.
- Even if specific acts of abuse are not present, growing up in a family at high risk for maltreatment is associated with developmental damage.
- Children who experience maltreatment may be at substantially increased risk for later delinquency, psychiatric disorders, school failure, self-destructive behavior, domestic violence, and sexual dysfunction, depending on the nature, age of onset, duration, and family climate of the maltreatment. How-

ever, existing research does not include sufficient large-scale, longitudinal, well-controlled studies to permit a definitive conclusion about the precise effects of maltreatment. Of particular concern are two issues: the role of sexual abuse in generating later sexually dysfunctional behavior, and the dynamic links between child maltreatment and juvenile delinquency.

This outline of current knowledge sets the stage for subsequent efforts in this article to focus attention on the crucial questions of whether, how and why handicapping conditions and maltreatment are connected in the lives of children. The issue of abuse/neglect as the cause of developmental harm will be addressed first.

CHILD MALTREATMENT AS THE CAUSE OF DEVELOPMENTAL HARM

As has been noted, a complete and unambiguous analysis of the outcomes of child maltreatment is certainly beyond the knowledge available at this point in the history of scientific inquiry into child abuse and neglect. Most of the existing research is retrospective, which limits the ability to detect causal relations. In the case of the link between child abuse and juvenile delinquency, for example, a review by Garbarino and Plantz[6] indicated that virtually all available studies were retrospective. Nonetheless, concern about the consequences of child maltreatment is justifiable on multiple grounds, empirical as well as clinical.

On the one hand, most professionals are convinced that child maltreatment has multiple and often severe consequences. On the other hand, it must be acknowledged that the prevalence of specific forms of harm, the mediators of damage and the mechanisms of influence are not as yet completely clear (to say the least). When discussing socioemotional consequences of physical abuse, Egeland and Sroufe assert that

> In the area of socioemotional development, even the obvious is often difficult to demonstrate. Uncovering the developmental consequences of child abuse is a prime example. Yet, no one can doubt that there are consequences of being physically abused.[7(p77)]

What are some of those consequences? Even a cursory review of the literature reveals numerous possibilities. These include death, permanent disability, developmental delay, speech and learning problems, impaired attachment relations, self- and other-directed aggression, psychosis (particularly multiple personalities), juvenile delinquency, depression, deficient social skills, and sexual dysfunction. Indeed it is difficult to identify any problem that has not been linked to child maltreatment on the basis of clinical observation, survey research, or informed speculation.

In a comprehensive review of the consequences of abuse and neglect, Martin[8] identified three major forms of harm: *medical problems*, ranging from nutritional deficiencies to hearing loss to brain damage; *developmental problems*, ranging from mental retardation to language deficiencies to impaired motor skills; and *psychological problems*, encompassing the extremes on most dimensions of personality (eg, being very shy and inhibited or very aggressive and provocative) as well as general unhappiness, poor attachment, and inadequate peer relations. Martin also sheds some light on the dynamics of the effect of abusive environment on development.[8] Sameroff and Chandler[9] include the idea that a pattern of transactions develops in which the damaged child elicits responses that reinforce the damage; for example, brain damage adversely affects personality, a pattern of entrapped parent–child conflict releases a pattern of abuse, mastery languishes, and increasingly iatrogenic interventions occur (eg, a foster placement that fails). All of this is plausible, and the reality of damage appears to be undeniable. It is the form, severity, prevalence, and duration of harm that remain at issue. Bear this in mind as the question is considered of whether handicapped children are at special risk for abuse and neglect, because some handicapping conditions may well result from maltreatment early in life and then become the cause of maltreatment in later interactions with parents, peers, teachers, and other caregivers.

ARE HANDICAPPED CHILDREN AT SPECIAL RISK FOR ABUSE AND NEGLECT?

The word "special" is used here with particular intent. While it may seem obvious that the main task at hand is to demonstrate that handicapped children and youths are disproportionately represented among the victims of maltreatment, this is neither the only nor the best way to express the issue. For one thing, it must be determined that the maltreatment experienced by handicapped children follows from their handicaps rather than vice versa. This is often difficult, if not impossible, to establish because cause and effect are intertwined. But even this is not the only empirical challenge to be faced in this area.

The real challenge lies in specifying the ways in which the factors that produce or prevent maltreatment in the lives of nonhandicapped children operate for handicapped children. This focus on children in their social context underlies the present article. Some handicapped children may be at greater risk than nonhandicapped children would be in the same situation, while others might well be at reduced risk. For example, if a child's handicap elicits greater nurturance, surveillance, and resources being brought to bear on a child's family, then the child in such a situation might be at less risk for abuse than a nonhandicapped child in the same family. At the same time, difficulties with comprehension and communication and heightened dependence on caregivers might render a handicapped child less able to seek protection from maltreatment when it does occur. Thus the degree of risk for handicapped children may derive from the very meaning and community implications of being "special," for that label may invoke extra resources in some settings and rejection in others.

No simple compilation of statistics reporting the incidence of maltreatment among handicapped versus nonhandicapped children is sufficient. Embry[10] highlighted this when he observed that the higher stress experienced by the family of a handicapped preschool child, who lacks the behaviors that normal children use to attract caretaking and attention and who has a developmental history that decreases mother–child bonding, increases the risk for severe family dysfunction, which may in turn exhibit itself in the most extreme form, child abuse.[11-13] Thus a family that would have established a successful, supportive relationship with a normal child or children can develop serious problems when a child with special needs enters the family system. Finally, dysfunctional family interactions appear to exacerbate a child's developmental delay. Given the nexus of developmental difficulties facing the handicapped child, not only does the task of intervention become far more complex but the risks of nonintervention become much more severe.[10] It is not enough to know what differences there are in the treatment of handicapped versus nonhandicapped children by their families. The effects of these differences among families are of paramount importance to the development of the handicapped child.

The etiology of maltreatment

Many studies report that handicapped children, particularly mentally retarded children, account for more than their proportionate share of the total number of abused and neglected children and youths,[8] while others do not.[14] Some report high levels of handicap among maltreated children. In one study, 43% of the abused children had handicaps, and 65% of the handicapped children were abused.[15] Sandgrund et al[16] reported that serious mental retardation was eight times more common among abused and neglected children than among socioeconomically and demographically similar children who were not maltreated. However, other studies report no significant difference between maltreated and comparison groups[14] and offer the hypothesis that child maltreatment is implicated primarily as a cause rather than an effect of handicap.[7]

It is generally accepted that approximately 12% of all children and youths are handicapped, with about 60% of these handicaps occurring after birth.[17] The incidence of handicap appears to be higher for low-income families, however, a fact that makes it difficult to know exactly whom to use as comparison groups in research on this topic. What is more, some handicapping conditions (eg, mental retardation) have a significant genetic component that functions through intergenerational transmission. This compounds research difficulties by making it even more troublesome to disentangle cause from effect.

The fact that handicapped children are likely to elicit special resources for their families from some communities means that the "expectable rate of abuse" (in a supportive community) is higher than the observed actual rate. Thus one might expect that the strength of any causal relationship between handicap and child maltreatment varies from time to time and place to place as a function of the over-all resource implications of being and having a special child.

It is known that abuse and neglect early in life (even prenatally) can produce physical damage. Experts estimate that only about 40% of all handicaps are attributable to prenatal and genetic conditions.[17] Deafness, mental retardation, blindness, and other handicapping conditions can all result from maltreatment. Such damage may then predispose the child to further victimization by impairing the child's ability to meet parental expectations, by requiring special care that exceeds parental resources, by leading a parent to reject the child, or by causing the parent to institutionalize the child (a factor that can itself be a cause of maltreatment).

Factors that increase the risk of maltreatment

Similarly, handicapping conditions may be linked to other factors that are the real causes of maltreatment. Researchers and clinicians have long sought to identify factors that increase the likelihood that a child will be maltreated. Their efforts have identified five broad categories of risk, two of which refer primarily to individual members of the family. The first concerns parents. Individual adults may not possess the personal resources that they need to function adequately as parents, particularly if they are subjected to greater than normal demands. One such personal characteristic identified in research on abuse is the lack of empathy (ie, the ability to perceive and appreciate the feelings and motives of others). Depression and apathy figure prominently as personal risk factors in cases of neglect. A second category of individual risk factors concerns characteristics of children or youths that make them especially challenging or difficult to care for, including fussiness, a chronic illness that requires special care, and delinquent and aggressive behavior.

A third documented risk factor involves aspects of the relationship between a particular adult and a particular child or youth that produce a deteriorating pattern of interaction, whether escalating conflict or progressive withdrawal. The fourth risk factor concerns elements of the immediate situation that stimulate abuse or neglect (eg, by increasing the level of stress beyond tolerable limits or by isolating the adult–child relationship from the support of spouse, friends, relatives, or professional helpers). A fifth risk factor is any feature of the culture or the society that encourages maltreatment or permits it to occur, such as values and institutions that approve of harsh physical punishment as a form of normal discipline or that define children as the disposable property of parents. Each of these five factors plays a role in the maltreatment of children and youths, although all are not necessarily present in any single case.

Handicapped children and youths may be at special risk for maltreatment because of any or all of these five factors. They appear to be particularly vulnerable to maltreatment when faced with parents who are themselves lacking in important personal resources. Raising a handicapped child is a challenge that makes great demands on parents. Thus parents who lack the ability to empathize, for example, pose a special threat to the handicapped child or youth, who usually requires a parent with heightened rather than diminished ability to understand feelings and respond sympathetically.

With respect to the second risk factor (ie, characteristics of children that increase the likelihood of maltreatment), it is again apparent that handicapped children and youths may be at special risk under some conditions. The very existence of a handicap that reduces the ability to communicate, to respond, and otherwise to meet parental and community expectations can make some children more vulnerable. They become simultaneously more likely to experience maltreatment and less able to respond in such adaptive ways as accommodating a parent's needs, offsetting the effects of neglect by caring for oneself, or seeking assistance from adults and peers outside the family. Diminished coping resources similarly explain the distinctions being drawn between the abuse of infants versus the abuse of adolescents. Infants represent "perfect victims" in that they are easily victimized and have few self-protective resources, and enjoy a broad base of public sympathy, whereas adolescents are less easily victimized but are viewed with suspicion by the public at large.

Characteristics of parents and children alike, then, can play a role in heightening the risk that a particular parent–child relationship will become enmeshed in a negative cycle that leads to escalating conflict (and thus to abuse) or to progressive withdrawal (and thus to neglect). Similarly, the presence of a handicapped child or youth within a family may raise the level of stress beyond the family's ability to cope, leading to a process of social withdrawal and estrangement that produces the kind of social isolation in which maltreatment flourishes. Indeed research has repeatedly identified a pattern in which families with handicapped children evince progressive social isolation.[10] The combination of fewer social contacts and increased reliance on relatives, when coupled with stress, has been identified as a correlate of elevated family violence.[18]

An important hypothesis emerges from research and clinical reports: It appears that the presence of a handicapped child tends to push families toward the opposite extremes of unusually strong and positive family interaction or particularly negative functioning. Like all such special circumstances, the presence of a handicapped child can act as a growth-inducing challenge or as a stressful event that erodes normal functioning. This is true of economic events (eg, unemployment) as well as of such sociopsychological circumstances as the birth of a handicapped child.

Social support

Certainly one key to how well a family responds is their overall level of functioning. A second is the level of accessible social support (ie, nurturance and guidance), which is especially important for families with handicapped offspring. Not surprisingly, research and clinical evidence indicate that handicapped children and youths experience maltreatment primarily when their families are isolated from such formal and informal social support systems, or when they isolate themselves.[10]

The availability and accessibility of social support for families with handicapped children and youths are not simply personal or even family matters, but reflections of the community's willingness and ability to provide such support and to assume responsibility for all children. Culture plays a role in the formation of and policies toward classes of children who are designated as "damaged" or otherwise less desirable than normal children.[19] Damaged children can include illegitimate or racially mixed offspring as well as handicapped children. The existence of a culturally derived stigma appears to heighten the risk for maltreatment among handicapped children and youths. It leads to a lowering of standards of care and to a kind of tacit license to abuse them. This can be seen most clearly by examining the problem of institutional abuse and neglect.

Institutional maltreatment

A recent federally funded study of institutional abuse conducted under the auspices of Ohio State University concluded that "there are factors inherent in institutions not necessarily found in family homes that may result in abuse or neglect (eg, emotionally detached caretakers, use of psychotropic drugs, large numbers of resident children)."[20(p2)] This and other findings about the incidence of institutional maltreatment have a special relevance for handicapped children because they are disproportionately likely to be institutionalized at some point in their lives.

Handicapped children and youths are at special risk for institutional maltreatment in the three forms that have been identified by investigators: institutional child abuse, including corporal punishment, misuse of psychotropic drugs, isolation exceeding two hours, and restraint by mechanical device; institutional child neglect, including failure to provide specific services, negligence in the administration of psychotropic drugs, and failure to notify the placing agency when a child's continued residence is detrimental to him or her; and wrongful abrogation of rights, including tampering with mail, racial or other improper segregation, restricting visitation and other contact, and interference with a resident's ability to consult with outside agents.

If handicapped children experience such maltreatment, they face special difficulties in seeking and receiving protection and assistance, both because of their difficulties in communicating and because they and their families may be highly dependent on the institution for essential services (eg, deaf or blind students enrolled in the only school that is geographically or financially available to them). In such conditions of heightened dependence, handicapped children and youths require special protective services.

•   •   •

All in all, it seems clear that handicapped children and youths are at special risk for maltreatment. "Special" here has several meanings. Many handicaps observed in children are probably themselves the result of earlier maltreatment. Many handicapped children experience heightened risk of abuse and neglect (or additional abuse and neglect). Many maltreated children exhibit handicaps. However, under some conditions, handicapped children may actually be at lower than usual risk, as when born to or adopted by highly motivated and competent parents who have special resources for caring for handicapped children. A strongly positive community response geared to the special needs of the family with a handicapped child can alter the context in which the handicap-maltreatment dynamic operates.

Beyond drawing conclusions about the levels and conditions of risk for handicapped children, we must recognize and deal with the special issues involved in preventing maltreatment or, failing that, in identifying cases of actual maltreatment and designing effective interventions. The task before us is to protect handicapped children and youths by modifying the conditions under which they are at special risk and by correcting problems when they do occur.

REFERENCES

1. Garbarino J: What kind of society permits child abuse? *Infant Ment Health J*. 1980;1:270–280.
2. Garbarino J, Gilliam G: *Understanding Abusive Families*. Lexington, MA: Lexington Books; 1980.
3. Garbarino J: What we know about child maltreatment. *Child Youth Services Rev*. 1983;5:1–6.
4. Garbarino J: What have we learned about child maltreatment? In *Perspectives on Child Maltreatment in the Mid '80s*. DHHS publication no (OHDS) 84–30338, Washington, DC: US Department of Health and Human Services; 1984:6–7.
5. Garbarino J: Can we measure success in preventing child abuse? Some issues in policy, programming, and research. *Child Abuse Neglect*. 1986;10:143–156.

6. Garbarino J, Plantz M: Child maltreatment and juvenile delinquency: What are the links? In Garbarino J, Schellenbach C, Sebes J, et al, eds.: *Troubled Youth, Troubled Families.* New York: Aldine; 1986:27–39.

7. Egeland B, Sroufe A: Developmental sequelae of maltreatment in infancy. *New Dir Child Dev.* 1980;45:1–64.

8. Martin H: The consequences of being abused and neglected: How the child fares. In Kempe CH, Helfer R, eds.: *The Battered Child,* ed 4. Chicago: University of Chicago Press; 1980: 347–365.

9. Sameroff A, Chandler M: Reproductive risk and the continuum of caretaking casualty. In Horowitz F, ed.: *Review of Child Development Research.* Chicago: University of Chicago Press; 1975: vol 4, 187–244.

10. Embry L: Family support for handicapped preschool children at risk for abuse, in Gallagher J, ed.: *New Directions for Exceptional Children.* San Francisco: Jossey-Bass; 1980: vol 4, 29–57.

11. Farber B, Jenne W: Interaction with retarded siblings and life goals of children. *Marriage Fam Living.* 1963;25:96–98.

12. Kempe CH, Helfer R, eds.: *The Battered Child,* ed 3. Chicago: University of Chicago Press; 1976.

13. Martin H: *The Abused Child.* Cambridge, MA: Ballinger; 1976.

14. Starr R, Dietrich K, Fischoff J, et al: The contribution of handicapping conditions to child abuse. *Top Early Child Spec Educ.* 1984;4:55–69.

15. Lightcap J, Kurland J, Burgess R: Child abuse: A test of some predictions for evolutionary theory. *Ethology Sociobiol.* 1982;3:61–67.

16. Sandgrund A, Gaines R, Green A: Child abuse and mental retardation: A problem of cause and effect. *J Mental Defic Res* 1975;19:327–330.

17. Garbarino J, Brookhouser P, Authier K, et al: *Special Children Special Risks: The Maltreatment of Children with Disabilities.* New York: Aldine; 1987.

18. Straus M: Stress and child abuse. In Kempe CH, Helfer R, eds.: *The Battered Child,* ed 4. Chicago: University of Chicago Press; 1980:86–103.

19. Korbin J, ed.: *Child Abuse and Neglect: Cross-Cultural Perspectives.* Berkeley: University of California Press; 1981.

20. Rindfleisch N: *Identification, Management and Prevention of Child Abuse and Neglect in Residential Facilities.* Columbus, Ohio: Ohio State University Research Foundation, 1984.

Parent–infant interaction in neonatal intensive care units: Implications for research and service delivery

Sheryl Ridener Gottwald, MS
Instructor
Department of Speech/Language/
    Hearing

Kenneth Thurman, PhD
Professor
Special Education Program
Department of Psychological Studies
    in Education
Temple University
Philadelphia, Pennsylvania

RECENT ADVANCES in medical science and technology have led to increased survival rates among preterm infants. Infants born as early as 24 weeks gestation and weighing under 500 gms are no longer beyond the grasp of neonatology expertise. They may survive, however, with a multitude of problems including physical trauma, neurologic insult, and iatrogenic effects of treatment for their prematurity. Thus, many infants who survive hospitalization in a neonatal intensive care unit (NICU) are at increased risk for achieving less than optimal development. Behaviorally, these infants are generally less active, initiate fewer interactions, and provide less feedback to their caregivers than normally developing peers.[1-3] Furthermore, these infants maintain less eye contact with their parents, avert their gaze more, smile less,[5,8] use more unclear signals,[4,9] and are more difficult to cuddle and console than their term peers.[10] As a result, the development of their social interactions may also be compromised.[4]

PARENT–INFANT INTERACTION WITH THE PREMATURE OR ILL INFANT

Parents of premature or ill infants respond differently to their children than parents of full-term, well infants. For example, they are less actively involved, make less body contact,[11] spend less time in face-to-face contact,[12] and smile, touch and talk to their infants less.[2,5,11] Greene, Fox and Lewis[10] have reported that mothers showed decreased affective expression to their preterm infants at three months of age. Other researchers, however, have indicated that mothers of these infants show more affectionate behavior with the infant.[13] In another study, premature infants and their mothers were less able to coordinate their cycles of affective behavior during social interaction.[14] Increased maternal efforts to engage the premature infant have been associated with increased gaze aversion by the infant.[4,7] As a result, their pattern of interaction is often much less synchronous and reciprocal than that of mothers with their healthy term infants.

Inf Young Children, 1990; 2(3): 1–9
© 1990 Aspen Publishers, Inc.

The initial interactions of many premature infants and their parents are influenced by factors associated with the NICU. If one accepts the transactional approach originally promulgated by Sameroff and Chandler,[15] it is reasonable to suggest that the nature of these early interactions in the NICU helps to define the nature of interaction patterns throughout the first year or two of life. Thus, better understanding of the factors that influence these early interactions can provide direction to practitioners and researchers concerned with the development of high-risk infants. The remainder of this paper focuses on these factors. Specifically, this article examines the nature of the NICU environment and its potential effects on patterns of parent–infant interaction. Moreover, research examining the specific nature of parent–infant interaction in the NICU is discussed. Finally, based on this discussion, recommendations are offered to caregivers and researchers interested in the earliest development of interaction patterns between high-risk infants and their parents.

THE NICU ENVIRONMENT

The NICU provides the neonate with a habitat for growth starkly different from the intrauterine environment.[16,17] The intrauterine environment is replaced by the bright lights,[18,19] high noise level,[19] and intrusive medical procedures characteristic of high technology treatment.[20] Several features of the NICU have been identified as factors that may affect the nature of parent–infant interactions. These include the constant stimulation provided by lighting and equipment sounds, the continuous and often unpredictable interventions provided by caregivers, the acute and rapidly changing nature of the infant's medical status, as well as the intimidating presence of the medical apparatus needed to maintain infant stability.

Although lighting must always be sufficient to conduct medical procedures,[19] light levels may be too bright or glaring for infants to gaze at their parents for any period of time—such gazing behavior is an important interactional signal.[21] Jones[18] observed two NICUs around the clock for three weeks. She reported that infants on "warmer beds" kept their eyes closed for all but an average of 48 min per day, perhaps in direct response to the intense light and heat to which they were continually exposed. Linn and colleagues[22] suggested that stimulation in the NICU was at sufficient levels, however, it was not contingent on infant behavioral or state conditions. Rather than lacking stimulation, per se, an infant's readiness to interact did not match the type and amount of stimulation provided.

Large amounts of auditory stimulation are present in the NICU as well. As a result, infants may receive distorted signals or unclear sounds, and may have difficulty integrating information about sound that can be used in a productive way for communication. Jones[12] described the incubator as significantly distorting the high sound levels continuously present in the NICU. Not only did the incubator tend to impair transmission of speech frequencies, it also deflected them, making it difficult for the infant to find the source of the sound. Lawson, Daum, and Turkewitz[19] reported that during the five 24-hour periods that they observed the NICU, nonspeech sounds were clearly audible in and out of the incubator 100% of the time. Other authors[22] have reported that adult speech and mechanical and activity sounds comprised between 45% and 65% of the total amount of background sounds that were clearly audible during the daytime hours. Sound-intensity levels in NICUs have been measured at an average of 70–80 decibels with frequent fluctuations.[23]

The number of people who have contact with infants in the NICU also may affect parent–infant interaction. For example, Sherman[20] pointed out that numerous health care providers interact with the infant in order to maintain medical stability. The necessary care of nurses, physicians, social workers, and physical, respiratory, speech-hearing, and occupational therapists may interfere with a parent's attempt to initiate and maintain interaction with the infant. Finally, Linn et al,[22] found that toys—which might provide a focus for shared parent–infant interaction—were often positioned in the isolette so the infants could not see them.

Another variable that may have potential effects on parent–infant interaction in the NICU is the medical status of the infant and the medical interventions necessary to maintain the infant. Als[24] identified the critical nature of the infant's health and the rapidly changing condition of that health as necessarily impinging on the development of an interactional relationship. In a study conducted by Minde and colleagues,[25] seriously ill infants showed less movement and opened their eyes less during acutely ill periods. As they became medically more stable, their behavior approximated the behavior of well infants. The mothers of the "sick" infants touched and smiled at their infants significantly less than mothers of otherwise healthy preterm infants. This passivity and reluctance of the mothers to interact persisted even after infants' medical condition stabilized and they began behaving like their 'well' counterparts.

Marton, Dawson & Minde,[26] observed that premature infants received a little over eight minutes of contact time per hour from ward personnel, and most of those contacts were for medical procedures. Other researchers have documented that medical treatment, as well as caregiving activities, increase infant arousal state.[16] These authors examined videotapes of caregiver–infant activity over a 24-hour period at six specific times for 102 infants. They found that infants tended to remain aroused long after aversive medical procedures, such as injections and suctioning. Blackburn and Barnard[16] described the physiologic changes that the infant in an aroused state experiences, including cardiorespiratory irregularities, color changes, and more irregular motoric responses. In this state of behavioral disorganization, the infant may be unavailable for interaction.[24] In addition, Jones[18] has reported that infants with respiratory distress syndrome (RDS) were discouraged by staff from crying, one of the most powerful early communication signals.

Parental characteristics may also affect the development of parent–infant interaction. Jones[18] found that the amount of time that the parents spent in the NICU was inversely related to how far they lived from the hospital. Since many NICUs are regionally based, parents may be unable to spend the amount of time with their infant that is necessary to learn to read the infant's signals and develop more successful interaction.

Sherman[20] described a number of potential reactions that parents may experience in response to having a sick or premature infant. As parents adjust to the discrepancy between their expectations and reality, they may feel an overpowering sense of grief, guilt, and anger that may make it difficult to engage with the infant.[27,28] They may express feelings of inadequacy through ambivalence that could limit the number of times they attempt interaction with the infant. Sherman[20] suggested that the father may have to provide family stability early in the NICU treatment process, since the mother may be recuperating from a medically invasive birth. This altered role may give the father unique responsibility for being the first parent to interact with the infant on a regular basis.[22]

PARENT–INFANT INTERACTION IN THE NICU

Early parent visits to the NICU have been described as infrequent and tenuous.[30,31] In a study reported by Minde, Trehub, et al,[32] mothers appeared to be less confident and more passive with their infants during this early period, preferring to look at the infants rather than interact more actively. Those mothers who visited more frequently and for longer periods were also those who interacted more dynamically. Over time, mothers visited more frequently and became more actively involved. They used essentially the same interactive behaviors during early and later visits; however, the number of occurrences of those behaviors significantly increased. Others have reported that mothers who were more active on the NICU were also more actively involved with the infant during the first three months at home.[30]

Psychologic well-being of the mother has been identified as a variable affecting the quality of mother–infant interaction on the NICU. In a study conducted by Minde, Marton, et al,[30] mothers were interviewed by a child psychiatrist three to four weeks after the infant's admission to the NICU and received a composite psychologic risk score. Those mothers who were judged to be more hesitant in interacting with their infants on the NICU had much lower psychologic well-being scores than mothers who tended to be more assertive in their interaction behavior. The combination of such factors as socioeconomic status, maternal age, gestational age of the infant, and perinatal medical complications added significantly less to the accuracy of prediction.

Using time-lag sequential analysis, Marton, Minde, and Ogilvie[33] determined that mothers modified their behavior in response to the infant's signals. Mothers who were more responsive smiled more in response to an infant's stretch and touched the infant more frequently when the infant's eyes were opened. Mothers who tended to interact less actively did not respond immediately to the infant signals of ''stretch'' and "eyes open."

Research examining parent–infant interaction on the NICU has focused primarily on the mother. A small number of studies have investigated the role fathers play during interactional sequences with their preterm infants. Marton, Minde, and Perotta[29] presented data that suggest that mothers talk to their infants more than fathers do and that infants behave differently when fathers rather than mothers are present. In a study conducted by Thurman and Korteland[34] fathers were more disengaged during their visits to the NICU and interacted with their infants in a more remote fashion than the mothers, who were more affectionate. Each parent communicated more with the infant when alone than when they visited together.

Data presented by Levy-Shiff, Shari, and Molgari[35] examined parent–infant interaction behavior when the infant was transferred from intensive care to transitional care. Initially, mothers continued to be more involved than fathers during interaction by exhibiting more caretaking, talking, and holding behavior. At the time of the infant's discharge from the transitional unit, however, both mother and father were equally active with the infant. Mothers tended to assume more caregiving responsibility whereas fathers played with and stimulated the infants

---

Variables That May Affect Parent–Infant Interaction In the NICU*

Infant variables
Medical status
Degree of prematurity
Neurologic integrity

Parent variables
Distance from the NICU
Emotional reactions
Altered roles
Psychologic well-being
Social support

NICU environmental variables
Noncontingent sensory stimulation from light, sound, heat
Medical interventions
Activity flow

*These variables are cited in references included within the text.

more. Although mothers in this study felt that the infants were more difficult to handle than fathers did, the mothers reportedly enjoyed the infants more. When infants were more physically mobile and alert, parent involvement became more passive. When the infants became distressed or were less active, the parents responded in a more active way by stimulating, playing with, or talking more to the infant.

Numerous factors that may affect parent–infant interaction in the NICU have been identified in the preceding review. These factors are summarized in the boxed material. The complex interaction of these factors may complicate the development of social interaction between parent and infant. Modifications in one or more of these variables may affect the development of parent–infant interaction.

Having identified these factors, it is possible to draw implications for both research and service delivery. The remainder of this article addresses these implications.

IMPLICATIONS FOR SERVICE DELIVERY AND RESEARCH

According to Gorski[36] the developing preterm infant progresses through three stages in the NICU: the "interning" stage, the "coming out" stage, and the "reciprocity stage." During the interning stage, infants are directing all of their energy to sustaining behavioral organization and, therefore, have little strength remaining to direct socially. These infants are generally unresponsive to the communicative environment. Attempts from caregivers to intrude on the infant's efforts to maintain stability may disrupt the physiologic balance the infant is fighting to maintain.[27]

Gorski[36] suggests that during the coming out and reciprocity stages, infants begin to tolerate brief interchanges with the environment. In the reciprocity stage, infants become increasingly able to send and receive interactive signals. These signals have been described as vague and subtle, often making them difficult to interpret and respond to appropriately.[9] Consequently, caregivers need to observe the infant over time and identify those infant behaviors that communicate information. In addition, caregivers must determine when those behaviors are more likely to occur. Early interactive signals might include physical movement of the head or extremities, visual gazing, and vocalizations.[28,37]

Because of their immature central nervous system, infants have difficulty maintaining their equilibrium and may require excessive effort to return to a state of behavioral organization following stimulation.[38] As a result, caregivers must respond to an infant's need for frequent respites from active interaction. They must also tailor their interaction style so that infants can integrate new behaviors. For example, one may speculate that the characteristics of 'motherese,'[39] which include higher pitch, exaggerated intonational contour, and increased affective tone often used by caregivers with normally developing infants, may be inappropriate for the preterm infant in the NICU. Instead, caregivers may initiate communication slowly and quietly, minimize the stimulation provided by sound and touch, and gradually increase that stimulation as the infant becomes more tolerant.[27]

Some behaviors of preterm infants have been identified as consistent indicators of distress (eg, limb hyperextension, rapid state changes).[38] Directions for future research on infant variables should focus on developing a better understanding of early warning signs associated with behavioral disintegration. Additional research could also help elucidate the interventions that facilitate behavioral reintegration. Blackburn and Barnard[16] have presented data examining whether rocking infants and the sounds of simulating heartbeats help infants maintain stability, while others have also examined the positive effects of proprioceptive and kinesthetic input.[40,41]

An assessment of parent strengths and needs would provide direction for enhancing parent interaction with infants on the NICU. For some parents, basic needs such as transportation and financial management (to deal with the expenses incurred during the infant's hospital stay) may preempt attempts to develop parent interaction skills.[42] For other parents, an opportunity to have their questions answered may reduce their stress and allow them to approach interaction more positively.[43] In a study by Bustan and Sagi[44] mothers of NICU infants who received education, counseling, and emotional support played with their infants in a more assertive, vigorous fashion. Infants of these mothers vocalized more and cried less than the infants in the control group. Juntii[43] described the successful use of the Brazelton Neonatal Assessment Scale to educate parents about infant behavior. Continued research to understand the counseling and information needs of parents with NICU infants should be undertaken so that intervention techniques can be developed to better meet these concerns.

Parents whose infants are in the NICU experience an increased amount of personal stress.[45] The relationship between stress and social isolation has been documented in the literature.[46] Furthermore, research has indicated that parents who have access to a variety of family resources and social supports are more likely to participate successfully in interventions for their children and feel more positively about their own well-being.[47] Minde et al[38] presented data that indicated that the mothers who were relatively inactive during interaction with their NICU infant were the mothers who had minimal social support resources.

Considering the usefulness of a wide-based social support system, caregivers interested in facilitating parent–infant interaction in the NICU should help parents use both formal and informal social support networks. Smith[48] described a parent volunteer group which, through the administration of a social worker and nursing care supervisor, allowed parents of infants previously treated in the NICU to provide support to parents of infants currently being treated. In addition, parents can be encouraged to bring extended family members with them to the NICU and to their medical appointments. Further research should be directed to understanding how parents with NICU infants can be encouraged to take advantage of a variety of social supports. One approach to enhancing social support and responding to identified family needs in the NICU has recently been described by Thurman, Cornwell, and Korteland.[49] This approach, The Liaison Infant Family Team (LIFT), is based on an ecologic model that focuses on the development of an "adaptive fit" among families, infants, and service delivery systems.

Most research examining parent–infant interaction in the NICU has focused on the mother. Research to date suggests that fathers talk less to their infants than mothers do and that the infants respond differently to the father. Future study should be directed to understanding paternal needs and patterns of interaction. In addition, it remains to be determined how satisfied fathers are with their interaction attempts and how behaviorally responsive infants are to them. More information about fathers is critical to identify new directions for intervention.

Many NICUs are regionally based, and therefore parents who are required to drive long distances to visit the infant may visit less frequently. Without ongoing contact and the resulting lack of familiarity, these parents may experience more difficulty establishing an interactional bond with their infants.[50] Caregivers interested in enhancing parent–infant interaction will need to develop living arrangements closer to the hospital to accommodate the parents' need to be close to their infant. Likewise, social services may help parents address other daily living needs such as finding babysitters for siblings and getting temporary leave from work. Continued research can clarify the relationship between parent visitation and parent–infant interaction. Rosenfield[31] reported a relationship between more alert and active infant state levels and increased frequency of visiting by the mothers; however, the direction of this relationship is not clear. With further study, the frequency and pattern of parental visiting may be used to identify families at risk who may require psychologic intervention.[33]

Parents can learn interaction skills that facilitate contact with their infant when they are ready.[51] Parents can learn how to read their infant's interaction signals during the preterm and neonatal period.[52] When an infant indicates readiness to interact, the parents can learn to respond slowly, with modulated tone and minimal stimulation, and gradually increase the dynamics of the interaction to match the infant's level of endurance. Physical contact can also be encouraged for those infants able to tolerate it. White-Traut[41] presented data that indicated that teaching mothers how to stimulate their infants through massage positively affected the quality of mother–infant interaction.

Continued research may identify subtle cues parents have used successfully to interact with their preterm infants; these cues may prove useful to other parents with similar infants.

Alteration of the physical environment in the NICU may also facilitate more optimal parent–infant interaction.[24] The bright lights and loud, often distorted auditory input could be modulated to better match the infant's cycles of arousal and to provide less distractions to the parent. Background noise from radios or from groups of caregivers conferring about an infant can be altered with simple modifications, while the frequent auditory disruptions imposed by medical alert equipment may be less easily adjusted. Blanket rolls added to the infant's warmer bed or incubator may provide the infant's feet and sides with necessary support and thus enhance behavioral integration and interaction potential. Through observation of the infant's status over time, hospital staff and parents may be better able to match caregiving and medical routines to an infant's cycles of arousal, and to cluster those interventions to decrease the number of times the infant is required to manage stimulation that will stress his current level of organization.

When providing medical and caregiving interventions, staff should be encouraged to accompany this contact with nurturant behavior and to interact socially with the infants independent of medical and caregiving tasks. In a study conducted by S.K. Thurman, et al (unpublished data, May 1989) only 4.1% of the observed behavior of physicians and nurses was directed solely to nurturant or communicative contact to infants. Also, very low percentages of the observed medical (3.1%) and caregiving (9.4%) contacts of physicians and nurses to infants were coupled with communicative behavior.

Little is known about the stimulating effects of the NICU environment on the quality of parent–infant interaction.[53] Infant responses to changes in environmental stimulation, such as dimmed lighting and elimination of nonessential auditory input, will need to be monitored. Many NICUs are now also attempting to synchronize caregiving and medical procedures with infant cycles of arousal. Identifying strategies for determining which cycles are the best interaction periods for the infant is essential. Researchers must begin to monitor the efficacy of this approach by measuring such variables as frequency and depth of infant distress as well as speed of recovery. Finally, Blackburn and Barnard[16] observed that social interaction occurred much less frequently than medical and caregiving procedures. The effects of increased social interaction and infant arousal attempts should be measured, and the best means for decreasing arousal when it threatens behavioral integration of the infant should be identified. High and Gorski[53] noted that the infants in the NICU they monitored had long periods without contact from the environment, and this may have enhanced the infants' ability to remain behaviorally integrated.

• • •

This article has focused on the interactive relationship between parents and their infants in neonatal intensive care. A search of the literature revealed that relatively little research has been done that specifically studies this relationship. Nonetheless, the present article has identified a number of variables that may be important in determining the degree and nature of parent–infant interactions in the NICU. The significance of these interactions cannot be emphasized enough if one accepts the premise that early parent–infant interactions are critical to the formation of attachment and help to determine the character of later relationships between parents and their children. Clearly, more research is needed to understand these variables and their interaction in determining the nature of the earliest interactions between preterm and seriously ill infants and their parents.

The passage and implementation of Public Law 99-457 sets the stage to provide services at birth to handicapped and significantly at-risk infants and their families. This means that service delivery models must be developed that respond to the needs of infants and their parents in the very earliest days of life.

REFERENCES

1. Cunningham CE, Reular E, Blackwell J, Deck J. Behavioral and linguistic development in the interactions of normal and retarded children with their mothers. *Child Dev.* 1981;52:62–70.
2. DiVitto B, Goldberg S. The effects of newborn medical status on early parent–infant interaction. In Field TM, ed. *Infants Born At Risk: Behavior and Development.* Jamaica, NY: SP Medical and Scientific Books; 1979:311–332.
3. Walker J. Social interactions of handicapped infants. In: Bricker D, ed. *Intervention With At-Risk Handicapped Infants: From Research to Application.* Baltimore: University Park Press; 1982:217–232.
4. Crnic K, Ragozin A, Greenberg M, Robinson N, Basham R. Social interaction and developmental competence of preterm and full-term infants during the first year of life. *Child Dev.* 1983;54:1199–1210.
5. Brooks-Gunn J, Lewis M. Temperament and affective interaction in handicapped infants. *J Div Early Child.* 1982;5:31–41.
6. Buckhalt J, Rutherford R, Goldberg K. Verbal and nonverbal interactions of mothers with their Down syndrome and nonretarded infants. *Am J Mental Def.* 1978;82:337–343.
7. Field T. Effects of early separation, interactive deficits, and experimental manipulations on infant mother face-to-face interactions. *Child Dev.* 1977;43:763–771.
8. Jones CL. Criteria for evaluating infant care environments in hospitals. *J Assoc Care Child Hosp.* 1979;1:3.
9. Yoder PJ. Relationship between degree of infant handicap and clarity of infant cues. *Am J Mental Def.* 1987;91(6):639 641.
10. Greene JG, Fox NA, Lewis M. The relationship between neonatal characteristics and three month mother-infant interaction in high risk infants. *Child Dev.* 1983;54:1286–1296.
11. Leifer A, Leiderman P, Barnett C, Williams J. Effects of mother-infant separation on maternal attachment behavior. *Child Dev.* 1972;43:1203–1218.
12. Klaus M, Kennell J, Plumb M, Zuehlke S. Human maternal behavior at the first contact with her young. *Pediatrics.* 1970;46:187–192.
13. Crawford JW. Mother-infant interaction in premature and full-term infants. *Child Dev.* 1982;53:957–962.
14. Lester BM, Hoffman J, Brazelton TB. The rhythmic structure of mother-infant interaction in term and preterm infants. *Child Dev.* 1985;56:15–27.

15. Sameroff AJ, Chandler MJ. Reproductive risk and the continuum of caretaking casualty. In: Horowitz FD, Hetherington M. Scarr-Salapatek S, Siegel G, eds. *Review of Child Development Research (Vol. 4).* Chicago: University of Chicago Press; 1975:187–243.

16. Blackburn S, Barnard K. Analysis of caregiving events relating to preterm infants in the special care unit. In: Gottfried A, Gaiter J, eds. *Infant Stress Under Intensive Care.* Baltimore: University Park Press; 1985:113–129.

17. Wolke D. Environmental and developmental neonatology. *J Repro Inf Psychol.* 1987;5:17–42.

18. Jones CL. Environmental analysis of neonatal intensive care. *J Nerv Ment Dis.* 1982;170:130–142.

19. Lawson K, Daum C, Turkewitz G: Environmental characteristics of a neonatal intensive-care unit. *Child Dev.* 1977;48:1633–1639.

20. Sherman M. The neonatal intensive care unit. *Psychiatr Clin of North Am.* 1982;5(2):433–443.

21. Rosetti L. *High Risk Infants: Identification, Assessment and Intervention.* Boston: Little, Brown; 1986.

22. Linn PL, Horowitz FD, Buddin BJ, Leake JC, Fox HA. An ecological description of a neonatal intensive care unit. In: Gottfried AW, Gaiter JL, eds. *Infant Stress Under Intensive Care.* Baltimore: University Park Press; 1985:83–112.

23. Gottfried AW, Wallace-Lande P, Sherman-Brown S, King J, Coen C, Hodgman JE. Physical and social environment of newborn infants in special care units. *Science.* 1981;214(6):673–675.

24. Als H. A synactive model of neonatal behavioral organization: framework for the assessment and support of the neuro-behavioral development of the preterm infant and his parents in the environment of the neonatal intensive care unit. In: Sweeney JK, ed. *The high-risk neonate: Developmental therapy perspectives. Physical and Occupational Therapy in Pediatrics.* 1986;6(34):3–55.

25. Minde KK, Whitelaw A, Brown J, Fitzhardinge P. Effects of neonatal complications in the premature nursery on early parent–infant interactions. *Dev Med Child Neur.* 1983;25:763–777.

26. Marton PL, Dawson H, Minde KK. The interaction of ward personnel with infants in the premature nursery. *Inf Behavior Dev.* 1980;3:307–313.

27. Als H, Lawhon G, Brown E, Gibes R, Duffy FH, McAnulty G, Blickman JG. Individualized behavioral and environmental care for the very low birth weight preterm infant at high risk for bronchopulmonary dysplasia: Neonatal intensive care unit and developmental outcome. *Pediatrics.* 1986;78(6):1123–1132.

28. Peterson N. *Early Intervention for Handicapped and At-Risk Children.* Denver: Love Publishing; 1987.

29. Marton P, Minde K, Perotta M. The role of the father for the infant at risk. *Am J Orthopsych.* 1981;51:672–679.

30. Minde KK, Marton P, Manning D, Hines B. Some determinants of mother-infant interaction in the premature nursery. *J Am Acad Child Psych.* 1980;19:1–21.

31. Rosenfield AG. Visiting the intensive care nursery. *Child Dev.* 1980;51:939–941.

32. Minde KK, Trehub S, Corter C, Boukydis C, Celhoffer L, Marton P. Mother-child relationships in the premature nursery. *Pediatrics.* 1978;61:373–379.

33. Marton P, Minde K, Ogilvie J. Mother-infant interactions in the premature nursery: a sequential analysis. In: Friedman SL, Sigman M, eds. *Pre-term Birth and Psychological Development.* New York: Academic Press; 1981:179–205.

34. Thurman SK, Korteland C. The behavior of mothers and fathers toward their infants during neonatal intensive care visits. *Children's Health Care*, in press.

35. Levy-Shiff R, Shari H, Molgari MB. Mother- and father-preterm infant relationship in the hospital preterm nursery. *Child Dev.* 1989;60:93–102.

36. Gorski PA. Premature infants behavioral and physiological responses to caregiving interventions in the intensive care nursery. In: Call JD, Galenson E, Tyson KL, eds. *Frontiers in Infant Psychiatry.* New York: Basic Books; 1983:256–263.

37. Yoder PJ. Clarifying the relationship between degree of infant handicap and maternal responsivity to infant communicative cues: Measurement issues. *Inf Mental Health J.* 1986;7:281–293.

38. Gorski PA, Hole WT, Leonard CH, Martin RJ. Direct computer recording of premature infants and nursery care: Distress following two interventions. *Pediatrics.* 1983;72:198–202.

39. Snow C. The development of conversation between mothers and babies. *J Child Lang.* 1977;4: 1–22.

40. Powell LF. The effect of extra stimulation and maternal involvement on the development of lowbirth-weight infants and or maternal behavior. *Child Dev.* 1974;45:106–113.

41. White-Traut RC. Maternal-infant interaction as a function of maternal stimulation of the premature infant initiated at twenty-four hours of infant age. *Dissert Abstr*, June, 1983.

42. Turnbull A. The challenge of providing comprehensive support to families. *Educ Train Mental Retarded.* 1988;23(4):261–272.

43. Juntii MJ. Use of the Brazelton Neonatal Assessment Scale to educate parents of high risk infants. *Inf Mental Health J.* 1982;3:180–183.

44. Bustan D, Sagi A. Effects of early hospital-based intervention on mothers and their preterm infants. *J Applied Dev Psychol.* 1984;5:305–317.

45. Affleck G, Tennen H, Rowe J, Roscher B, Walker L. Effects of formal support on mothers' adaptation to the hospital-to-home transition of high-risk infants: The benefits and costs of helping. *Child Dev.* 1989;60:488–501.

46. Wahler RG. The insular mother: Her problems in parent-child treatment. *J Applied Beh Analysis.* 1980; 13:207–219.

47. Dunst CJ, Leet HE, Trivette CM. Family resources, personal well-being and early intervention. *J Spec Educ.* 1988;22(1):108–116.

48. Smith AV: Parent outreach in a neonatal intensive care nursery. *Social Work.* 1986;31(1):69–73.

49. Thurman SK, Cornwell JR, Korteland C. The Liaison Infant Family Team (LIFT) Project: An example of case study evaluation. *Inf Young Children.* 2(2):74–82.

50. Field T, Widmayer S, Stringer S, Ignatoff E. Teenage, lower class, black mothers and their preterm infants: An intervention and developmental follow-up. *Child Dev.* 1980;51:426–431.

51. Stengel TJ. Infant behavior, maternal psychological reaction, and mother-infant interaction issues associated with the crisis of prematurity: A selected review of the literature. *Physical Occup Ther Pediatr.* 1982; 2(213):3–24.

52. Als H, Lester BM, Brazelton TB. Dynamics of the behavioral organization of the premature infant: a theoretical perspective. In: Field TM, Sostek AM, Goldberg S, Shuman HH, eds. *Infants Born At Risk: Behavior and Development.* New York: SP Medical and Scientific Books; 1979:173–192.

53. High PC, Gorski PA. Recording environmental influences on infant development in the intensive care nursery. In: Gottfried A, Gaiter J, eds. *Infant Stress Under Intensive Care.* Baltimore: University Park Press; 1985:131–155.

Attachment in infants at risk: Theory, research, and practice

Susan Goldberg, PhD
Psychiatric Research Unit
The Hospital for Sick Children
Department of Psychology and
    Faculty of Medicine
University of Toronto
Toronto, Ontario, Canada

THE NATURE OF THE infant–caregiver relationship and its significance in subsequent development have been sources of fascination and speculation for both researchers and clinicians. In the past 20 years, there has been a dramatic proliferation of empiric work in this domain, much of it highly relevant to clinical practice. The purpose of this article is to summarize that work, particularly studies of infants with developmental or medical problems, and to highlight its significance for clinicians. The history and theory of attachment as outlined by John Bowlby and others are briefly reviewed, the laboratory techniques developed to study attachment are explained, and the research with normal and biologically at-risk infants is summarized. Finally, the clinical implications of this research are detailed.

ATTACHMENT THEORY AND ORIGINS

The three most common terms in the literature on infant–caregiver relationships are "object relations" (in psychoanalytic theory), "dependency" (in social learning theory), and "attachment" (in Bowlby's[1-4] ethologic theory). Efforts to observe and study these relationships have occurred within each of these theoretic frameworks, but it is the last of these that has engendered the most recent wave of empiric studies.

In his theoretic work, Bowlby[1-4] sought to integrate concepts from psychoanalysis and ethology. His work has been elaborated and tested empirically, first by Ainsworth et al[5,6] and later by others. Bowlby argued that the affectional ties between infant and caregiver have biologic underpinnings that must be viewed in an evolutionary context. Because the survival of infants depends on adult caregiving, infants are genetically "biased" to behave in ways that enhance and maintain proximity to the caregiver, and caregivers are biased to behave reciprocally. Over the course of the first year, the infant's proximity-promoting behaviors (including orienting to the caregiver, signals such as cries and vocalizations, and direct actions such as approaching and clinging) become organized into a goal-corrected system focused on a specific caregiver. The mother is usually the first such attachment figure, but other caregivers can also serve this role. However, since the majority of studies were concerned with infant–mother relationships, this discussion will focus on mothers. When the attachment system is in its goal state (ie, has adequate proximity and contact), attachment behaviors subside; when the goal state is threatened, attachment behaviors are activated. Further-

Inf Young Children, 1990; 2(4): 11–20

more, because the attachment system operates in the context of other interrelated systems (eg, exploration), the goal is adjusted to the context. Thus, for a healthy infant in a familiar (safe) environment, the goal may be to remain in the same room with the attachment figure, but if the infant is tired or ill, or if the environment is unfamiliar, the goal is adjusted to the attainment of greater proximity.

When considering attachment in infants with medical or developmental problems, it is necessary to bear in mind the possibility that the goals of the dyad may differ from those in dyads including low-risk infants. As the child matures and develops more complex skills, the goal is adjusted to accept more frequent, more distal, and longer separations. The overall goal remains felt security,[6] but the conditions conducive to meeting the goal change with development. Once again, this shift in goals may progress at a different rate or have a different developmental end point when medical or developmental problems are present.

ASSESSMENT OF ATTACHMENT

A major step in attachment research was taken when Ainsworth et al[5,6] used Bowlby's ideas to develop a standardized methodology, known as the "strange situation procedure," for assessing the quality of attachment to the mother in infants 12 to 18 months old. This procedure focuses primarily on the infant and is thought to reflect the infant's understanding and expectations of the mother's behavior.

The strange situation procedure is the laboratory observation of eight episodes in which the caregiver and a female stranger interact with, depart from and reunite with the infant in an environment that offers the child opportunities for exploration. As the episodes proceed to a first and then second separation from the caregiver, the child is assumed to be more stressed and to have increased needs for proximity. The extent to which the child is successful in coping with these needs and the strategy chosen to do so is considered indicative of the quality of attachment. Scoring depends on detailed review from videotapes of the changing balance of exploratory and attachment behaviors. The infant is rated for features of caregiver-directed behavior:
- contact seeking,
- contact maintaining,
- distance interaction,
- avoidance, and
- resistance to contact.

From this information, the dyad is classified into one of eight subtypes that fall into three broad categories (Table 1). Although behavior throughout the entire session is considered, reunion behaviors have been shown to be the most salient feature distinguishing these patterns.[5]

Table 1. Attachment classifications

	A (two subgroups) insecure (avoidant)	B (four subgroups) secure	C (two subgroups) insecure (ambivalent/ resistant)
Preseparation behavior	Little attention to mother, explores freely	Explores freely but "checks in" with mother	Preoccupied with mother, little exploration
Behavior to stranger	May be more sociable to stranger than mother	Responds with interest to stranger, looks at or moves toward mother while doing so	May cling to mother and reject or withdraw from stranger
Behavior at separation	Little distress	May or may not be distressed, makes concrete efforts to contact mother (eg, follow to door, call, search)	Extreme distress, may make some search efforts, may be angry or helpless
Behavior at reunion	Snubs or ignores mother or is slow to warm up to her invitations	Greets mother positively, if distressed makes physical contact and is comforted	Ambivalent response, seeks and rejects contact, refuses to be comforted

These three major patterns reflect strategies used by the infant to manage affective arousal in the context of interactions with, separations from, and reunions with the caregiver. In some dyads, there does not appear to be an identifiable coherent strategy. Main and Solomon[7] developed a system for scoring the extent to which the predominant strategy is well organized (and classifiable in the traditional scheme) or poorly organized (and not classifiable as one of the three predominant strategies). In the latter case, the predominant feature is identifiable only as disorganized/disoriented attachment (D). Preliminary data suggest that this represents a very insecure pattern, as it was first identified in maltreated children and those with depressed parents.[8-10] The D scheme may be especially relevant to use with infants at risk, as several groups of investigators[11-13] have found that a high proportion of at-risk infants and toddlers are not readily classifiable in the traditional scheme. However, reasons for classification difficulty other than disorganization (eg, immature behavior, motor handicaps) also affect the assessments of at-risk infants.

In samples of healthy, middle-class children in North America,[5] two of three are secure, two of nine are insecure-avoidant, and one of nine is insecure-ambivalent.

Moreover, the statistical analysis[14] of 39 studies from eight countries (admittedly weighted by a large number of North American studies) indicated that, in close to 2,000 healthy developing children, the same distribution of these three major types of attachment was observed (65% secure, 21% avoidant, 14% ambivalent).

NORMATIVE DATA ON ATTACHMENT: VALIDITY OF THE STRANGE SITUATION

Identification of consistent patterns is not sufficient evidence that strange situation procedure behavior is a good indicator of quality of attachment. Investigators need to know that there is some consistency or stability in the child's behavior over time, that there is a relation between behavior in the strange situation procedure and caregiver–child interaction in real life, and that strange situation procedure behavior is related to other aspects of child development and family functioning in theoretically expectable ways. This evidence is summarized.

Consistency or stability

Because the strange situation procedure is both salient and moderately stressful for infants and toddlers, it is not feasible to repeat the procedure within a short interval.[7] However, under stable life conditions, patterns of attachment remain stable in both short-term (eg, 6 months)[15] and long-term (eg, up to 5 years)[16] follow-ups. These data refer to attachment to the same caregiver assessed on different occasions. A number of studies[16–18] have compared child behavior with different caregivers (mother and father), and the patterns of attachment to mother and to father are found to be independent. Thus, patterns of behavior in the strange situation procedure reflect qualities of distinct relationships rather than a trait of the child.

Behavior and interaction

Patterns of attachment behavior in the strange situation procedure are related to both prior and concurrent behavior in the home. Mothers of secure infants have been rated more sensitive, responsive, accessible, and cooperative at home in the first year than mothers of insecure infants.[5,19–23] Although there is some evidence that infant characteristics and/or behaviors may also predict the subsequent quality of attachment,[24,25] those findings have been less consistent than those on maternal behavior. This suggests that the mother plays a more influential role than the infant in shaping the quality of the relationship.

A discussion has been ongoing in the literature as to the extent to which infant temperament affects attachment.[16,26–29] The most recent evidence[16,29] indicates that, whereas some aspects of behavior in the strange situation are related to temperament (eg, the amount of distress at separation), security per se is independent of temperament. Main et al[16,30] found that the "states of mind" of parents regarding their own attachment experiences are related to the attachment patterns of their infants. Parents whose infants are avoidant dismiss their own attachment experiences as unimportant, and idealize past relationships or cannot recall them. Parents with ambivalent infants appear to be enmeshed with their own parents, while those with securely attached infants value attachments and have achieved a realistic view of their own attachments. Those with disorganized infants were most likely to be coping with the unresolved loss of attachment figures.

Development and family functioning

An increasing number of studies[5,16,31-38] show that secure infants are more competent than insecure infants in a variety of subsequent cognitive and social skills up to age 6 years. There have been several studies assessing the relation between early attachment and subsequent behavior problems. Sroufe[29] and Sroufe and Egeland[39] found that up to age 8, children who as infants were securely attached to their mothers were less likely to have behavior problems than those who were insecurely attached. Lewis and colleagues[40] earlier reported a similar finding, but only for boys. However, at least one longitudinal study[41] produced conflicting data showing that early attachment was not related to preschool behavior problems. More recently, Greenberg et al[42] reported that, among children with conduct disorders, 85% were concurrently insecurely attached. (Infancy data for this sample were not available.) Thus, although data are accumulating to suggest that early insecure attachment as assessed in the strange situation procedure is associated with subsequent behavior problems, the connection is not yet fully convincing. Many current studies are focused on this question.

Although there is a propensity for early attachment patterns to persevere, changes are also possible and may be highly likely when the family environment changes. Therefore, it would be useful to have measures of attachment at ages beyond infancy. While the strange situation procedure has been in use for infants for over 20 years, parallel measures for preschoolers,[43] children 5 to 7 years old,[44] and adults[45] have only been recently developed and are currently being standardized and validated. It will soon be possible to study developmental changes in attachment over a broad age span, but at present there are only limited data about the relation between early attachment and later parent–child relationships.

Although the strange situation procedure and related procedures have contributed to a valuable and coherent body of data, there have also been methodologic and theoretic criticisms.[26,46-48] Space does not permit a thorough review of these, as the purpose of the present article is to review the research within the attachment framework. The interested reader is referred to the sources above for this purpose.

ATTACHMENT IN INFANTS AT BIOLOGIC RISK

Preterm infants

There have been numerous studies of attachment in infants with various medical and developmental problems. Many were motivated by the expectation that such infants would be particularly vulnerable to insecure attachments, which in turn, partly stems from the expectation that stress and family disruption associated with such problems would be associated with inadequate parental care. Infants born prematurely have most commonly been the subject of these studies. It has been shown that the early social interaction styles of preterm and full-term mother–infant pairs differ.[49] However, the majority of studies that used the strange situation procedure with preterm infants reported[20,50–52] that the distribution of attachment patterns did not differ significantly from the norms. Only one such study[53] diverged from this pattern, in finding that preterm, low birth weight infants who were more seriously ill were more likely to be ambivalently attached. This finding contrasts with the data of Goldberg et al,[20] in which more serious neonatal illness in a similar low birth weight group was found to characterize secure rather than insecurely attached infants. The reasons for this discrepancy are not clear. In addition, it was found[20] that the pattern of relations between attachment and prior home observations over the first year differed from the patterns generally reported in the full-term population. Although mothers of very secure infants (B_2, B_3) had received the highest ratings for sensitivity and responsiveness (as expected), those of ambivalent and resistant (insecure) infants had received intermediate ratings, and the lowest ratings had been given to mothers of secure infants with some signs of avoidance or ambivalence (B_1, B_4).

More recently, the original strange situation procedure videotapes were reviewed using the Main and Solomon[7] criteria for disorganization,[12] because it was felt that many of the infants had been difficult to score. This review indicated that, in comparison with a healthy control group, the proportion of securely attached infants in the preterm sample was significantly lower (54% v 74%; ie, some "previously secure" infants were now considered "disorganized"). Because other studies of preterm infants have not used the D scheme, it is not clear whether this will be a consistent finding. However, there is some consensus among the above investigators that preterm infants are often difficult to classify and that it is necessary to assess preterm infants at the older end of the 12- to 18-month period (with correction for prematurity), when cognitive and motor skills basic to organization of attachment are sufficiently mature.

Developmental delay

Several studies have used the strange situation procedure with toddlers or preschoolers with developmental delays. Cicchetti and Serafica[54] provided descriptive data on the behavior of toddlers with Down syndrome in the strange situation process, but did not use classifications. More recently, Goldberg[11] and Vaughn[13] reported difficulties in using the standard classification scheme with toddlers and preschoolers with developmental delays. In each case, about a third of the sample were not initially classifiable. In this study, with the addition of a mixed avoidant/ambivalent category (A/C) described by Crittenden[8] and Radke-Yarrow et al,[9] classification of all but eight children in a group with Down syndrome, neurologic impairments, or delays of unknown etiology was possible. With the exception of the A/C group (7%), the distribution of the remaining subjects did not differ from the normative distribution ($2/3$ secure), nor was there any indication of diagnostic group differences in patterns of attachment.[11] (The mixed A/C pattern has previously been associated with very inadequate child care by a depressed mother[9] or in a family with known maltreatment problems[8,10] and is considered to be a very insecure attachment pattern. It is also now considered one pattern of disorganized/disoriented attachment,[7] as it captures a dyad with a mixture of conflicting strategies rather than a coherent strategy.) Vaughn's findings[13] were somewhat different, as the proportion of securely attached toddlers in his Down syndrome group was lower than expected from the normative predictions.

Infants with physical handicaps

Two studies of neurologically impaired[55] and physically handicapped infants[56] also reported the use of the standard classification scheme with atypical populations, in which the distribution of attachment patterns was similar to that of the normative data. However, because the infant's locomotion relative to the attachment figure is used in scoring, it is clear that the strange situation procedure and the standard classification scheme are not appropriate for infants and toddlers with very limited motor skills. Recently, two attempts to adapt the strange situation procedure for such children were reported. Siera[57] observed 28 infants with mild to moderate cerebral palsy. Modifications were made in the interactive rating scales to facilitate classifications, and with this modification, she found an increased proportion of avoidant infants (43%) and a new subgroup of avoidant infants described as "passive-avoidant." In general, the securely attached infants demonstrated higher levels of developmental competence. Pianta and Marvin[58] described a modified procedure for assessing infants with severe motor impairments, which includes a series of graded mother–infant separations before maternal departure, including cessation of physical contact and proximity and the infant being handed to a friendly stranger. In a pilot study with 15 infants, none was able to tolerate maternal departure. However, with appropriate modifications in classification criteria to take into account their limited motor skills (eg, greater reliance on visual and manual exploration and greeting) all infants could be classified and half were considered secure.

Chronic illness in infants

The author and colleagues have begun to study attachment in two groups of infants with chronic illness: those with cystic fibrosis (CF) and those with congenital heart disease (CHD). CF is a lethal genetic disease affecting 1 in 2,000 white births. It is marked by abnormal mucous secretions that interfere with pancreatic function, which results in the malabsorption of nutrients. CF also affects the lungs, interferes with breathing, and increases vulnerability to infection. Most infants are relatively healthy once treated, but the burden of treatment is very demanding of parents. The disease is also progressive, and these seemingly healthy infants face increasing impairment and a shortened life span. Attachment assessments of 40 infants diagnosed with CF within the first year indicated that the distribution of avoidant, secure, and ambivalent attachment conformed to the normative pattern. However, scoring for disorganization distinguished this group from healthy controls (58% secure *v* 74%).[20]

CHD is the most common chronic problem diagnosed in infancy and covers many different conditions. The subjects studied were restricted to the four most common diagnoses: ventricular septal defect (a hole that can vary in size), transposition of the great arteries (a life-threatening condition requiring corrective surgery), tetralogy of Fallot (a cluster of malformations requiring surgery that can vary in success), and coarctation (constriction) of the aorta (that can vary in severity and may also be surgically corrected). Thus, the sample is a very heterogeneous group with respect to initial presentation treatment, and prognosis. Observation of 40 infants with CHD in the strange situation procedure indicated that attachment distribution differed from the norms: 36% were avoidant, 48% were secure, and 16% were ambivalent. Further review using the D criteria indicated that 37% of these already classified infants were best considered primarily disorganized.

In summary, the majority of studies have found that the distribution of attachment patterns among infants at risk is very similar to that found in the normative data. However, in many cases, the procedures and scoring schemes have had to be adapted, and there is some preliminary evidence of more frequent signs of disorganized/disoriented attachment. A smaller number of studies[12,13,20,53,57] have reported increased rates of insecure attachment.

CLINICAL IMPLICATIONS

Blacher and Myers[59] reviewed studies of attachment in handicapped children and argued that there is a major clinical need for attachment assessments of handicapped children. In particular, decisions about placement out of home, readiness for centerbased programs, and parent replacement by respite services would benefit from information about parent–child relationships. While the strange situation procedure had not been widely used in these groups, they felt it to be the most promising tool for the purpose. The studies previously discussed demonstrate that, for many groups of infants, it can be used or adapted for research purposes. However, the extent to which the strange situation procedure is a viable clinical tool has not been established. A preliminary step in such consideration is the evaluation of the features of the strange situation that contribute to its power as a research tool, as well as of its limitations.

The data above indicate that the strange situation procedure and Ainsworth's scheme for classification have been remarkably successful in capturing qualities of infant–caregiver relationship that reflect interaction history and predict subsequent developmental competence. Many other efforts to demonstrate these continuities have been less successful. What accounts for the dramatic success of the strange situation procedure?

1. The strange situation methodology relies on the identification of patterns of behavior rather than of single behaviors or global ratings. The organization of behavior rather than behavior alone is assessed. This reaches a closer approximation to the complexity of the underlying phenomenon than coding of discrete behaviors or ratings would do.
2. Caregivers fulfill many roles for infants (eg, social partner, teacher, attachment figure), and different assessment schemes measure different roles or aspects of these roles. The success of the strange situation procedure and its derivation from Bowlby's theory of attachment suggests that the underlying formulation (that identifies the attachment role as a key element for subsequent socioemotional development) has advantages over alternative theoretic approaches.
3. Classification of strange situation procedure behavior is based on detailed review of videotapes and demands an amalgamation of strong clinical skills with detailed objective research criteria. The strengths of two complementary approaches are combined.
4. The procedures focus on the organization of a system under stress and styles of coping, which may well be the key to both demonstrating and understanding individual differences.
5. Although the dyad is the object of study, caregiver behavior is constrained by the self-consciousness of adults and by instructions. The focus is on the

infant (who is less self-aware) as the more revealing participant. Even more important, the emphasis is on reunions in which the infant's behavior before the caregiver acts reveals the infant's expectations, which represent an important component of the infant's "working model" or cognitive scheme of the relationship. It is currently believed that this representation of the dyadic relationship plays a major role in subsequent development.

In spite of all these strengths, the strange situation procedure also has many limitations, particularly as a clinical tool. (1) It was not intended as a clinical tool, and the time required to conduct the assessment and score the tape limits its cost-effectiveness. (2) Current research indicates only that this has been a successful method for group prediction. The use of the strange situation in individual assessment and prediction has been very limited and does not justify its use without additional contextual data.[60,61] (3) The studies previously discussed indicate that, for infants with developmental and medical problems or handicaps, there are further limitations. In general, without modification, the strange situation procedure is not suitable for children whose mental and motor skills are below the 1-year level. Even in those whose functioning meets that criterion, poorly organized behavior may result in classification difficulties. The use of the Main and Solomon D scale[7] is a relatively recent addition to the methodology, and it is not yet clear how well it selects out organization in attachment from general behavioral organization. Although early studies[8,9,62] suggested that disorganized attachment is a more insecure pattern than any of the others, those data are limited relative to the extensive work with the traditional scheme over a 20-year period, and investigators are not in a position to evaluate the clinical significance of disorganized/disoriented attachment. As clinicians look increasingly at atypical infants, they are likely to see more unusual forms of attachment, and further modifications and additions to the traditional scheme will be needed .

Thus, while the strange situation procedure may appear to be a quick and simple way to assess infant–caregiver relationships, it cannot be used without supporting information and may be of limited use for many at-risk groups. However, there are broader uses of the strange situation procedure and attachment research. Because this research tradition has relied so heavily on detailed observations and clinical judgments, it has served to develop concepts and methods that are easily integrated with clinical practice. Indeed, some clinicians will find that Bowlby's concepts, Ainsworth's methods, and the body of empiric information they have generated provide a coherent framework for organizing their current efforts. Others may find that exposure to the rigorous training that researchers undergo in learning to code strange situation procedure videotapes sharpens their clinical intuitions about infant–caregiver dyads.

The data reviewed here have particular implications for clinicians working with medically compromised infants. Although there has been much discussion of the extent to which physical problems or handicaps place infants at risk of impaired caregiving, the majority of studies indicate that there are few examples of deviant distribution of attachment patterns that are attributable to infants' biologic problems. This, coupled with many observations that parents of infants with developmental or medical problems use styles of interaction that differ from those used with healthy infants, should lead us to be very cautious about concluding that "different" necessarily means "maladaptive." The evidence of normal attachment data suggests that some of these patterns are, in fact, well adapted to extraordinary infant needs.

•   •   •

As a result of the last 20 years of attachment research, there is a growing body of empiric support for tenets that have been working assumptions of clinicians about early social relations. Although this may not change actual practice, it provides a common ground for clinicians and researchers to overcome their mutual skepticism. While clinicians often feel that research does not address issues of clinical importance (or does so in a sterile way), and researchers often feel that clinical work is without an empiric foundation, early attachment is one area in which this is no longer the case. It is clear that clinicians and researchers can profitably inform each other.

REFERENCES

1. Bowlby J. The nature of the child's tie to his mother. *Int J Psychoanal.* 1958;39:350–373.

2. Bowlby J. *Attachment and Loss: Attachment.* New York: Basic Books; 1969.

3. Bowlby J. *Attachment and Loss: Separation.* New York: Basic Books; 1973;2.

4. Bowlby J. *Attachment and Loss: Loss, Sadness and Depression.* New York: Basic Books; 1980;3.

5. Ainsworth MDS, Wittig BA. Attachment and exploratory behaviour of one-year-olds in a strange situation. In: Foss BM, ed. *Determinants of Infant Behaviour.* London: Methuen; 1969;4.

6. Ainsworth MDS, Blehar MC, Waters E, et al. *Patterns of Attachment: A Psychological Study of the Strange Situation.* Hillsdale, NJ: Erlbaum; 1978.

7. Main M, Solomon J. Discovery of an insecure/disorganized/disoriented attachment pattern. In: Brazelton TB, Yogman MW, eds. *Affective Development in Infancy.* Norwood, NJ: Ablex; 1986.

8. Crittenden P. Maltreated infants: vulnerability and resilience. *J Child Psychol Psychiatry.* 1985;26:85–96.

9. Radke-Yarrow M, Cummings EM, Kuczynski L, et al. Patterns of attachment in two- and three-year-olds in normal families and families with parental depression. *Child Dev.* 1985;56:591–615.

10. Spieker SJ, Booth C. Maternal antecedents of attachment quality. In: Belsky J, Nezworski T, eds. *Clinical Implications of Attachment.* Hillsdale, NJ: Erlbaum; 1988.

11. Goldberg S. Risk factors in attachment. *Can J Psychol.* 1988;42:173–188.

12. Goldberg S, Fischer-Fay A, Simmons R, et al. Effects of chronic illness on infant–mother attachment. Paper presented at the Biennial Meeting of the Society for Research in Child Development, Kansas City, Missouri, April 1989.

13. Vaughn B. Assessing attachment quality in a Down syndrome sample. Paper presented at the Biennial Meeting of the Society for Research in Child Development, Kansas City, Missouri, April 1989.

14. Van Ijzendoorn MH, Kroonenberg PM. Cross cultural patterns of attachment: a meta-analysis of the strange situation. *Child Dev.* 1988;59:147–156.

15. Waters E. The stability of individual differences in infant–mother attachment. *Child Dev.* 1978;49:483–494.

16. Main M, Kaplan N, Cassidy J. Security in infancy, childhood and adulthood: a move to the level of representation. *Monogr Soc Res Child Dev.* 1985;50(1–2, Serial No. 209):66–104.

17. Belsky J, Rovine M. Temperament and attachment security in the strange situation: an empirical rapprochement. *Child Dev.* 1987;58:787–795.

18. Main M, Weston D. The quality of the toddler's relationship to mother and father: related to conflict behavior and the readiness to establish new relationships. *Child Dev.* 1981;52:932–940.

19. Belsky J, Rovine M, Taylor DG. The Pennsylvania Infant and Family Development Project, 3: the origins of individual differences in infant–mother attachment: maternal and infant contributions. *Child Dev.* 1984;55:718–728.

20. Goldberg S, Perrotta M, Minde K, et al. Maternal behavior and attachment in low birthweight twins and singletons. *Child Dev.* 1986;57:34–46.

21. Grossmann K, Grossmann KE. Maternal sensitivity and newborns' orientation responses as related to quality of attachment in northern Germany. *Monogr Soc Res Child Dev.* 1985;50(1–2, Serial No. 209):233–256.

22. Main M, Tomasini L, Tolan W. Differences among mothers of infants judged to differ in security. *Dev Psychol.* 1979;15:472–473.

23. Maslin CA, Bates JE. Anxious attachment as a predictor of disharmony in the mother–toddler relationship. Paper presented at the International Conference on Infant Studies, Austin, Texas, 1982.

24. Connell DB. *Individual Differences in Attachment: An Investigation into Stability, Implications and Relationships to Structure of Early Language Development.* Syracuse, New York: Syracuse University; 1976. Dissertation.

25. Waters E, Vaughn B, Egeland B. Individual differences in infant–mother attachment relationships at age one: antecedents in neonatal behavior in an urban economically disadvantaged sample. *Child Dev.* 1980; 51:208–216.

26. Chess S, Thomas A. Infant bonding: mystique and reality. *Am J Orthopsych.* 1982;52:213–222.

27. Crockenberg SB. Infant irritability, mother responsiveness, and social support influences on security of infant–mother attachment. *Child Dev.* 1981;52:857–865.

28. Goldsmith HH, Alansky JA. Maternal and infant temperamental predictors of attachment: a meta-analytic review. *J Consult Clin Psychol.* 1987;55:806–816.

29. Sroufe LA. Attachment classification from the perspective of infant–caregiver relationships and infant temperament. *Child Dev.* 1985;56:1–14.

30. Main M, Hesse E. The disorganized/disoriented pattern in infancy: precursors and sequelae. In: Greenberg M, Cicchetti D, Cummings EM, eds. *Attachment in the Preschool Years: Theory, Research and Intervention.* Chicago: University of Chicago Press; in press.

31. Arend R, Gove , Sroufe LA. Continuity of individual adaptations from infancy to kindergarten: a predictive study of ego resiliency and curiosity in preschoolers. *Child Dev.* 1979;50:950–959.

32. Bell S. The development of the concept of object as related to infant–mother attachment. *Child Dev.* 1970;41:291–311.

33. Lieberman A. Preschooler's competence with a peer: relations with attachment and peer experience. *Child Dev.* 1977;48:1277–1287.

34. Londerville S, Main M. Security of attachment, compliance, and maternal training methods in the second year of life. *Dev Psychol.* 1981;17:289–299.

35. Matas L, Arend RA, Sroufe LA. Continuity and adaptation in the second year. The relationship between quality of attachment and later competence. *Child Dev.* 1978;49:549–556.

36. Sroufe LA, Fox N, Pancake V. Attachment and dependency in developmental perspective. *Child Dev.* 1983;54:1335–1354.

37. Waters E, Wippman J, Sroufe LA. Attachment, positive affect, and competence in the peer group: two studies in construct validation. *Child Dev.* 1979;50:821–829.

38. Erickson MF, Sroufe LA, Egeland B. The relationship between quality of attachment and behavior problems in a preschool high-risk sample. *Monogr Soc Res Child Dev.* 1985;50(1–2, Serial No. 209):147–166.

39. Sroufe LA, Egeland B. Early predictors of psychopathology. Paper presented at the Biennial Meeting of the Society for Research in Child Development, Kansas City, Missouri, April 1989.

40. Lewis M, Feiring C, McGuffog C, et al. Predicting psychopathology in six-year-olds from early social relations. *Child Dev.* 1984;55:123–136.

41. Bates JE, Bayles K. Attachment and the development of behaviour problems. In: Belsky J, Nezworski T, eds. *Clinical Implications of Attachment.* Hillsdale, NJ: Erlbaum; 1988.

42. Greenberg M, DeKlyen M, Speltz M. The relationship of insecure attachment to externalizing behavior problems in the preschool years. Paper presented at the Biennial Meeting of the Society for Research in Child Development, Kansas City, Missouri, April 1989.

43. Cassidy J, Marvin RS. Attachment organization in three- and four-year-olds: coding guidelines, 1988. Department of Psychology, Charlottesville, University of Virginia.

44. Cassidy J, Main M. The relationship between infant–parent attachment and the ability to tolerate belief separation at six years. In: Tyson R, Galenson E, eds. *Frontiers of Infant Psychiatry.* New York: Basic Books; 1985; 2.

45. Kaplan N, Main M. Internal representations of attachment at six years as indicated by family drawings and verbal responses to imagined separations. Paper presented at the Biennial Meeting of the Society for Research in Child Development, Toronto, Ontario, April 1985.

46. Kagan J. *Psychological Research on the Human Infant: An Evaluative Summary.* New York: W.T. Grant Foundation; 1982.

47. Lamb ME, Thompson RA, Gardner WP, et al. Security of infantile attachment as assessed in the strange situation: its study and biological interpretation. *Behav Brain Sci.* 1984;7:127–147.

48. Campos JJ, Barrett KC, Lamb ME, et al. Socioemotional development. In: Mussen PH, ed. *Handbook of Child Psychology.* 4th ed. New York: Wiley; 1983;2.

49. Goldberg S, DiVitto B. *Born Too Soon. Preterm Birth and Early Development.* New York: W.H. Freeman; 1983.

50. Brown J, Bakeman R. Early interaction: consequences for social and mental development at 3 years. *Child Dev.* 1980;51:437–447.

51. Rode SS, Chang RO, Fisch R, et al. Attachment patterns of infants separated at birth. *Dev Psychol.* 1981;13:188–192.

52. Frodi A. Attachment behavior and sociability with strangers in premature and full-term infants. *Inf Ment Health J.* 1983;4:13–22.

53. Plunkett J, Meisels S, Stiefel G, et al. Patterns of attachment among preterm infants of varying biological risk. *J Am Acad Child Psychiatry.* 1986;25(6):794–800.

54. Cicchetti D, Serafica FC. Interplay among behavioral systems: illustrations from the study of attachment, affiliation, and wariness in young children with Down syndrome. *Dev Psychol.* 1981;17:36–49.

55. Stahlecker JE, Cohen MC. Application of the strange situation attachment paradigm to a neurologically impaired population. *Child Dev.* 1985;56:502–507.

56. Wasserman G, Lennon M, Allen R, et al. Contributors to attachment in normal and physically handicapped infants. *J Am Acad Child Adolesc Psychiatry.* 1987;26:9–15.

57. Siera AM. The assessment of attachment in infants with mild to moderate cerebral palsy. Paper presented at the Biennial Meeting of the Society for Research in Child Development, Kansas City, Missouri, April 1989.

58. Pianta RC, Marvin RS. Procedures for assessing and classifying attachment behavior of children with moderate to severe motor impairments. Paper presented at the Biennial Meeting of the Society for Research in Child Development, Kansas City, Missouri, April 1989.

59. Blacher J, Myers CE. A review of attachment disorder and formation in handicapped children. *J Ment Defic.* 1983;87:359–371.

60. Lieberman A, Pawl J. Clinical applications of attachment theory. In: BelskyJ, Nezworski T, eds. *Clinical Implications of Attachment.* Hillsdale, NJ: Erlbaum; 1988.

61. Greenspan S, Lieberman A. A clinical approach to attachment. In: Belsky J, Nezworski T, eds. *Clinical Implications of Attachment.* Hillsdale, NJ: Erlbaum; 1988.

62. Lyons-Ruth C, Connell D, Zoll D, et al. Infants at social risk: relations among infant maltreatment maternal behavior, and infant attachment Behavior. *Dev Psychol.* 1987;23:223–232.

Mental health intervention with infants and young children with behavioral and developmental problems

Dennis Drotar, PhD
Professor of Psychology

Lynne Sturm, PhD
Assistant Professor of Psychology
Departments of Psychiatry and
    Pediatrics
Case Western Reserve University
    School of Medicine
MetroHealth Medical Center
Cleveland, Ohio

INFANTS AND YOUNG children with developmental disabilities, including mental retardation, evidence behavioral disorders that are serious enough to disrupt their social and emotional development. In addition, such problems often interfere with their response to developmental intervention and, in some cases, threaten their physical health.[1–3]

Evidence from several sources underscores the scope and salience of behavioral problems among developmentally delayed children. Blackman and Cobb[4] found that compared with parents of normal children, parents of developmentally at-risk children reported significantly more behavioral problems during the child's first year of life and a longer duration of problems. Clinicians also have identified a wide spectrum of behavioral disorders in young children with developmental disabilities. For example, feeding problems have been estimated to occur in as many as 6% to 33% of individuals with handicaps.[1] Specific problems include selective food refusal and preferences or prolonged insistence on soft or pureed foods. Rumination (repeated mouthing of partially digested food) and pica (ingestion of nonnutritive materials) are also prevalent in the developmentally disabled population.

Behavioral disturbances such as stereotypic motor movements (eg, repetitive hand, head, or trunk movements) and self-injurious behavior (eg, head banging, head or face slapping) can seriously interfere with the developmentally disabled child's acquisition of new skills and social acceptance. Aggressive behavior, temper tantrums, and hyperactivity also are encountered frequently in developmentally disabled populations.[3] Finally, autism, which includes serious impairments in social relations and communication deficits, often is accompanied by some degree of mental retardation.[5]

Although many young children with developmental disorders have compelling behavioral problems that are very difficult to manage, clinical assessment and intervention approaches for this population have not been well described. Moreover,

Preparation of this manuscript was supported in part by grant number MCJ-390557 awarded by the Bureau of Maternal and Child Resources Development, Health Resources and Services Administration, Department of Health and Human Services.

similar to behavioral problems in general childhood populations,[6-10] behavioral problems in young developmentally impaired children may not be recognized until the problems have become severe enough to cause substantial family stress. For this reason, there is a need to inform parents and professionals concerning issues related to the identification and management of behavioral disorders in infants and young children with developmental problems. This article describes clinical assessment and mental health intervention with this population.

IDENTIFICATION AND REFERRAL

Identification of behavioral disorders

In many cases, parents are the first to question whether their developmentally delayed child's behavior is abnormal. Parents may consider their young child's behavior to be problematic for several different reasons; for example, the behavior may interfere with their relationship or ability to teach the child or with the child's interactions with others, or the parent may consider a particular behavior to be deviant or strange. Parents may be reluctant to act on their concerns because they do not regard the problem as serious and feel that their child may grow out of it, because they believe that their child's behavior relates directly to their developmental problem, or because they or other family members are reluctant to label their child as having a mental disorder.

Consequently, parents of young children with developmental and behavioral disorders often need advice and support from professionals to evaluate the developmental impact of their child's problem and to effectively consider options for assessment and treatment. Because of their continuing access to the young child's development in the first years of life, pediatricians and nurse practitioners are in a primary position to identify behavioral problems in young children. In addition, early childhood educators, occupational and physical therapists, and speech–language pathologists are often in an excellent position to identify behavioral problems in young children with developmental problems because of their contact with them in diagnostic, treatment, and educational programs. In the authors' experience, many developmentally delayed children with behavioral problems are initially identified by speech or occupational therapists who note that the child has a highly unusual response to assessment or treatment.

Referral for mental health intervention

Although there are no hard-and-fast rules for referral, parents and professionals may wish to consider the following three questions in deciding whether it is necessary to refer a young developmentally delayed child for an evaluation of his or her behavioral problems:

1. Is the child's behavior problem interfering with his or her capacity to negotiate developmental tasks considered appropriate for the child's mental age and level of cognitive development? A preschooler whose aggressive behavior disrupts many areas of his or her life to the point that he or she is not learning at an expected rate and is alienating others has a much greater priority for referral than a toddler with oppositional behavior that is not significantly hindering developmental progress.

2. Is the child's behavior interfering with response to early education or developmental services? A young child's behavior problem should be evaluated if parents and practitioners are frustrated by the lack of progress in speech, physical, or occupational therapy services caused by behavioral difficulties such as problems forming relationships with others.

3. Are the child's parents highly anxious or stressed about their child's psychologic or interpersonal functioning? Even if the child's behavioral problem does not appear to be especially serious to professionals, if the parent perceives it as a significant problem, a referral and evaluation can be helpful to the family.

As a general rule, a "yes" answer to any one of the above questions warrants an evaluation of a young child's behavioral problem and treatment recommendations. Given the importance of early identification and preventive intervention with behavioral disorders, parents and professionals might profit from seeking an evaluation even when they doubt that the child's problem is serious. Even if the evaluation indicates that the child's behavioral problems do not require ongoing treatment, the referring parent or professional receives the useful benefits of reassurance, support, and advice concerning management of the child's problem.

Professional qualifications

To identify professionals who are adequately trained to provide services for young children with behavioral and developmental problems, parents and professionals should not hesitate to ask practitioners about their professional training background and recent clinical experience with this population. It should be noted that generic professional training in the mental health specialties of psychology, psychiatry, or social work does not necessarily equip professionals to work effectively with infants with developmental and behavioral disorders.[11] Diagnostic and treatment experiences with this heterogeneous population are critical to enable clinicians to conduct informed treatment planning and to differentiate normal variations in developmentally delayed children's behavior from problems that warrant treatment. Thus, professionals who work with this population should have general training in assessment and intervention with infants and young children as well as specialized training with children who have both developmental disabilities and behavioral problems.[11]

CLINICAL ASSESSMENT

Infants and young children with developmental delays who are referred because of concerns about behavioral problems require a thorough assessment that ideally should document the nature and severity of the child's behavioral problem, assess possible etiologic influences, inform parents and professionals about findings and recommendations, and help the family obtain recommended intervention services. Although specific diagnostic procedures may be tailored to the needs and presenting problems of individual children, the assessment should begin with intellectual testing[12] using standardized instruments such as the Bayley Scales of Mental Development,[13] the Stanford-Binet Intelligence Scale,[14] or the Kaufman Assessment Battery for Children.[15] Other assessment tools can include parent interview, behavioral observation, and information from other professionals.

Parent interview

Most young children with developmental disorders are too young to be interviewed about their problems or to be given standardized assessments of their emotional functioning. As a consequence, interviewing parents concerning their perceptions of their child's presenting problem, developmental history, and level of psychologic functioning is especially important. Most clinicians use a series of open-ended interview questions that cover each of the above areas. It is also useful to supplement interview data with information from standardized parent report instruments that assess the child's adaptive functioning (eg, Vineland Adaptive Behavioral Scales[16]) and behavioral symptoms (eg, Child Behavior Checklist[17,18]) compared to norms.

Informed practitioners also will inquire about parents' impressions of their relationship with their child, attitudes and experiences concerning discipline, family stress, and resource problems. In the authors' experience, it is particularly helpful to pay special attention to what prompted the parents to seek help for their child's problem, what they expect from the evaluation, and how they perceive their prior experiences with professional help.

The authors' experience also suggests that involving fathers and extended family members in their children's diagnostic and treatment planning process has several important advantages. First, it communicates a clear message that the management of the child's behavioral problem is a family responsibility, rather than solely a maternal responsibility. Second, a family-centered approach to diagnosis can provide information concerning family members' involvement in the child's care, relationship with the child, and attitudes about the child's problem and family relationship patterns that can be critical to treatment planning. During the course of the assessment, the professional may observe serious relationship problems between the parents that may disrupt the family's capacity to follow through with intervention. Alternatively, professionals may uncover hidden family strengths, such as fathers and grandparents who are available to provide support for an overburdened mother.

Behavioral observation

Observation of the child's behavior in free play or in structured intellectual tests provides information about the child's ability to organize his or her behavior and focus on tasks and his or her social responsiveness. Behavioral rating scales, such as the Bayley Infant Behavior Record,[19] will help organize these observations.

Observation of parents' and children's interactions in free play or structured problem-solving or compliance tasks also provides a clinically relevant assessment of the quality of their relationship, especially the quality of attachment and affective engagement.[20-22] Observation of the mother's ability to direct her child in carrying out a structured task may be especially useful in assessing children with oppositional behavior.

Although office-based observational assessment is the most feasible, observation of a young child's behavior in naturalistic situations is usually very helpful.[23,24] The authors have found that home observation can be particularly informative in assessing interactions between developmentally delayed young children and multiple family members, documenting family resources and interactional patterns, and clarifying unusual or confusing findings obtained from office-based developmental or behavioral assessment.[23,24] Finally, observation of the child's social interactions with peers and teachers in preschool settings provides useful diagnostic information concerning the child's capacity to engage in social relationships.

Information from other professionals

Professionals already providing services to the child with developmental problems contribute important observations concerning the child's behavior in various situations and should be contacted, with parental consent, to communicate their impressions and concerns about the child, test findings, and referral questions. A mutually respectful relationship between the mental health evaluator and the child's early intervention therapists is critical to subsequent implementation of specific suggestions that may result from the evaluation.

Informing parents and professionals about evaluation results

Based on their assessment, mental health practitioners develop a working diagnosis of the nature and severity of the child's behavior problem, recommend additional evaluations (eg, medical, speech–language) and interventions to manage the child's behavioral problem. Diagnostic findings and recommendations are generally discussed with parents in a feedback interview and communicated to parents and professionals in a written report. Close communication with parents and other professionals throughout the process of treatment planning is very important to ensure their effective collaboration in the child's treatment. Parents should be treated as respected participants and colleagues, and their opinions, questions, and emotional reactions to diagnostic impressions and treatment recommendations should be actively elicited and addressed. When parents have difficulty accepting treatment recommendations for their child's behavioral problem, priorities for treatment will need to be negotiated.

APPROACHES TO MENTAL HEALTH INTERVENTION

Interventions for young children with behavioral and developmental problems vary considerably as a function of the child's presenting behavioral disorder, including whether the problem is focused or generalized, the child's age and developmental capacities, and the availability of community and family resources. Options for intervention include family-centered guidance, training, and support; relationship-based intervention with parents; psychoeducational interventions; individual psychotherapy; pharmacotherapy; and out-of-home treatment.

Family-centered guidance, training, and support

Interventions for young children with behavioral and developmental problems are most frequently directed toward their parents. Parents can benefit from advice concerning ways to manage their child's behavior problem and to limit the family stress caused by the problem. In situations where parents are locked into maladaptive interactional patterns with their developmentally disabled children, practitioners need to help parents consider and use alternative approaches to disciplining and promoting adaptive behavior. In addition to the benefits provided by specific child-rearing advice, parent guidance can offer emotional support for the parents and help them appreciate the impact of their child's temperament, personality, or medical condition on all family members and family development. In some cases, family or marital therapy may be needed to assist the family in balancing the needs of siblings or the parents' marital relationship with the demands of the child's management.

In some cases, it may be effective to target parent guidance to the child's specific behavioral symptoms and to formally train parents in behavioral management techniques. Key ingredients of behavioral parent training approaches include an objective assessment of the child's behavioral problems, targeting of specific problems, therapy based on reinforcement principles, and objective and detailed evaluation of presenting problems and progress. Behaviorally oriented programs have been shown to be effective with a wide range of childhood behavioral problems associated with developmental disorders[25-28] and can be implemented in office or home settings.[27,29]

Relationship-based interventions with parents

Intervention with parents of young children with behavioral and developmental problems also focuses specifically on enhancing the quality of parent–child relationships.[22,30] For example, in parent–infant psychotherapy, a form of parent guidance based on psychoanalytic principles, parents are helped to develop more adaptive relationships with their child by addressing the impact of prior childhood conflicts on their relationships.[22] This model of intervention has been used most frequently in cases where the child's behavioral and developmental problems reflect a serious relationship or parenting problem such as child abuse, neglect, or failure to thrive.[22] However, as noted by Seligman,[31] the principles of this intervention model (eg, close attention to the quality of parent–child relationships, detailed observation of parent–child interaction, emphasis on parental empathy, communication with their infants and young children) appear to be generally applicable to children with developmental and behavioral disorders.

Psychoeducational interactions

Parent groups and parenting classes can provide a helpful adjunct to treatment, especially for parents who want to obtain the support of other parents and share their experiences with children with behavioral and developmental problems. However, many behavioral disorders in young children require more intensive, individualized interventions than can be provided in a group. For this reason, parent groups usually are not the primary treatment for this population.

In some communities, comprehensive psychoeducational programs that provide socialization experiences and stimulation for the child and guidance for parents are the primary resource for preventive intervention for behavioral problems for infants and preschoolers with developmental problems. Some communities also have developed specialized early intervention programs for children with developmental and behavioral disorders. For example, in Cleveland, the Early Intervention Center provides both behaviorally oriented guidance for parents of young children with developmental and behavioral problems and preschool experience for the child. An interesting feature of this particular program is the "payback" system, in which parents who have completed the program work with other parents of children with similar problems.

Individual psychotherapy

In most cases, developmentally delayed infants' and preschoolers' limited verbal repertoire limits the effectiveness of individual play therapy in treating for behavioral disorders. However, in cases where the child is verbal or productive in imaginative play and presents with anxiety disorders, depression, or inhibition of feelings, play therapy may be useful. In some instances, play therapy also can be used to help the child adjust to new or stressful social situations.

Pharmacotherapy

In the authors' experience, pharmacotherapy is not extensively used with young developmentally delayed children with behavioral disorders largely because the efficacy of drug treatments generally has not been demonstrated with this population and because of concern with side effects. However, in selected cases, methylphenidate hydrochloride (Ritalin) may be helpful to some preschool children with severe attentional and behavioral problems as an adjunct to behavioral management.[3,32] Medication may also be helpful in some cases of self-injurious behavior.[33]

Out-of-home treatment

Home- and office-based interventions are applicable to the majority of infants and young children with behavioral and developmental disorders. However, some problems (eg, severe behavioral disorders that parents cannot manage at home, self-mutilative behaviors that seriously injure the child, or feeding problems that seriously affect the child's physical health and nutritional status) may require treatment outside the home. One option for comprehensive diagnosis and intensive treatment of behavioral and developmental disorders is hospitalization in specialized pediatric or psychiatric units. For example, Sigman[34] has described a comprehensive and specialized program for inpatient psychiatric treatment for children and adolescents with emotional disorders and developmental disabilities. Although such programs are rare, especially for young children, they have the advantage of specially trained staff skilled in dealing with the mental health problems of developmentally disabled children. Disadvantages of inpatient programs include isolation of the child from his or her community or family. Many inpatient facilities provide services on a time-limited basis for several months at most. Serious and intractable behavioral problems may necessitate longer-term residential treatment in a state or private facility.

CASE ILLUSTRATIONS OF INTERVENTION APPROACHES

The following case examples illustrate mental health services that are provided to young children with behavioral and developmental problems in the context of comprehensive developmental intervention.

Case 1

Amy was a 20-month-old toddler with cerebral palsy who presented with head banging, hair pulling, and sleep problems. Amy's mother's negative perception of her daughter was striking, and she felt that Amy could never get enough of her time or attention. Amy attended a developmental intervention center two mornings per week, where her mother participated in a parent support group and occasionally saw a social worker for counseling for herself.

Home observation revealed that Amy's self-abusive behavior followed periods during which she was expected to play independently and had minimal interaction with her mother. Amy's mother had particular difficulty accepting her daughter's need for stimulating activities and preferred that she play independently despite her clear inability to do so. Amy's severe deficits in language expression intensified her frustration and aggravated her difficulties with her mother. Marital interviews eventually revealed that Amy's father was minimally involved with her and that parental arguments frequently centered around how to manage Amy .

Interventions included environmental support to decrease the frequency of Amy's self-abusive behavior and to improve her communication skills. Amy's attendance at the center was increased to three mornings per week, and a communicative system was introduced using picture cards. Amy's mother began to obtain adapted toys from a Lekotec Center (a national program that provides a toy-lending "library"), and a senior citizen volunteer began visiting twice a week to play with Amy. Amy's father was receptive to encouragement to extend his role in his daughter's life and he began to participate in one-on-one time with Amy in the evening, which relieved her mother of sole responsibility for her care.

Case 2

Tony was a 2-year-old former preterm infant with chronic bronchopulmonary dysplasia and developmental delay. He lived with his mother, who had a long history of psychiatric problems, his father, and a 5-year-old sister. During a pediatric admission for failure to thrive, observation of his feeding interactions with his mother and staff revealed a severely restricted range of accepted foods and frequent battles with parents concerning food.

Developmental testing indicated cognitive functioning in the mild range of mental retardation and a marked deficit in expressive language. A home visit indicated that mealtime was one of the few times that Tony received one-on-one attention from his mother, who responded to his oppositional feeding behavior. Because Tony's father worked long hours, had minimal involvement with his son, and felt that Tony had "no problems," a treatment plan was developed solely with Tony's mother's input.

Tony was referred to the local County Board of Mental Retardation preschool for a daily educational program. The mental health professionals felt that Tony's mother's psychologic vulnerabilities would prevent her from being effective as the primary agent of behavioral intervention. For this reason, his teacher and occupational therapist were encouraged to develop a simplified behavioral program to reward Tony's adaptive eating behavior and to institute brief time-out from social interaction whenever food refusal occurred. A caseworker from the developmental center also made home visits to teach Tony's mother how to reduce between-meal snacks, to decrease Tony's intake of junk food, and to increase his interest in nutritionally sound foods.

SPECIAL ISSUES

Diagnosis and classification

In an interesting discussion of the classification of behavioral disorders in infancy, Anders[35] differentiated between occasional behavioral disruptions that occur within a normally evolving parent–child relationship and more rigidly fixed parent–child relationships in which parent and child are unable to achieve a stage-appropriate relationship. The problem of differentiating temporary, normative symptoms from more serious and chronic behavior problems is particularly difficult for practitioners who work with children with developmental disorders. Such practitioners must be very familiar with the characteristics of developmental disorders in young children to avoid mislabeling symptoms such as benign autism (keeping to oneself) or nonobsessive repetitive behaviors that are frequently encountered in this population but that could reflect serious psychiatric symptoms in children of normal intelligence.[36]

The presence of a developmental disorder complicates the assessment of behavioral problems in other ways. For example, a behavioral problem may appear in less elaborate form in some children with developmental delays. In addition, the label of mental retardation may overshadow the significance of other psychological problems. For example, professionals may be less likely to diagnose a mental disorder when the patient had been previously labeled as mentally retarded. [37,38] Finally, some children with mental retardation also have vision or hearing impairments that affect their behavior and that should be taken into account in their diagnostic assessment.[3,39] The close interrelationship of cognitive, language, and behavioral deficits also complicates diagnosis and management.[40,41]

Many young children with developmental disorders are very difficult to adequately classify within existing psychiatric diagnostic systems such as the *Diag-*

nostic and Statistical Manual of Mental Disorders (third edition, revised),[42] the most commonly used diagnostic classification system for children's behavioral disorders. The difficulties of diagnosing pervasive developmental disorder (PDD), which includes impairments in reciprocal social interaction, communication skills, and imaginative activities and intellectual abilities, provide a case in point.[43] The general category of PDD subsumes a heterogeneous group of problems and is not generally helpful in treatment planning. For this reason, some clinicians have advocated alternative classification approaches for young children's psychologic disorders based on detailed observation of functional impairment in young children's social relationships, play, or attachment.[44] Others have argued that the classification of parent–child relationship disorders more adequately captures the essence of psychologic problems in infants and young children[35] than diagnoses of individual psychopathology.

Priorities for intervention

Because young children with behavioral and developmental problems have multiple and, in some cases, extensive problems, mental health practitioners need to carefully set treatment priorities to avoid overwhelming parents' emotional and financial resources. It is helpful for practitioners to carefully specify primary versus secondary targets of intervention and to conduct the treatment in stages. For example, problems such as extreme self-injurious behavior that threatens the child's safety and physical health would deserve primary treatment priority. Parental concerns about the child's behavior also should be strongly considered in setting priorities for treatment planning.

With the passage of Public Law 99-457 (Education of the Handicapped Act, Amendments of 1986), Individualized Family Service Plans (IFSPs) are now a required component of many community-based programs. IFSPs are intended to help families identify a broad array of needs as they pertain to their children's development and to identify and obtain access to resources for meeting those needs.[45,46] IFSPs can assist the evaluator in summarizing family members' goals for the child's treatment and perceptions of their child's strengths and weaknesses. Hence, priorities for management of behavioral problems should be set in accord with family service plans to which parents may already be committed.

Barriers to mental health intervention

Parental reactions can be a substantial barrier to recommended intervention. Some parents are reluctant to accept the diagnosis of a psychologic disorder because they feel that it implies they are responsible for causing it. Others may experience the diagnosis of an emotional disorder as added insult to the personal "injury" that they have already experienced concerning their child's developmental impairment. Practitioners who are insensitive to parental needs or quick to label parental adaptational patterns as pathologic may intensify parental anxiety and guilt and create barriers to treatment.

Treatment of young children's behavioral problems can involve a considerable amount of time or expense for parents, especially if they are already involved in medical care and other services for the child's developmental problems, as is so often the case. For all these reasons, many parents of children with behavioral and developmental problems need ongoing support from professionals to enable them to accept the need for intervention for their child's problem.

The scarcity of high-quality community resources for the treatment of young children's behavioral problems is another salient barrier to intervention. To make informed referrals and treatment recommendations, professionals need to develop a first-hand knowledge of practitioners and agencies that have specialized diagnostic and treatment expertise with this population by visiting agencies and programs, talking with practitioners, and obtaining feedback from parents concerning their satisfaction with services.

Serious family dysfunction or parental psychopathology also can interfere with the family's ability to comply with recommended interventions for their child's behavior problems. In such cases, practitioners may need to reduce their expectations and modify their priorities for treatment.

• • •

Interdisciplinary didactic and clinical training programs are needed to provide training in the special diagnostic and treatment problems posed by young children with developmental and behavioral disorders.[11] Empirical data concerning incidence, prevalence, and prognosis of preschool children with behavioral and developmental disorders must be generated to enhance clinicians' ability to predict effectively the course of a given disorder and to determine appropriate treatment. Finally, assessment of the efficacy of mental health interventions for preschoolers with developmental and behavioral problems also should be a research priority.

REFERENCES

1. Ginsberg AJ. Feeding disorders in the developmentally disabled population. In: Russo DC, Kedesdy JH, eds. *Behavioral Medicine with the Developmentally Disabled.* New York, NY: Plenum; 1988.

2. Sigman M, ed. *Children with Emotional Disorders and Developmental Disabilities.* New York, NY: Grune & Stratton; 1985.

3. Mattson JL, Frame CL. *Psychopathology among Mentally Retarded Children and Adolescents.* Beverly Hills, Calif: Sage; 1986.

4. Blackman JA, Cobb LS. A comparison of parents' perceptions of common behavioral problems in developmentally at-risk and normal children. *Child Health Care.* 1988;18:108–113.

5. Ungerer J. The autistic child. In: Sigman M, ed. *Children with Emotional Disorders and Developmental Disabilities.* New York, NY: Grune & Stratton; 1985 .

6. Larson CP, Pless IB, Miettinen O. Preschool behavioral disorders: Their prevalence in relation to determinants. *Pediatrics.* 1988;113:278–285.

7. Campbell SB, Ewing LJ, Breau AM, Szumowks EK. Parent–referred problem three-year-old: Follow up at school entry. *J Child Psychol Psychiatry.* 1986;27:473–488.

8. Miller S, Scarr S. Diagnosis of behavioral problems in young children. *J Clin Child Psychol.* 1989;18:290–298.

9. Costello EJ, Pantino T: The new morbidity: Who should treat it? *J Dev Behav Pediatr.* 1987;8:288–291.

10. Lerner JA, Invi TS, Trupin EW, Douglas E. Preschool behavior can predict future psychiatric disorders. *J Am Acad Child Psychiatry.* 1985;24:42–48.

11. Drotar D, Sturm LA. Training psychologists as infant specialists. *Inf Young Child.* 1988;2(2):58–66.

12. Shelton T. The assessment of cognition/intelligence in infancy. *Inf Young Child.* 1989;1(3):10–25.

13. Bayley N. *The Bayley Scales of Mental Development Manual.* New York, NY: Psychological Corp; 1969.

14. Thorndike RL, Hagen EP, Sattler JM. *The Stanford-Binet Intelligence Scale.* 4th ed. Chicago, Ill: Riverside Publishing; 1986.

15. Kaufman AS, Kaufman NL. Kaufman Assessment Battery for Children Manual. Circle Pines, Minn: American Guidance Service; 1983.

16. Sparrow SS, Balla DA, Cicchetti DC. *Interview Edition Survey Form Manual: Vineland Adaptive Behavior Scales.* Circle Pines, Minn: American Guidance Service; 1984.

17. Achenbach T, Edelbrock C. Empirically-based assessment of the behavioral/emotional problems of 2–3 year old children. *J Abnorm Child Psychol.* 1987;15:629–650.

18. Garrison WT, Earls F. The child behavior checklist as a screening instrument for young children. *J Am Acad Child Psychiatry.* 1985;24:76–80.

19. Wolf AW, Lozoff B. A clinically interpretable method for analyzing the Bayley Infant Behavior Record. *J Pediatr Psychol.* 1985;10:199–215.

20. Greenspan SI, Lieberman AF. Infants, mothers, and their interactions: A quantitative clinical developmental approach to assessment. In: Greenspan SI, Pollock GH, eds. *The Course of Life: Psychoanalytic Contributions Toward Understanding Personality Development, I.* Washington, DC: National Institute of Mental Health; 1980.

21. Call JD, Marschak M. Styles and games in infancy. *J Am Acad Child Psychiatry.* 1966;5:193–210.

22. Fraiberg S, ed. *Clinical Studies in Infant Mental Health.* New York, NY: Basic Books; 1980.

23. Drotar D, Crawford P. Using home observation in the clinical assessment of children. *J Clin Child Psychol.* 1987;8:342–349.

24. Budd KS, Fabry PL. Behavioral assessment in applied parent training: Use of a structured observation system. In: Dangel RF, Polster RA, eds. *Parent Training: Foundations of Research and Practice.* New York, NY: Guilford; 1984.

25. Breiner J. Training parents as change agents for their developmentally disabled children. In: Schaefer CE, Briesmeister JM, eds. *Handbook of Parent Training: Parents as Cotherapists for Their Children's Behavioral Problems.* New York, NY: Wiley; 1989.

26. Cunningham CE. A family system based training program for parents of language delayed children with behavioral problems. In: Schaefer CE, Briesmeister JM, eds. *Handbook of Parent Training: Parents as Cotherapists for Their Children's Behavioral Problems.* New York, NY: Wiley; 1989.

27. Christopherson ER, Sykes BW. An intensive homebased family training program for developmentally delayed children. In: Hamerlynk LA, ed. *Behavioral Systems for the Developmentally Disabled: School and Family Environments.* New York, NY: Brunner/Mazel; 1979.

28. Lewis C, Drabman RS. Training parents in behavioral medicine techniques for the chronic care of their developmentally disabled children. In: Russo DC, Kedesdy JH, eds. *Behavioral Medicine with the Developmentally Disabled.* New York, NY: Plenum; 1988.

29. Howlin P, Merchant R, Rutter M, Berger M, Hersov L, Yule W. A home based approach to the treatment of autistic children. *J Autism Child Schizo.* 1973;3:308–336.

30. Affleck G, McGrade BJ, McQueeney M, Allen D. Relationship focused early intervention in developmental disabilities. *Except Child.* 1982;49:259–261.

31. Seligman S. Concepts in infant mental health: Implications for work with developmentally disabled infants. *Inf Young Child.* 1988;1(1):199–215.

32. Payton JB, Bunkart JE, Hersen M, Helsel WJ. Treatment of ADDH in mentally retarded children: A preliminary study. *J Am Acad Child Adolesc Psychiatry.* 1989;28:761–767.

33. Schroeder SR. Behavioral assessment technology for pharmacotherapy in developmental disabilities. In: Russo DC, Kedesdy JH, eds. *Behavioral Medicine with the Developmentally Disabled.* New York, NY: Plenum; 1988.

34. Sigman M. Individual and group psychotherapy with mentally retarded adolescents. In: Sigman M ed. *Children with Emotional Disorders and Developmental Disabilities.* New York, NY: Grune & Stratton: 1985.

35. Anders TF. Clinical syndromes, relationship disturbances, and their assessment. In: Sameroff AJ, Emde RN, eds. *Relationship Disturbances in Early Childhood: A Developmental Approach.* New York, NY: Basic Books; 1989.

36. Menolascino FJ. Valuable approaches to difficult problems. Presented at Symposium: Mental Health Controversies in Mental Retardation; April 1, 1990; Cleveland, Ohio.

37. Weiss S, Levitan GW, Szyszko J. Emotional disturbance and mental retardation: Diagnostic overshadowing. *Am J Ment Defic.* 1982;86:567–574.

38. Levitan GW, Reiss S. Generality of diagnostic overshadowing across disciplines. *Appl Res Ment Retard.* 1983;4:511–524.

39. Wachs T, Sheehan R, eds. *Assessment of Young Developmentally Disabled Children.* New York, NY: Plenum; 1988.

40. Prizant BM, Audet LR, Burke GM, Hummel LJ, Maher SR, Theodore G. Communication disorders and emotional behavioral disorders in children and adolescents. *J Speech Hear Disord.* 1990;55:179–192.

41. Cantwell DP, Mattison RE. The prevalence of psychiatric disorder in children with speech and language disorder. *J Am Acad Child Psychiatry.* 1979;18:450–461.

42. American Psychiatric Association. *Diagnostic and Statistical Manual of Mental Disorders.* 3rd ed, rev. Washington, DC: APA; 1987.

43. Cohen DJ, Paul R, Volkmar F. Issues in the classification of pervasive and other developmental disorders: Toward DSM-IV. *J Am Acad Child Psychiatry.* 1986;25:213–220.

44. Sherman M, Shapiro T, Glassman G. Play and language in developmentally disabled preschoolers: A new approach to classification. *J Am Acad Child Psychiatry.* 1983;22:511–524.

45. Dunst C, Trivette CM, Deal AG. *Enabling and empowering families.* Cambridge, Mass: Brookline Books; 1988.

46. Deal G, Dunst CJ, Trivette CM. A flexible and functional approach to developing individualized family support plans. *Inf Young Child.* 1989;4:32–44.

Identifying maternal depression in an early intervention setting

Shelley Ross, PhD
Senior Clinician
Child Psychiatry
Western Psychiatric Institute and
   Clinic

Kay Donahue Jennings, PhD
Assistant Professor of Child
   Psychiatry
Department of Medicine
University of Pittsburgh

Sally D. Popper, MS, MEd
Graduate Student
Clinical Psychology
University of Pittsburgh
Pittsburgh, Pennsylvania

PARENTAL DEPRESSION has been a continuing focus of attention, in part because early studies indicated that it was a significant risk factor for adverse infant development and because depression is prevalent. The effects of parental psychopathology on children's development have been investigated in a number of clinical studies.[1-10] In infants, toddlers, and older children, parental depression has been linked to negative affective, behavioral, and cognitive child outcomes, especially when the depression is severe and when there are multiple family risk factors (eg, economic disadvantage, marital discord, poor social support). The effects of parental depression on a medically fragile or developmentally delayed child may be particularly strong, because the child is already at risk for difficulties in development.

Maternal depression in the postpartum period is of particular concern because the developing relationship between infant and mother is associated with the quality of mother–child interactions. These interactions, which are sometimes difficult with an ill or delayed child, may be further compromised by maternal depressive disorders. Depressive disorders are characterized by symptoms that may inhibit the display of usual maternal interactive behaviors (eg, smiling, exaggerated facial expressions, modulated vocalizations). These interactive behaviors are believed to be functionally important in gaining and maintaining infants' attention and positive affect in interaction.[11-13] Negative effects of maternal depression on children's behavior and development have been demonstrated when comparing groups of depressed and nondepressed mothers.[7,14-18]

In this article, information on clinical depression that a clinician working in an early intervention setting should know is reviewed. Guidelines to help a clinician assess whether a depressed mother should be referred for an evaluation are also presented. Although maternal depression is the focus of this article, depression in fathers and other significant family members influences family functioning and

P6718951. *Parts of this article were presented at the Seventh Biennial National Training Institute of the National Center for Clinical Infant Programs, December 1991, Washington, DC.*

Inf Young Children, 1993; 5(3): 12–21

should be assessed as well. The authors' experience with depression in parents of young children comes from their clinic, the Pregnancy and Infant/Parent Center, a family-focused assessment and treatment program for families with children under 3 years of age.[19] The Pregnancy and Infant/Parent Center is part of the psychiatric outpatient program at the University of Pittsburgh Medical Center. Because there are a number of informative articles[8,20–24] on the prediction and course of depression, this information is not reviewed in depth. Likewise, the issue of how depression interacts with the special stresses related to caring for a child with special needs will not be discussed in depth because this subject was covered in a recent article in this journal.[25] Instead, focus will be placed on practical issues of use to a clinician working in an early intervention setting.

PREVALENCE AND COURSE OF POSTPARTUM DEPRESSION

Postpartum depression is a significant mental health problem. In a review of epidemiologic studies of emotional disorders during the postpartum period, Coble and Day[20] reported that 15% to 20% of all childbearing women have emotional disturbances, primarily depression. Campbell and colleagues[26] reported that 10% of a large, middleclass sample with healthy infants experienced a clinically significant depression. For families experiencing more stressful circumstances, the frequency of depression is probably higher. The risk of subsequent depression (not related to pregnancy or birth) following a postpartum depression is 40%.[27]

RISK OF DEVELOPING DEPRESSION

Although 10% to 20% of mothers will become depressed in the postpartum period, it is difficult to predict which mothers will become depressed. O'Hara, Neunaber, and Zekoski[23] found that the following variables predicted occurrence and symptomatology of postpartum depression: personal and family history of depression, depression during pregnancy, and stressors specific to childbirth and child care. Gotlib and associates[22] also found that a history of depression predicted the occurrence of postpartum depression. Approximately half of the depressed mothers in the authors' clinic have had depressive episodes in the past. Thus the postpartum period may be a vulnerable period for both the first episode of depression and a recurrence. Women who have experienced difficult deliveries or whose child is demanding may also be at increased risk for depression .

One question that clinicians in an early intervention setting may ask is: Who should be screened for depression? Certainly anyone with a personal history of depression should be screened. In addition, there are a number of risk factors associated with depression and maladaptive parenting behavior. For example, the stressful circumstances that accompany economic disadvantage are important risk factors in depression. Low social support has also been related to negative infant outcomes,[28] especially in mother–child pairs in which infants have irritable temperaments.[29] Clearly the process of single parenting, which frequently is accompanied by other stressors such as financial difficulty and low social support, needs to be better understood. Marital discord has been implicated as both a cause and an effect of maternal depression.[3,4,6,22,30,31] In addition there is evidence that marital discord has direct and indirect effects on parenting behavior.[3] Because past research has focused on marital discord, however, there is little research on the expected protective or positive influence of support from husbands. One possible mediator of the effects of many of these risk factors on maternal behavior is a mother's sense of self-efficacy.[32] Families with ill or developmentally delayed children may experience more of these factors that place them at risk for depression.

IDENTIFYING DEPRESSION IN AN EARLY INTERVENTION SETTING

Clinicians in an early intervention setting are likely to encounter a substantial number of families in which a mother is clinically depressed. There are many emotional and functional changes in the postpartum period, and these changes are more difficult in families with a child with special needs. Parents of children with special needs report higher levels of depressed mood and lower self-esteem.[33–35] They also report more stress and less security in their role as parents.[33,35–37] These factors increase the likelihood that a vulnerable parent will suffer a clinical depression.

Most lay people think of "depression" as equivalent to depressed mood or feelings. Indeed, even from the psychologic and psychiatric views, depressed mood is the hallmark of a depressive syndrome. Mothers will often describe their depressed mood as feeling sad, blue, or down in the dumps. Depressed feelings may also be described at times as a loss of interest and pleasure in usual activities (known as anhedonia in psychiatric terms). Because so many mothers expect the postpartum period to be a joyous time, the lack of enjoyment in usual activities and in the baby may be the most prominent feelings for the mother. Although anhedonia is usually accompanied by depressed mood, when severe it may indicate a clinical depression even when a person does not endorse sad feelings per se. Similarly, persistent irritability may also indicate depression. Thus, in a clinical situation it is important to ask mothers about depressed mood, anhedonia, and irritability. Any of these three states, if persistent, indicates the possible presence of clinical depression and should be further discussed.

Almost everyone experiences some fleeting feelings of sadness or depression, often when there has been a stressful or sad event in their lives. Since childbirth, the presence of young children, and caring for an ill or developmentally delayed child are all significant stressors, the question arises, What is a significant level of depressed mood? Although there are many ways to answer this question, the best definition is one that the mother provides. That is, when a mother experiences her depressed feelings to be excessive, to interfere with her enjoyment of parenting, or simply feels very different from her "normal self," then her depressed feelings are significant. Unfortunately, because many mothers expect to have a brief period of blues or tearfulness following the birth of the child, those with more significant feelings of depression often assume that the feelings are not important and will quickly diminish. Also, because some mothers feel guilty about being depressed during a time when others expect them to be happy, they may minimize their true feelings. When notable depressed feelings last for at least 2 weeks, they are considered, from a psychiatric point of view, to be clinically significant. Depressed feelings often do not abate quickly, and there is little evidence to suggest that depression in the postpartum period is qualitatively different from depressions that are not childbirth related.[38] As in depressions occurring at other times, postpartum depression is often accompanied by significant anxiety or periods of panic.

Other symptoms that may accompany depressed mood include fatigue, poor concentration, changes in sleep and appetite, feelings of guilt or worthlessness, physical agitation or retardation, and suicidal thoughts or behaviors. The most severe depression, called "major depression" in psychiatric diagnosis,[39] is comprised of depressed mood or anhedonia and at least four of the symptoms listed in the box entitled "Diagnostic Criteria for Diagnosis of Major Depression." Other psychiatric diagnoses related to depression include dysthymia, which is a more chronic depression that has fewer symptoms than major depression, and adjustment disorder with depressed mood, which is a period of depressed mood following a stressor. A related syndrome is "bipolar disorder," in which periods of elevated or irritable mood, as well as depressed periods, occur. Women with a history of bipolar disorder appear to be particularly vulnerable to developing symptoms during the postpartum period.[40] Psychosis in the postpartum period is very uncommon. It occurs in only 1 or 2 women per 1,000 deliveries, and it usually begins within 2 weeks of delivery.[41–43] The symptoms of psychosis include confusion, disorganization, bizarre behavior, rapid mood changes, rambling speech, distractibility, hearing voices or seeing things that are not really present, and increased activity.[44]

A clinician in an early intervention setting may want to ask a mother questions about her symptoms of depression to get a rough picture of the level of her depression. This process allows the clinician to make an appropriate referral for evaluation and treatment and to provide the mother with some educational information about postpartum adjustment.

Diagnostic Criteria for Diagnosis of Major Depression

I.   Depressed mood or loss of interest or pleasure. Must be change from normal mood and persist for at least 2 weeks.

II. Symptoms (at least four for major depression)
1. Decreased or increased appetite with or without associated weight gain or loss
2. Sleep disturbance with loss of sleep, or much more sleep than usual
3. Fatigue
4. Guilt
5. Poor concentration or difficulty making everyday decisions
6. Anhedonia—loss of pleasure or interest in life
7. Psychomotor retardation or agitation
8. Suicidal ideation or plans

III. Impairment in daily functioning or help-seeking because of distress.

Reprinted with permission from *American Psychiatric Association: Diagnostic and Statistical Manual of Mental Disorders*, Third Edition, Revised. Washington, DC, American Psychiatric Association, 1987.

Some symptoms of depression are difficult to distinguish from normal postpartum adjustment. In a depressive syndrome, sleep and appetite may either increase or decrease. It is important to judge whether these changes are the usual changes seen in the postpartum period, especially if the mother is breastfeeding (thus increasing appetite) and if the child's sleep–wake pattern disrupts the mother's sleep schedule. Thus, what is "normal" for the mother must be judged according to what is expected given her postpartum status. In the authors' clinic, significant symptoms that are typically seen include mothers who are breastfeeding but have little appetite and interest in food, and mothers who are not able to fall asleep or stay asleep, even when the infant is sleeping.

Significant levels of fatigue are also difficult to assess in the postpartum period. Again, one must judge fatigue in relation to other factors, especially how much the mother is sleeping. One expects some fatigue if sleep is not adequate, and fatigue at expected levels is not considered a symptom of depression. If a mother is getting a reasonable amount of sleep, however, but feels she has no energy at all, and has difficulty caring for the infant, then she is significantly fatigued. If the infant requires special care, or is difficult and irritable, however, it may be nearly impossible to judge whether a mother's fatigue is more severe than expected.

Difficulty concentrating may be experienced as forgetting things, losing track of conversation or the plot of a television program, or wanting to accomplish a task but being unable to focus on it.

It may also manifest itself in difficulty making everyday decisions that are typically easy. Anhedonia, as mentioned previously, is defined as loss of interest in usual activities. Many mothers become so interested in their child, however, that they lose interest in hobbies, and this condition is a substitution of interest, not a loss of interest.

Feelings of guilt are often reported by mothers who feel "bad" about something. This feeling is a frequent and passing one for many people, but is not clinically significant at this level. Most mothers whose children have had difficulties in the early months will feel guilty, but usually they can keep their feelings in perspective and are not preoccupied by the guilty thoughts. When guilt is overwhelming, when the mother believes that she is a bad or worthless person, or when she holds herself responsible for outcomes over which she had no control, guilt is clinically significant.

Three other symptoms rarely occur outside of depression and anxiety syndromes. These are psychomotor agitation, psychomotor retardation, and suicidal thoughts or behaviors. Agitation, which is often accompanied by feelings of anxiety, is a restlessness manifest in frequent pacing, fidgeting, or picking. Retardation is a general feeling of being slowed down, as in slowed speech or body movements. Suicidal indicators may include thoughts that one would be better off dead, suicidal thoughts with or without plans, or actual attempts. Clearly, suicidal thoughts or behaviors are important to assess in all depressed mothers; it will therefore be discussed in more detail.

Other features that are frequently seen include persistent thoughts or behaviors that are unwanted, intrusive, and often senseless. (These thoughts or behaviors may also be symptoms of obsessive-compulsive disorder, another serious psychiatric syndrome.) A small but significant group of mothers have thoughts that something bad will happen to their child, or that they themselves will harm the child, even though they know that they would never do such a thing. These thoughts appear to come out of the blue and are quite disturbing because mothers worry about why they are having such awful thoughts. (Only a very small number of women harm their child, and most of these women have a psychotic disorder.) Repetitive compulsive behaviors that depressed mothers report include checking the stove repeatedly (eg, every 10 minutes) to see that the gas is off, cleaning the infant's room several times a day, or tapping the floor when passing a certain location in the house.

Of course, anyone who is considerably depressed and experiences a number of symptoms, or who asks for a referral, should be referred for evaluation and treatment. Clinicians in an early intervention setting should also consider the mother's ability to provide adequate care, the child's development, and the child's emotional adjustment when considering whether to discuss referral with a depressed mother. Again, assessing depression in all members of a high-risk family should be considered.

EFFECTS OF DEPRESSION ON PARENT–CHILD INTERACTION AND PARENTING

Because parental depression may be manifest in many different ways, depending in part on the particular symptoms experienced, one cannot predict that a depressed mother will exhibit a particular pattern of behavior with her child. For example, research has shown that some depressed mothers are withdrawn, while others are intrusive and overstimulating with their children.[45] In addition, it is important to remember that some very depressed mothers are able to interact appropriately with their children.

Because depression can have an adverse effect on the parent–child relationship, the relationship should be assessed either formally or informally. The authors routinely observe mother–child interaction in two types of situations. First, behavior is assessed in relatively nonstressful situations. For example, face-to-face play is observed with infants 2 to 5 months of age. In this situation, infants sit in an infant seat facing the mother and they play without toys for 3 minutes. For infants over 5 months of age, free play is observed in which the mother and child play together as they normally do at home with toys. Second, behavior is observed in situations in which the mother places a demand on the child, as often occurs in everyday situations at home. The mother is asked to interest her child in a toy or in reading a book. The "demand" situation often precipitates negative interactions that are typical for the dyad, whereas nonstressful interactions allow both parties to be "on their best behavior." In evaluating the interaction, both the mother's and the infant's behavior are important, while keeping in mind that an infant's behavior may be quite variable depending on the infant's age, transient state (eg, sleepiness), and environmental cues (eg, presence of interesting toys in the room). Mothers' behavior is also variable and depends on many factors. It is always important to remember that any clinical assessment necessarily views only a small sample of behavior. At the same time, a clinician should be concerned about a mother who is quite withdrawn from interaction or intrusive with her child (even when she is aware that she is being observed). If repeated assessments indicate continuity in nonoptimal behaviors, referral is warranted.

REFERRING A MOTHER FOR ASSESSMENT AND TREATMENT

Referring a mother for psychologic or psychiatric evaluation can be difficult. A clinician should be prepared to make referrals to a number of mental health professionals when a mother raises concern about her adjustment. When a clinician suspects that a mother is depressed, it is best that the clinician discuss his or her perceptions with the mother. There is no clear symptom "threshold" for making a referral, but clearly a referral should be macle when the influence of maternal psychopathology on individual or family functioning is apparent. In addition, when a mother has suicidal thoughts or behavior, a referral should be made. Any mother suffering from depression should know that help is available and is usually effective.

Mothers can be referred to many different types of mental health–promoting services. When the clinician believes that a mother is hesitant to seek professional services, referral can be made to self-help groups. Frequently these groups can provide emotional support and referral based on first-hand experience. Hotlines can refer to a broad range of services, and mothers should be made aware of the crisis intervention support that hotlines can provide. Referrals can also be made to professionally led psychotherapy groups, local hospitals, community mental health centers, other clinics, or private practitioners. A self-help group for postpartum mothers, called Depression After Delivery, has a national telephone number for information and local referrals within the United States. In addition, the National Institute of Mental Health (NIMH) sponsors a Depression Line for information on depression and treatment.

One way of approaching the question of referral with a hesitant mother is to assess how she has been feeling and then to provide some information on postpartum depression. Some educational materials come from the Depression Awareness, Recognition, and Treatment Division and the Office of Scientific Education of NIMH (see the box entitled "Information and Support Services"). Three frequently used questionnaires to assess the level of depression are the Center for Epidemiological Studies of Depression Questionnaire (CES-D),[46] the Beck Depression Inventory (BDI),[47] and the Inventory to Diagnose Depression (IDD).[48,49] The IDD is particularly useful because it allows the clinician to identify specific

---

Information and Support Services

- Depression Awareness, Recognition, and Treatment (DART)
  National Institute of Mental Health
  Room 15C-05
  5600 Fishers Lane
  Rockville, MD 20857
- National Institute of Mental Health Depression Line
  (800) 432-BLUE
- Depression After Delivery
  (215) 295-3994
  Depression After Delivery is a nationally based network of local support groups. A call to the main office will put you in touch with the local group nearest you.

symptoms of depression. The questionnaires are quite easy to complete and score and can be administered routinely as part of an assessment package. It is important to explore the mother's experience with those mothers who have elevated scores on any of these instruments. It is also helpful to review data on the prevalence of postpartum depression with the mother, and to explain how a mother's symptoms fit (or do not fit) the depression syndrome. This explanation helps a mother understand that her experience is, in fact, quite common, and (in most cases) has little to do with her feelings about the infant and parenting. The authors also review their belief in the "biopsychosocial" model of depression, emphasizing biologic vulnerability, coping resources, stressors, and social and marital support. The authors emphasize that, when an infant is difficult to care for, the stress of parenting greatly increases.

Referrals can also be difficult in high-risk situations in which a mother is suicidal or has placed the child at significant risk (eg, neglect). In these cases, the authors typically talk to the mother about her feelings and ask her permission to discuss the situation with her and a close relative. This discussion often helps when a mother has to be admitted to a psychiatric hospital but is hesitant to do so voluntarily. By informing a member of the family (typically the husband) that the depression is quite severe and by discussing the possibility of suicide, the family member can become a source of both emotional and instrumental support during the hospitalization. In many cases, even though a husband is quite concerned about his wife's condition, he takes no action because the wife minimizes the extent of her depression. The husband is often quite relieved to hear that someone else can "see" the depression and can offer help. Pressure from the family member may also help the mother accept hospitalization voluntarily. In an emergency situation, such as when a mother is suicidal, and no family member is available, the clinician should call the local psychiatric hospital to discuss how to proceed. One may also have to consult with community social services about the children if they have to be placed in temporary foster care. An adult can be involuntarily committed to a psychiatric hospital if he or she is a danger to self or others. Even if a mother is not hospitalized, however, the safety and health of the children must be assessed. Possible neglect or compromised safety must be sympathetically explored; community resources can be enlisted when appropriate.

TREATMENT OPTIONS

A number of options are available for treatment of depression. It may be helpful to review these with a depressed mother, as many people have unwarranted fears of treatment. Research has documented that most depressed people can be successfully treated within a relatively short period of time.[50] The two most common modes of therapy are psychotherapy ("talking therapy") and psychopharmacology (antidepressant medication). There are a vast number of different approaches to psychotherapy. Three therapies that research has shown to be useful in the treatment of depression are cognitive therapy, behavioral therapy, and interpersonal therapy. *Cognitive therapy* focuses on changing negative ways of thinking and behaving and developing problem-solving strategies. *Behavioral therapies* help depressed people unlearn patterns of behaving and relating to others that perpetuate negative experiences. *Interpersonal therapy* involves changing dysfunctional personal relationships that may intensify the depression. Many, perhaps most, therapists use a variety of treatment techniques rather than a single approach. Furthermore, there is research evidence that treatment of major depression by combining medication and psychotherapy is more effective in preventing relapse than either therapy alone.[51,52]

Many patients are concerned that antidepressant medication will be habit-forming and that it will interfere with their "normal" thinking process. Tricyclic antidepressants, the most frequently used antidepressants, are quite safe and not habit-forming. Antidepressant medication works by changing the balance of specific brain chemicals called neurotransmitters. Annoying side effects, such as dry mouth or constipation, may occur; serious side effects are rare. Usually it takes a few weeks for these medications to become effective. It is important that the medication be prescribed in adequate dosage and that the medication be continued for a period of time sufficient for beneficial effects. In addition, there is some evidence that continuing medication and therapy may help delay the onset of future major depressive episodes.[51] A recent study of a small group of mothers has shown that breastfeeding mothers may take some antidepressant medications with little risk to the infant,[53] but mothers who are breastfeeding should consult with their physician about the use of antidepressant medication.

•   •   •

Maternal depression is a prevalent mental illness that may adversely affect a child's development. Clinicians working in an early intervention setting can expect to have a few depressed mothers in their caseload. In order to best help these families, it is important for the clinician to recognize possible symptoms of depression and feel comfortable discussing these symptoms and mood disturbances with the mother. By understanding the symptoms and treatment of depression, the clinician working with the family can more effectively refer mothers for treatment and feel confident about possible ways of handling any mental health crises that may arise. The infant or young child who is the primary focus of the clinician's intervention will clearly benefit from the clinician's attention to the mother's need for help with depression.

REFERENCES

1. Cohler BJ, Musick JS. Psychopathology of parenthood: implications for mental health of children. *Inf Ment Health J.* 1983;4:140–164.

2. Cole PM. Maternal psychopathology and its influence on children's emotional development. Presented at the American Psychological Association Meeting; August 1989; New Orleans, La.

3. Downey G. Coyne JC. Children of depressed parents: an integrative review. *Psychol Bull.* 1990;108: 50–76.

4. Gelfand DM, Teti DM. The effects of maternal depression on children. *Clin Psychol Rev.* 1990;10: 329–353.

5. Hammen C, Gordon D, Burge D, Adrian C, Jaenicke C, Hiroto D. Maternal affective disorders, illness, and stress: risk for children's psychopathology. *Am J Psychiatry.* 1987;144:736–741.

6. Hops H, Biglan A, Sherman L, Arthur J, Friedman L, Osteen V. Home observations of family interactions of depressed women. *J Consult Clin Psychol.* 1987;55:341–346.

7. Lyons–Ruth K, Zoll D, Connell D, Grimebaum HU. The depressed mother and her one-year-old infant: environment, interaction, attachment, and infant development. In: Tronick EZ, Field T, eds. *Maternal Depression and Infant Disturbance.* San Francisco, Calif: Jossey-Bass; 1986.

8. Phillips LHC, O'Hara MW. Prospective study of postpartum depression: 4½-year follow-up of women and children. *J Abnorm Psychol.* 1991;100:151–155.

9. Sameroff A, Seifer R, Zax M. Early development of children at risk for emotional disorder. *Monogr Soc Res Child Dev.* 1982;47:7. Serial no. 199.

10. Sameroff A, Seifer R, Barocas R. Impact of parental psychopathology: diagnosis, severity, or social status effects? *Inf Ment Health J.* 1983;4:236–249.

11. Schaffer HR. *Studies in Mother–Infant Interaction.* London, England: Academic Press; 1977.

12. Schaffer HR. *The Child's Entry into a Social World.* London, England: Academic Press; 1984.

13. Stern D. *The Interpersonal World of the Infant.* New York, NY: Basic Books; 1985.

14. Cohn JF, Tronick EZ. Specificity of infants' response to mothers' affective behavior. *J Am Acad Child Adolesc Psychiatry.* 1989;28:242–248.

15. Field T. Early interactions between infants and their postpartum depressed mothers. *Inf Behav Dev.* 1984;7:5 17–522.

16. Field T, Healy B, Goldstein S, Guthertz M. Behavior-state matching and synchrony in mother–infant interactions of nondepressed versus depressed dyads. *Dev Psychol.* 1990;26:7–14.

17. Field T, Healy B, Goldstein S, et al. Infants of depressed mothers show "depressed" behavior even with nondepressed adults. *Child Dev.* 1988;59:1569–1579.

18. Fleming AS, Ruble DN, Flett GL, Shaul DL. Postpartum adjustment in first-time mothers: relations between mood, maternal attitudes, and mother–infant interactions. *Dev Psychol.* 1988;24:71–81.

19. Jennings KD, Wisner KL, Conley BA. Serving the mental health needs of families with children under three: a comprehensive program. *Inf Ment Health J.* 1991;12:276–290.

20. Coble PA, Day NL. The epidemiology of mental and emotional disorders during pregnancy and the postpartum period. In: Cohen RL, ed. *Psychiatric Consultation in Childbirth Settings: Parent and Child-Oriented Approaches.* New York, NY: Plenum; 1988.

21. Gitlin MJ, Pasnau RO. Psychiatric syndromes linked to reproduction in women: a review of current knowledge. *Am J Psychiatry.* 1989;146:1413–1422.

22. Gotlib I, Whiffen VE, Wallace PM, Mount JH. Prospective investigation of postpartum depression: factors involved in onset and recovery. *J Abnorm Psychol.* 1991;100:122–132.

23. O'Hara MW, Neunaber DJ, Zekoski EM. A prospective study of postpartum depression: prevalence, course, and predictive factors. *J Abnorm Psychol.* 1984;93:158–171.

24. Olioff M, Aboud FE. Predicting postpartum dysphoria in primiparous mothers: roles of perceived parenting self-efficacy and self-esteem. *J Cognitive Psychother.* 1991;5:3–14.

25. Short-DeGraff MA, Healy SM. Postpartum depression related to care for the child with special needs. *Inf Young Children.* 1989;2:24–36.

26. Campbell SB, Cohn JF, Ross S, Elmore M, Popper S. Postpartum adjustment and postpartum depression in primiparous women. Presented at the International Conference on Infant Studies; April 1990; Montreal, Canada.

27. Davidson J, Robertson E. A follow-up study of postpartum illness 1946–1978. *Acta Psychiatr Scand.* 1985;71:451–457.

28. Crnic KA, Greenberg MT, Slough N. Early stress and social support influences on mothers' and high-risk infants' functioning in late infancy. *Inf Ment Health J.* 1986;7:19–33.

29. Crockenberg SB. Infant irritability, mother responsiveness and social support influences on the security of infant–mother attachment. *Child Dev.* 1981;52:857–865.

30. Feiring C, Fox NA, Jaskir J, Lewis M. The relation between social support, infant risk status, and mother–infant interaction. *Dev Psychol.* 1987;23:400–405.

31. Rutter M, Quinton D. Parental psychiatric disorder: effects on children. *Psychol Med.* 1984;14:853–880.

32. Teti DM, Gelfand DM. Maternal depression, parenting and maternal self-efficacy: a longitudinal study of mothers and infants. Presented at the International Conference on Infant Studies; April 1990; Montreal, Canada.

33. Cummings ST, Bayley HC, Rie HE. Effects of the child's deficiency on the mother: a study of mothers of mentally retarded, chronically ill, and neurotic children. *Am J Orthopsychiatry.* 1966;36:595–608.

34. Gallagher JJ, Beckman P, Cross AH. Families of handicapped children: sources of stress and its amelioration. *Except Children.* 1983;50:10–19.

35. Kazak AE, Marvin RS. Differences, difficulties, and adaptation: stress and social networks in families with a handicapped child. *Fam Relations.* 1984;33:67–77.

36. Quittner AL, Glueckauf RL, Jackson DN. Chronic parenting stress: moderating versus mediating effects of social support. *J Pers Soc Psychol.* 1990;59:1266–1278.

37. Tavorima JB, Boll TJ, Dunn NJ, Luscomb RL, Taylor JR. Psychosocial effects on parents of raising a physically handicapped child. *J Abnorm Child Psychol.* 1981;9:121–131.

38. Whiffen VE. The comparison of postpartum depression with non-postpartum depression: a rose by any other name. *J Psychiatr Neurosci.* 1991;16:160–165.

39. *Diagnostic and Statistical Manual of Mental Disorders.* 3rd ed, rev. 1987.

40. Wisner KL, Day NL, Mezzich JE, Peindl K. Psychiatric disorders related to childbearing. Presented at Jeanette Hospital; May 1990; Jeanette, Pa.

41. Brockington IF, Winokur G, Dean C. Puerperal psychosis. In: Brockington IF, Kumar R, eds. *Motherhood and Mental Illness.* London, England: Academic Press; 1982.

42. Pugh TF, Jerath BK, Schmidt WM, Reed RB. Rates of mental disease related to childbearing. *N Engl J Med.* 1960;268:1224–1228.

43. Thomas CL, Gordon JE. Psychosis after childbirth: ecological aspects of single impact stress. *Am J Med Soc.* 1959;238:363–388.

44. Kendell RE, Chalmers JC, Platz C. Epidemiology of puerperal psychoses. *Br J Psychiatry.* 1987;150:662–673.

45. Cohn JF, Matias R, Tronick EZ, Connell D, Lyons–Ruth K. Face-to-face interactions of depressed mothers and their infants. In: Tronick EZ, Field T, eds. *Maternal Depression and Infant Disturbance.* San Francisco, Calif: Jossey-Bass; 1986.

46. Radloff LS. The CES-D scale: a self-report depression scale for research in the general population. *Appl Psychol Measurement.* 1977;1:385–401.

47. Beck AT, Ward CH, Mendelson M, et al. An inventory for measuring depression. *Arch Gen Psychiatry.* 1961;4:561–571.

48. Zimmerman M, Coryell W. The inventory to diagnose depression (IDD): a self-report scale to diagnose major depressive disorder. *J Clin Consult Psychol.* 1987;55:55–59.

49. Zimmerman M, Coryell W, Corenthal C, Wilson S. A self-report scale to diagnose major depressive disorder. *Arch Gen Psychiatry.* 1986;43:1076–1081.

50. Keller MB, Klerman GL, Lavori PW, Coryell W, Endicott J, Taylor J. Long-term outcome of episodes of major depression. *JAMA.* 1984;252:788–792.

51. Frank E, Kupfer DJ, Perel JM, et al. Three-year outcomes for maintenance therapies in recurrent depression. *Arch Gen Psychiatry.* 1990;47:1093–1099.

52. Klerman GL. Treatment of recurrent unipolar major depressive disorder. *Arch Gen Psychiatry.* 1990;47:1158–1162.

53. Wisner KL, Perel JM. Serum nortriptyline levels in nursing mothers and their infants. *Am J Psychiatry.* 1991;148:1234–1236.

Strategies for building resilience in infants and young children at risk

Marie Kanne Poulsen, PhD
Clinical Associate Professor
Department of Pediatrics
University Affiliated Program
Children's Hospital Los Angeles
Los Angeles, California

BIOLOGIC, ENVIRONMENTAL, and psychosocial circumstances combine in various ways to either enhance or stress the healthy development of infants and young children. The resulting constellations of needs, strengths, and vulnerabilities uniquely combine to produce the individuality that is inherent in all human beings.

INFLUENCES ON RISK AND RESILIENCE

Positive perinatal biologic, environmental, and psychosocial circumstances set the stage for healthy development. When all circumstances are positive, the growing child is provided with a reserve of resiliency that will enable the child to handle daily challenges as well as be prepared in case of future adversity. No child is impervious to trauma. The construct of invulnerability or resilience refers to the notion that there is a continuum of potential resilience inherent in all children as a counterbalance to the now acknowledged zone of vulnerability[1] recognized in children at risk.

Children who are healthy, temperamentally easy, and developmentally competent, who are born into families that can provide rich relationships, appropriate expectations, and low environmental stress, tend to develop the internal resources that allow them to easily cope with the demands that are a part of all children's lives.

These resilient children develop the internal self-regulation to respond to and recover from environmental challenges.[2] They acquire a repertoire of responses, and they have the flexibility to respond in a manner that matches the situation in context and intensity.[3] Resilient children accomplish transitions smoothly and easily. They recover from stressful events in a period of time that matches the traumatic significance of the event. Stress and distress responses do not linger.[4]

To the extent a child expands his or her zone of resilience, the stressors that influence emotion and behavior will be better handled. *Resilience* refers to the child's capacity to overcome biologic, psychosocial, and environmental stressful events. Resilience thus is the capacity to withstand stressors, overcome adversity, and, in the process, achieve higher levels of self-mastery and self-esteem and internal harmony. Conversely, children who are born at biologic risk or who are living in families overwhelmed by psychosocial or environmental circumstance (or both) often confront daily challenges that stress them beyond their capacity to cope. Tempera-

Inf Young Children, 1993; 6(2): 29–40

mentally difficult children are more vulnerable to family stressors than are their temperamentally easy counterparts.[5] Without resilience-building intervention, vulnerable children are at higher risk than their nonrisk peers for negative developmental outcomes. When risks are multiple, children are in danger of becoming adolescents who are high school dropouts, teenage parents, juvenile offenders, substance abusers, runaways, and gang members.[6,7] The early identification of vulnerable children is essential as a first line of defense against negative adolescent outcome.[8,9]

Four principles about at-risk children need to be emphasized, however, to avoid the early identification of developmental risk becoming a self-fulfilling indicator of negative outcome:

1. Prenatal and perinatal biologic stressors, difficult temperamental characteristics, and negative environmental circumstance are risk factors contributing to potential developmental vulnerability, not indicators of negative developmental outcome.[10,11]
2. Infants at risk due to perinatal insult or constitutional temperamental vulnerability are more vulnerable to adverse environments than are nonrisk infants.[2,12]
3. Infants at risk can overcome or learn to compensate for early deficits.[13] The plasticity of infant and young child developmental function offers the potential for improvement as a response to a supportive, protective environment.[14]
4. Infant vulnerability significantly decreases when there is a "goodness of fit" between parental expectations, demands and opportunities, and the child's constitutional characteristics and special needs.[2] The single most important influence on the development of infants at risk is the psychosocial environment in which the child is reared.[15,16]

An understanding of the relationship of biologic, environmental, and psychosocial circumstances to the healthy development of children forms a framework for the provision of resources and services needed to buffer negative circumstance and build resilience in children at risk. Significant biologic and constitutional influences on developmental outcome include

- health,
- neurodevelopmental characteristics, and
- temperament.

Significant environmental influences on developmental outcome include

- family stressors and resources,
- developmental opportunities,
- community stressors and resources, and
- cultural context.

Significant psychosocial influences on developmental outcome include

- child–caregiver relationship, and

• goodness of fit of parental expectations.

Positive biologic influences endow the infant with internal resilience that impacts how the child perceives and responds to the world. Positive home, family, community, and environmental influences affect the infant directly. Of equal importance is the positive effect home, family, and community supports can have on the parenting figure. Parents can contribute to child resilience only if they are not emotionally overwhelmed by their interpersonal, family, and community lives. Essential parental and family resources are

- parental capacity to cope,[3]
- parental self-esteem,[17]
- parental emotional availability,[13]
- responsive caregiving,[3]
- appropriate developmental expectations and opportunities,[16]
- capacity to provide protection from overstimulation,[18]
- internal family harmony,[1]
- economic self-sufficiency: availability of food, shelter, medical care,[17]
- neighborhood safety and freedom from racial discrimination,[17] and
- social supports.[11]

Although parenting roles can be effectively provided by either the mother or the father, the preponderance of research concentrates on mother–child relationships. Thus, the psychosocial factors studied are those environmental factors that center on the quality of mother–infant interaction. The best predictor of later positive interpersonal relationship, personal competence, and self-reliance—the elements of child resilience—is the quality of infant–caregiver experience in infancy and early childhood.[19] Child resilience cannot be predicted independent of the caregiver–child relationship. Healthy mother–child attachment is the basis for later emotional, social, and cognitive functioning.[20–22] Competence in such domains in infancy predicts competence in adolescence.[23] In fact, the early mother–infant attachment relationship has been deemed the prototype for all later intimate relationships.[24]

Through rich relationships and appropriate developmental expectations, parents are the chief purveyors of resilience for their children.[25] A critical element of resilience is the young child's appreciation that there is a relationship between one's actions and the response from the environment. Through interacting with a caregiver responsive to social cues, the infant starts to develop feelings of self-efficacy.[9] In this manner, the infant becomes better able to regulate his or her behavior and the seeds of self-mastery and interpersonal relationship are sown.[19,26]

The well-matched mother can help her infant or young child recover from distress through physical comfort, emotional solace, and the removal of emotional and sensory overload that may contribute to distress. She helps her child learn to be resilient, however, through reassurance, encouragement, and the provision of developmental opportunities that match the child's capacity to adapt and achieve.

Mothers and infants each bring resources to the relationship. Mothers, as primary caregivers, are expected to operate as buffers between the infant and an intrusive, overstimulating environment as well as provide the early responsive caregiving needed for infants to thrive. Healthy mothers who are educationally and economically advantaged with available family and social supports are more likely to be able to protect their young from an overwhelming environment and facilitate healthy development. They can provide the cognitive stimulation and emotional support needed to build resilience in their offspring.[5] The well-endowed infant brings to the mother–child relationship an inborn capacity to initiate and respond to human interaction. The well-endowed child who has an easy temperament often can even relax and extract nurturance from an anxious, inexperienced mother.[27]

The most advantaged dyad is the healthy infant with inborn biologic resilience and the well-matched mother with emotional, social, and economic support. The vulnerable infant, who is paired with a "well-matched mother" who has available community resources to help her meet her child's special needs, is in a strategic position for positive developmental outcome. The high-risk dyad occurs when both mother and child are beset with biologic, environmental, and mismatched temperamental circumstances that make a rich relationship more difficult to initiate, establish, and sustain.[13]

BIOLOGIC RISK FACTORS

Genetic or environmental factors (or both) may result in prenatal, perinatal, or neonatal complications or conditions that place the newborn at risk. A biologic circumstance can be considered a risk condition when there is an increased probability that it may negatively impact the development of the child. The biologic insult itself is not necessarily an indicator that a problem will occur, but rather it is a marker that developmental function may be affected. With the exception of severe organic damage, no single biologic, psychosocial, or environmental stressor can predict outcome. The notion of cumulative risk, however, asserts that the greater the number of stressors, the greater the risk for later difficulties.[28]

Several prenatal and perinatal biologically based risk factors may delay or impair the neurodevelopment of the infant. These factors include prematurity,[29] sexually transmitted disease,[30] intrauterine growth retardation,[31] prenatal alcohol and other drug exposure,[15,32] toxic blood lead levels,[6] and perinatal asphyxia.[33]

These risk conditions may give rise to a number of biologically based infant characteristics that may interfere with the development of mother–infant attachment. These characteristics include poor self-regulation, abnormal muscle tone, abnormal sensory threshold, and depressive interactive behaviors. Infants who have been described as having difficult temperaments present very similarly to infants who are identified as having neurodevelopmental immaturities due to known perinatal events such as maternal substance abuse, low birth weight, intrauterine growth retardation, and malnutrition.

It is generally accepted that biologic risk factors, in contrast to established medical diagnoses, do not generally lead to major developmental disability, but rather place the child's development in jeopardy with respect to information processing and learning behaviors. Research[31,34] suggests that high-risk infants demonstrate a greater incidence of the more subtle signs of central nervous system dysfunction than nonrisk infants.

The infant at biologic risk is not only more susceptible to the stresses of daily living, but also has fewer internal capacities to deal with the challenges successfully. The infant at risk needs the buffer of positive early mother–child interactions and a protective environment in order to thrive. The confluence of negative biologic and environmental factors without these preventive intervention buffers can lead to later learning, behavioral, and social-emotional disorders.[35,36]

A number of investigators[16,28,37] have attempted to delineate certain combinations of variables that can be useful in predicting which infants are at risk for developmental difficulties. When an infant's neurodevelopmental functioning is poorly organized, delayed, or compromised, maternal intervention is essential to help the child learn to overcome, compensate for, or cope with the neonatal vulnerabilities. Mothers may need community services to assist in meeting the special needs of their at-risk infants.

Many children will overcome earlier neurodevelopmental vulnerability through the maturation process and the inborn compensating mechanisms inherent in plasticity of development.[34] Others will have early vulnerabilities ameliorated or resolved through early intervention. Even with intervention, not all children will overcome the internal stressors that impact their regulation of behavior, but all children can be helped to learn to deal with attention, learning, and regulatory problems. In this way, their vulnerabilities become developmental or educational inconveniences rather than disabling conditions.

ENVIRONMENTAL RISK FACTORS

Environmental factors have both a direct influence on the child and an influence on the quality of caregiving between the parents and child.[38] Environmental risk factors refer to the social-economic, cultural, and community circumstance that impact a family's capacity to provide safety, security, and nurturance for their children. Significant environmental circumstance include housing, recreation, nutrition, health care, employment, racial nondiscrimination, community harmony, and social supports. The literature[39-42] clearly documents the significance of poverty for developmental outcome.

Children of the homeless and unemployed, children with poor nutrition and health care, and children growing up in communities with violence, racial discrimination, or high concentration of lead exposure show higher incidences of school problems, reported maltreatment, foster care placement, and mental and emotional problems.[43,44]

The Erikson Institute in Chicago[43] studied how children cope in multirisk environments that include poverty, violence, and drugs. Three elements were deemed critical in order for children to develop resilience in very difficult environments: parental self-esteem, parent–child attachment, and basic needs of shelter, food, and medical care.

PSYCHOSOCIAL RISK FACTORS

There are numerous psychosocial maternal circumstances that can interfere with a woman's capacity to protect and nurture her infant[17,45,46] including:

- single parenthood without resources,
- substance abuse,
- spousal abuse,
- maternal adolescence,
- social isolation,
- mental illness,
- intellectual limitations, and
- history of child neglect.

The high-risk mother is the woman who because of intellectual or educational limitations and her own history of parental neglect, substance abuse, or emotional, social, and economic stressors cannot provide her infant with a protective environment and nurturing relationship. Children at highest risk are those with mothers who are emotionally unavailable or who have parenting styles that do not match the child's needs.[3]

A key strategy in developing resilience in children is to help the mother compensate for and cope with the stressors in her own life. The literature supports the notion that child resilience is significantly influenced by parental coping. A child's capacity to handle stressful events is determined to a great extent by how parents handle the trauma. Parents' coping skills not only allow them to be emotionally available for their children's needs, but also serve as models of coping.[1,17]

Biologic circumstance can place the infant at psychosocial risk if temperament or perinatal insult results in infant characteristics that interfere with mother–child relationship, developmental mastery, and feelings of self-efficacy.

PREVENTIVE INTERVENTION

The variability of outcome of infants born at risk due to poverty,[11] difficult temperament,[2] perinatal substance exposure,[15] low birth weight,[13] asphyxia,[33] and young children raised in stressful environments[17] supports the notion of resilience as a powerful counterbalance to risk. The literature has substantiated that early life experiences and a protective social and physical environment can buffer a child's response to biologic constitutional risk factors or stressful life events and in the process broaden the child's zone of resiliency.

Increase in child resilience occurs when the interaction between the child and the environment supports the child in the development of personal competency, self-sufficiency, physical and mental health, and positive interpersonal relationships. Resilience is enhanced when the child and family are exposed to fewer psychosocial and environmental risks and are provided with sources of support to build the personal competencies needed to overcome unavoidable stressors.

Infant neurodevelopmental risks

Intervention may be needed if neurodevelopmental characteristics of the infant place personal competence or the development of mother–infant bonding (or both) at risk. Infant risk indicators for early intervention include

- *Poor self-regulation.* Difficulty in the regulation of behavior may manifest in difficulty in consoling self, in receiving comfort, and in poor feeding and sleep patterns. The infant's capacity to control states of calm-focused alertness is crucial to allow for mother–infant engagement. Persistent poorly developed sleep and feeding patterns are added stressors for the infant, caregiver, and family. Difficulty in consoling self and in being consoled by others leaves the infant and caregiver with growing feelings of incompetence. Intervention strategies may be needed to help the young infant learn to self-regulate.
- *Abnormal muscle tone and motoric disorganization.* Under stress, the newborn may become motorically disorganized, becoming flaccid, hypertonic, or losing control of extensor flexor balance.[48] An increase or decrease in tone may be transient and level as the infant matures. Tone abnormalities may persist, however, and interfere with function. An increase in tone can interfere with the infant's nestling responses and can influence the attachment process. Inexperienced mothers may interpret that the infant does not "want" to be held. In addition, visual and tactile exploration of body parts and reaching for objects may be diminished due to the mild hypertonia. Mothers may need to be taught how to handle and position their at-risk babies more effectively to help these infants become better organized.

- *Abnormal sensory threshold.* Many infants with difficult temperament or neurodevelopmental immaturities are hypo- or hyperreactive to the world around them. Hyperreactive infants tend to become distressed easily by too much noise, light, movement, and commotion. They may respond with prolonged periods of intense crying if their sensitive sensory threshold is accompanied by poor control of emotional state (ie, self-regulatory difficulty). Parents may read cries as "leave me alone" cues rather than "protect me from overstimulation" cues. They may need strategies to help their infants to raise their sensory threshold gradually.
- *Depressed interactive behaviors.* If neurodevelopmental immaturities result in diminished eye contact, fewer vocalizations, muted smiles, and disorganized following of "love objects," the infant is likely to receive less adult attention. Responsive caregiving that is contingent on infant cues is crucial for the development of self-efficacy. Anxious, inexperienced, and overstressed mothers may need help in reading their infants' more muted, sporadic social signals. Without maternal intervention in recognizing and responding to subtle infant cues, there will be an overall decrease in mutual gazing, responsive smiling, vocal dialogue, and joint attention. These are the significant markers of human attachment.

Early interventionists; occupational, physical, and language therapists; developmental pediatricians; pediatric nurses; pediatric psychologists; and others must work with mothers to discover effective strategies to meet their infants' special needs. The box entitled "Caregiving Strategies for Building Resilience in Infants" includes caregiving strategies that build resilience in at-risk infants. The application of strategies must match the particular need of the infant.

Outcome factors

Many of the infants who present with risk indicators during the neonatal period will become healthy, intact toddlers. The process of maturation and the inborn biologic thrust toward health, development, and resilience will lead to the resolution of some risk indicators without intervention for a group of newborns.[14] Other risk indicators will resolve through significant maternal and community service delivery intervention efforts. A number of infants at risk, however, will remain at risk for developmental, learning, and behavioral problems during their toddler and early childhood years.

The outcome of individual infants is based on the interaction of several factors:
- degree of central nervous system dysfunction,
- emotional availability of mothers and fathers,
- match of parenting style to child's needs,
- number of changes of mothering figure,

Caregiving Strategies for Building Resilience in Infants

1. Availability of consistent emotionally responsive caregivers over time.
2. Appropriate maternal responses contingent on infant-initiated signals.
3. Protection from environmental overstimulation of noise, lights, people, touch, commotion.
4. Gradual introduction of small increments of environmental stimuli to build sensory threshold.
5. Use of swaddling to help with toleration of sensory stimulation, to enhance organization of behavior, and to increase the calm, focused alertness needed for environmental exploration and maternal engagement.
6. Use of vestibular proprioceptive stimulation to reduce sensitivity to stimulation, to enhance visual alertness and social interaction, and to calm crying states.
7. Use of handling and positioning to soothe, to improve muscle tone, to increase visual alertness and engagement, to encourage midline play, to support and maintain posture, to encourage movement, and to improve feeding.
8. Gradual reduction of "supportive" techniques as infant matures or learns to compensate.
9. Recognition of muted sporadic infant cues for social engagement or stress relief.
10. Appropriate maternal interaction in terms of speed, intensity, and tempo.
11. Appropriate response to infant "overload signals" (yawning, gaze aversion, crying, sneezing, hiccoughing, color change).

- number of stressors in family life, and
- availability of community resources and intervention services to mother and infant.

Toddler and young child risk indicators

It appears that the influence of prenatal and perinatal insult or environmental stress (or both) on central nervous system functioning creates a wider range of variability in the toddler and young child's capacity in several domains[49]:

1. *Organization of play and daily living activities.* The at-risk toddler and young child may be more distracted and less focused than peers and show less self-initiation and organized follow-through in play, learning, and self-help activities. These children are at risk for attention problems.
2. *Precision and direction of movement.* The at-risk toddler and young child may have difficulty with spatial relations or motor coordination (or both), seen in crayon use, block play, puzzle completion, and tricycle riding. These children are at risk for learning problems.
3. *Learning continuity and learning strategies.* The at-risk toddler and young child may show sporadic mastery (ie, masters a learning strategy, skill, or verbal concept one day and needs to re-learn it again and again). There may be an impairment in sensory information processing; and these children are at risk for learning disabilities.

4. *Sense of self and interactive behaviors.* The at-risk toddler and young child may have very low stress thresholds and be overreactive to stress. Children who experience multiple foster placements may lack the close attachments or relationships to adults that allow for the use of adults as sources of emotional comfort, security, object attainment, and information. These children are at risk for social and emotional problems.

5. *Language.* The at-risk toddler and young child may not use words to express needs, request comfort, solve problems, or resolve conflict. The at-risk toddler and young child may not respond to verbal prohibitions of behavior or verbal praise given at a distance or in a group situation.

The box entitled "Caregiver Strategies for Building Resilience in Toddlers and Young Children" presents caregiving strategies for building resilience in toddlers and young children at-risk. The application of strategies must match the particular need of the young child.

Social and community supports

An ecologic approach asserts that individual child intervention strategies are not enough. Harmony and positive influences within the family and community

---

Caregiver Strategies for Building Resilience in Toddlers and Young Children

1. Use of proximal behaviors in caregiver–child interactions, including call to attention, eye contact, and touch before verbal directions, prohibitions, information, and praise are given.
2. Protection from overfatigue by establishment of personalized bedtime rituals and routines.
3. Protection from overstimulation of too many children, adults, transitions, noise, light, commotion, and emotional distress.
4. Use of rituals for hellos, goodbyes, and daily transitions so child can predict behavior.
5. Modeling, encouragement, acknowledgment, labeling, and responding to child's expression of feeling while setting limits on harmful behavior.
6. Encouragement of autonomy and decision making by providing "limited" choice, whenever possible.
7. Teaching and guidance of social behavior; provision of language and process for peer conflict resolution.
8. Encouragement of self-dependence that matches child's functional level.
9. Modeling and provision of relaxing time, relaxing place, and relaxing activities for child.
10. Modeling and encouragement of representational play to express feelings and recreate significant events.
11. Observation of child's behavior, and intervention before behavior is out of control.
12. Timely response to toddler or young child's needs and initiation of social interaction.
13. Teaching the at-risk child to learn cause and effect in relationship by providing words that relate affect to action (eg, "You grabbed his toy. That makes him upset. Use your words and tell him it's your turn next.").
14. Personalized, one-to-one, child-centered time spent daily to build relationship.

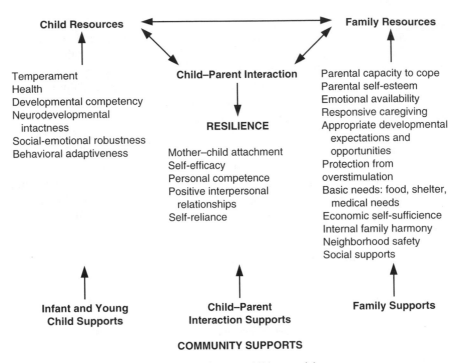

Fig 1. Building resilience in infants and young children at risk.

not only directly affect the developmental outcome of the child, but also influence parental capacity to contribute to child outcome.

The availability of family social supports is critical. The seminal work of Werner and Smith[11] underscored the importance of social supports. Their 30-year follow-up study of high-risk children indicated that those persons who remained at risk in adolescence and adulthood lacked some of the essential social bonds that appear to buffer stress. It has been found that social supports serve as buffers against parental stress when children are extremely challenging, allowing for positive repercussions for mothers, children, and mother–child interaction.[50] Social supports are informally provided by extended family, friends, and neighbors and through social structures such as clubs, church groups, and parent groups sponsored by schools.

The community needs to provide resources in the formal support of the family. These may include health care; transportation; Women, Infants, and Children (WIC) services; early intervention programs; Head Start programs; child care; latchkey programs; parks and recreation; mental health programs; social and drug recovery services; availability of job training and employment; low-cost housing; and protection against violence and racial discrimination.

Policy and quality service delivery issues

Fig 1 describes child and family resources needed to enhance the mother–child relationship. The box entitled "Community Resources to Support Families and Build Resilience in Children" illustrates how community services and resources can provide support for child, family, and mother–child relationships leading to resilience.

The provision of quality services to children and families is predicated on several principles including:
- proactive outreach to the underserved members of the community;
- early identification and intervention for infants at risk;
- services delivered in a culturally competent manner;
- available, accessible, coordinated, and family-focused services;
- colocation of services on a single site; and

Community Resources to Support Families and Build Resilience in Children

Infant or young child supports	*Child–parent interaction supports*	*Family supports*
Public health nurse	*Mother–child interaction supports*	Community health clinics
Neonatal intensive care unit follow-up	Developmental services	Family service clinics
Well baby clinics	Psychologist	Community mental health clinics
Health care	Early interventionist	Welfare and social services
Developmental screening	Communication specialist	Aid to Families with
Women, Infants, and Children Program	Feeding team specialist	Dependent Children
Early identification and referral (Child Find)	Mommy & me classes	Food stamps
Clinic-based, home-based, and center-based developmental services	Conjoint mother–infant therapy	Housing
Public Law 99-457, Part H services	*Parental support*	Medicaid
High-risk infant program	Parent support groups	Drug and alcohol recovery programs
Well baby clinics	Parent education	Job training and job counseling
Public health nurse	Parent counseling	Instrumental support for service delivery
Infant and child care	*Social supports*	child care
Head Start	Church mommy & me activities	transportation
Public school system	Library mommy & me activities	toy loan
Child guidance clinics	Parks and recreation mommy & me activities	translator
		Child development warm lines
		Job availability
		Community safety
		Freedom from discrimination

- availability of instrumental supports such as transportation, child care, toy loans, and so on.

Policy issues relating to building resilience in children must center on making community resources available to:

- enhance intra-child resources, including health, temperament, developmental competency, social-emotional robustness, and behavioral adaptiveness;
- enhance parental resources, including parenting skills, economic self-sufficiency, internal family harmony, community safety, and social supports; and
- enhance mother–child interaction through enhancing child and parental resources and intervention services for children and families with special needs.

Quality care to families requires that methods be created that will (1) ensure comprehensive resources and services are available in every community, (2) link at-risk children and families to community resources and services, and (3) improve collaboration and communication among service providers.[51]

REFERENCES

1. Murphy LB, Moriarty AE. *Vulnerability, Coping & Growth*. New Haven, Conn: Yale University Press; 1976.
2. Thomas A, Chess S. *Temperament and Development*. New York, NY: Brunner/Mazel; 1977.
3. Anthony EJ, Cohler BJ, eds. *The Invulnerable Child*. New York, NY: Guilford; 1987.
4. Trad PV. *Infant & Childhood Depression: Developmental Factors*. New York, NY: Wiley; 1987.
5. Baker PC, Mott EL. New York Longitudinal Study Child Handbook. Columbus, Ohio: Center for Human Resource Research, Ohio State University; 1989.
6. Needleman HL, Schell A, Bellinger D, Leviton A, Allred EN. The long term effects of exposure to low doses of lead in childhood. *N Engl J Med*. 1990;332:83–88.
7. Spencer M, Blumenthal J, Richards E. *Child care for at-risk children and the Family Support Act*. Presented at the Foundation for Child Development Forum on Children and the Family Support Act; November 1989; Washington, DC.
8. Constantino JN. On the prevention of conduct disorder: a rationale for initiating preventive efforts in infancy. *Inf Young Children*. 1992;5:29–41.
9. Losel F, Bliesner T. Resilience in adolescence: a study on the generalizability of protective factors. In: Hurrelmann K, Losel F, eds. *Health Hazards in Adolescence*. New York, NY: Walter de Gruyter; 1990.
10. Horowitz FD. *Exploring Developmental Theories: Toward a Structural/Behavioral Model of Development*. Hillsdale, NJ: Erlbaum; 1987.
11. Werner E, Smith S. *Overcoming the Odds*. New York, NY: Cornell University Press; 1992.
12. Gorski P, Davison MM, Brazelton TB. Stages of behavioral organization in the high risk neonate: theoretical and clinical consideration. *Semin Perinatol*. 1979;3:61–72.
13. Escalona S. Social and other environmental influences on the cognitive and personality development of low birth weight infants. *Am J Ment Defic*. 1984;88:508–512.

14. Rauh VA, Narcombe B, Ruff P, Jette A, Howell D. The Vermont infant studies project: the rationale for a mother–infant transition program. In: Bond LA, Joffe JM, eds. *Facilitating Infant & Early Childhood Development*. Hanover, NH: University Press of New England; 1982.

15. Johnson HL, Glassman MB, Fiks KB, Rosen TS. Resilient children: individual differences in developmental outcome of children born to drug abusers. *J Genet Psychol*. 1990;151:523–539.

16. Sameroff A, Seifer R, Barocas R, Lax M, Greenspan S. Intelligence quotient scores of 4 year old children: social environmental risk factors. *Pediatrics*. 1987;79:343–350.

17. Garbarino J, Dubrow N, Kostelny D, Pardo C. *Children in Danger: Coping with the Consequences of Community Violence*. San Francisco, Calif: Jossey-Bass; 1992.

18. Wallace IF. Socioeconomic issues in longitudinal research of high-risk infants. In: Vietz PM, Vaughn HG, eds. *Early Identification of Infants with Developmental Disabilities*. Philadelphia, Pa: Grune & Stratton; 1988.

19. Greenspan SI, Lieberman AF. Infants, mothers and their interactions: a quantitative clinical developmental approach to assessment. In: Greenspan SI, Pollock GH, eds. *The Course of Life: Psychoanalytic Contribution toward Understanding Personality Development, I*. Washington, DC: National Institute of Mental Health; 1980.

20. Arend R. Continuity of individual application from infancy to kindergarten. *Child Dev*. 1979;50:950–959.

21. Matas L, Arend R, Sroufe L. Continuity and adaptation in the second year: the relationship between quality of attachment and later competence. *Child Dev*. 1978;49:549–556.

22. Bell S. The development of the concept of objects as related to mother–infant attachment. *Child Dev*. 1970;41:291–311.

23. Sroufe LA. Pathways to adaptation and maladaptation: psychopathology on developmental deviation. In: Cicchetti, D, ed. *The Rochester Syr. posium on Developmental Psychopathology*. Hillsdale, NJ: Erlbaum; 1990.

24. Bowlby J. *Attachment & Loss: Vol I Attachment*. New York, NY: Basic Books; 1969.

25. Garmezy N, Rutter M, eds. *Stress Coping & Development in Children*. New York, NY: McGraw-Hill; 1983.

26. Rutter M. *Helping Troubled Children*. Middlesex, England: Penguin Books; 1975.

27. Alexsandrowicz M, Alexsandrowicz D. The molding of personality. *Child Psychiatry Hum Dev*. 1975;(5)4: 231–241.

28. Molfese VJ. *Perinatal Risk & Infant Development: Assessment and Prediction*. New York, NY: Guilford; 1989.

29. Vohr B. Preterm cognitive development: biologic and environment influences. *Inf Young Children*. 1991;3:20–29.

30. Dixson B. *Environmental Effects on Fetal Development*. Sacramento, Calif: California Department of Education; 1988.

31. Allen MC. Developmental implications of intrauterine growth retardation. *Inf Young Children*. 1992;3:13–28.

32. Streissguth AP, Barr HM, Sampson PD, Darby BL, Martin DC. IQ at age 4 in relation to maternal alcohol use and smoking during pregnancy. *Dev Psychol*. 1989;25:3–11.

33. Broman SH, Nichols PL, Kennedy WA. *Preschool IQ: Prenatal and Early Developmental Correlates*. Hillsdale, NJ: Erlbaum; 1975.

34. Horowitz FD. Using developmental theory to guide the search for the effects of biological risk factors on the development of children. *Am J Clin Nutr*. 1989;50:589–597.

35. Siegel LS. Home environmental influences on cognitive development in preterm and full term children during first five years. In: Gottfried AW, ed. *Home Environment and Early Cognitive Development*. Orlando, Fla: Academic Press; 1984.

36. Field TM, Dempsey JR, Shuman HH. Developmental follow-up of pre- and post-term infants. In: Friedman SL, Sigman M, eds. *Preterm Birth and Psychological Development*. New York, NY: Academic Press; 1981.

37. Johnson HL. Path analysis of variables affecting 36-month outcome in a population of multi-risk children. *Inf Behav Dev*. 1987;10:451–465.

38. Campbell S. *Behavior Problems in Preschool Children*. New York, NY: Guilford; 1990.

39. US Department of Health and Human Services, Family Support Administration. *Characteristics and Financial Circumstances of AFDC Recipients, FY 1987*. Washington, DC: US Government Printing Office; 1989.

40. Bassuk EL, Rubin L, Lauriat AS. Characteristics of sheltered homeless families. *Am J Public Health*. 1986;76:1097–1101.

41. Zeitel LV. Infant illness among New York's disadvantaged. In: Krasner MI, ed. *Poverty & Health in New York City*. New York, NY: United Hospital Fund of New York; 1989.

42. Wilson JW. *The Truly Disadvantaged: The Inner City, The Underclass and Public Policy*. Chicago, Ill: University of Chicago Press; 1987.

43. Garbarino J, Dubrow N, Kostelny K. *Progress Report*. Chicago, Ill: Erikson Institute; 1989.

44. National Center for Children in Poverty. *Five Million Children: A Statistical Profile of Our Poorest Young Citizens*. New York, NY: Columbia University School of Public Health; 1990.

45. Field T. Teenage, lower-class black mothers and their preterm infants: an international and developmental follow-up. *Child Dev*. 1980;51:426–435.

46. Finnegan L. *Drug Dependency in Pregnancy: Clinical Management of Mother and Child*. (NIDA Service Research Monograph Service). Washington, DC: US Government Printing Office; 1989.

47. Masten A, Garmezy N. Risk, vulnerability and protective factors in developmental psychopathology. In: Lahey DB, Kazdin AE, eds. *Advances in Clinical Child Psychology*. Vol. 8. New York, NY: Plenum; 1985.

48. Als H, Duffy FH. Neurobehavioral assessment in the newborn period: opportunity for early detection of later learning disabilities and for early intervention. *Birth Defects*. 1989;25:127–152.

49. Poulsen MK. *Schools Meet the Challenge: Educational Needs of Children at Risk Due to Prenatal Substance Exposure*. Sacramento, Calif: Special Resources in Education; 1992.

50. Honig AS. Stress and coping in children. *Young Child*. 1986;5:50–61.

51. US General Accounting Office. *Integrating Human Services: Linking At-Risk Families with Services More Successful Than System Reform Efforts*. Washington, DC: Human Resources Division, General Accounting Office; 1992.

Infant mental health: A consultation and treatment team for at-risk infants and toddlers

Jean M. Valliere, BCSW, ACSW
Program Manager
Consultation and Treatment Team for
   At-Risk Infants and Toddlers
Division of Infant, Child, and
   Adolescent Psychiatry
Louisiana State University Medical
   Center
New Orleans, Louisiana

YOUNG CHILDREN are the fastest growing segment of the homeless population today, representing approximately 30% of homeless individuals.[1] The majority of homeless families are headed by single women, and a growing number of these mothers are adolescents. Studies with adolescent parents over the years have consistently shown that their children are at increased risk for emotional disorders and lowered developmental outcomes, while characteristics thought to be protective for adolescent parents and their children, such as high levels of social support, are clearly not available to the homeless.[2-4] Additionally, profiles of homeless adolescents find a high prevalence of behavioral and emotional disorders and, frequently, histories of extreme emotional deprivation, all factors that can negatively affect parenthood even under more optimal circumstances.[5]

Adolescents find themselves homeless due to several factors, the most common being domestic violence, parental substance abuse, sexual abuse, and lack of financial resources.[6] A majority of homeless and runaway youths themselves come from single, female-headed families with multiple problems. Almost a third were formerly in foster care;[6] additionally, as many as 30% of homeless youth have substance abuse problems.[6]

This article will describe an infant mental-health consultation and treatment program for homeless infants (birth to 3), their adolescent parents, and the agency staff that serves them. The program is located in a shelter that provides short- and long-term residential services and a community-based service center. Each program component will be described.

INFANT MENTAL HEALTH TEAM

In 1991 an interdisciplinary infant mental-health team at the Louisiana State University Medical Center responded to a request to provide effective programming and treatment for families in a large shelter for homeless adolescents.

This program is supported by The Institute for Mental Hygiene, New Orleans, Louisiana. Appreciation is expressed to Charles Zeanah, MD; Julie Larrieu, PhD; Ana Fick, PhD; and Martin Drell, MD, for their assistance.

Inf Young Children, 1994; 6(3): 46–53

Funded by a private foundation for 3 years, the team provides consultation, training, direct services, and program evaluation to the agency and homeless infants (birth to 3 years) and their parents. The box entitled "Consultation and Treatment Team for At-Risk Infants and Toddlers" lists program components. The team consists of a psychiatrist, a developmental and a clinical psychologist, and a social worker. The program serves as a rotation for trainees in psychiatry, psychology, and social work in the Division of Infant, Child, and Adolescent Psychiatry. The team is funded to serve infants and their parents of either sex. Custodial parents have been mothers without exception so far. The team has also served several married couples and involves fathers at every opportunity.

The shelter, Convenant House, which opened in 1988, serves homeless and runaway youth between the ages of 16 and 21 years. The services provided are a short-term shelter program, a long-term residential program, and a community services center, where case management, GED classes, life skills, parenting classes, and limited child care services are offered. Approximately 50% of the youths receiving services are young women, and over 50% of these young women have one or more children or are pregnant during their stay at the shelter. In a given year, the agency serves about 260 children ages 3 years and under in the residential programs and approximately 170 through community services. Newborns are common, and several mothers have more than one child. Mothers with a substance abuse history (10% to 30%) are also served. Most mothers report histories of sexual, physical, or emotional abuse, with a significant number reporting suicide attempts. Approximately 70% of the families served are African-American and 30% White. Three percent are human immunodeficiency virus (HIV) positive. Length of stay can be from one night in the Crisis Center to up to 2 years in the long-term program. The agency also has an on-site health service staffed by registered nurses and volunteer physicians.

Consultation and Treatment Team for At-Risk Infants and Toddlers
Primary responsibilities

Consultation
    Intervention
        Educational support/training
            Program evaluation/research
Additional team goals
- Assistance with referral
- Improved identification of client needs
- Identification of appropriate interventions
- Data collection
- Assistance in securing future grants

CONSULTATION SERVICES

The team has the objective of offering consultative services to the shelter, for whom services to infants and parents are only part of the mission. The team provides ongoing program consultation, case consultation, and case conferencing with each of the three programs weekly.

During the first year of the grant, the team concentrated on efforts to work collaboratively with management and staff in designing programming for the parent/child population in residence. The team viewed this as an opportunity to use the milieu itself as a positive intervention for infant mental health. The first step was to survey and incorporate existing parent/child services within the agency and to make the physical environment child friendly. This included establishing a play area on both the girls' floor and the communal lounge area. A series of meetings to determine program parameters for infants and parents followed. The resulting schedule for the Family Life Program participants (all mothers and children) in the Short Term Shelter Program reflects the results of consultation (see the box entitled "Family Life Daily Schedule").

Homeless adolescent mothers are at increased risk for difficulties in parenting. Many teen mothers in the shelter may not know how to care for and support healthy development. For some mothers, their own emotional neediness often pre-

---

Family Life Daily Schedule

6:30 AM	Wake up
7:00 AM	
7:30 AM	Breakfast
8:00 AM	AM meeting/chores
9:30 AM	Snack Plus
10:00 AM	FOGIN
11:15 AM	Lunch
12 Noon	Nap/rest time
1:00 PM	Nap/rest time
1:30 PM	Nap/rest time
	Parent Education Program (PEP)
2:00 PM	PEP
2:30 PM	Snack Plus
3:00 PM	
4:00 PM	Father's Support Group (Th)
4:00 PM	Mother's Respite (M–F)
5:15 PM	Dinner
6:00 PM	Bathing, and grooming
7:00 PM	Babies' bedtime
8:00 PM	Personal care
9:00 PM	Night meeting

cludes their being able to play and respond to their children positively and to interpret their babies' communicative attempts.[2] Very few of the mothers in the shelter have had access to developmental information. Moreover, since they come from highly troubled families, they have had limited positive experiences on which to base healthy, culturally validated child-rearing practices. Toddlers who are beginning to individuate and separate from their mothers are especially at risk for being ignored and are frequently characterized as being "bad." Communicative attempts are often misread or unnoticed. Babies are frequently either held continuously or, conversely, are rarely held to avoid "spoiling" the child.

The team's goal is to facilitate the adolescents' development of a "parent" identity. To work toward this end, both the structure of the day and specific interventions were planned to increase the potential for enjoyable and empathic discovery of the infant as an individual and to further promote healthy and responsive interaction between mother and child. A series of daily activities, Snack Plus, Mother's Respite, and Family of Origin/Ghosts in the Nursery Group (FOGIN),[7] was implemented to support such growth. (A description of the FOGIN [7] group will be found in the information about the Direct Services component.)

Snack Plus is an activity that includes a healthy snack and guided interaction between mother and baby. Participants are provided with developmentally appropriate toys and are gently prompted to notice aspects of the child's response to the toy and to the mother in her attempts to play with her baby. A number of mothers have difficulty waiting for the baby to respond and following the baby's lead in play. To promote interaction, each family is seated at individual tables, and a volunteer may assist in the care of other children in the family. We found that mothers will sit together and talk to each other rather than play with their children without this support. In addition, many mothers with newborns will tend to focus on the baby and not attend to the older child, who is expected to be more independent and less in need of the mother's attention than it is realistic to expect. Toddlers are thought to be endowed with near-adult reasoning abilities and are often expected to anticipate their parents' needs. Indeed, "parentified" 3- and 4-year-olds are not unusual at Covenant House. Snack Plus is run by trained agency staff, with continuing consultation by a team member.

When it was pointed out that adolescent parents, often with more than one child, were weary of both the program demands and the demands of their role as parents, it became apparent that they needed some time for respite. So a daily Parent's Respite hour was created. During this hour, agency staff provide creative activities for the children, and the parent is free to use this time as he or she wishes. A team member provides consultation to this activity. Once developed, the respite hour was often attended by parents and other childless adolescents as well as the young children staying at the shelter. The team agreed that adolescents would be permitted to stay if they would play.

Team members also provide consultation to individual staff members upon request. Case managers often have difficulty dealing with a particular client. A young mother who woke up screaming every night frightened the staff and disrupted the shelter routine. As typical in such cases, agency staff considered discharging the young woman. A team member explained posttraumatic stress disorder and consulted with the night case manager on workable strategies for calming the resident. Instead of the resident being discharged, she was better understood and supported. In another example, an aggressive 2-year-old, who roamed around the shelter and tended to run from his mother, got a reputation for being "bad." In fact, the team realized that a lack of attention and poor behavior management techniques were responsible. A negative identification of the child was prevented by meeting with the mother to support and to increase her attending behavior to her son and by meeting with training shelter staff to discuss the developmental needs of 2-year-olds.

TRAINING

Training activities for shelter staff take place through staff seminars (monthly), hands-on activity training (Snack Plus, FOGIN, Parent's Respite), and cluster

---

Training Topics

Monthly Trainings

Behavior Modifications 1	Behavior Modifications 2
Postpartum Depression	Violence and Children
Adolescence	Adolescent Mothers
Eating Disorders	Grief
Setting Limits with Adolescents	Setting Limits with Toddlers
Ethnically Diverse Parenting Styles	Child Development: Early Childhood
The Importance of Family of Origin	Cultural Sensitivity and Ethnic Issues

Childhood Sexual Abuse—Implications for Adolescence
Working with Adolescents with Borderline Personality Disorder
Babies Whose Mothers Abused Substances During Pregnancy
The Hateful Resident (Transference and Countertransference)

Cluster Trainings

Series 1	Series 2
Environments for Infants and Toddlers:	Major Domains of Parent–Child Relation-
1. Supporting Cognitive and Language Development	ships
	Clinical Foci for Interventions in Infant
2. Supporting Social-Emotional Development	Mental Health
	Methods of Assessing Infants and Toddlers
3. Supporting Motor Development and Self-Help Skills	Individual, Family, and Group Interventions in Infant Mental Health

training for special interest topics (see box entitled "Training Topics"). Staff training topics are based on the results of an agency-wide needs assessment combined
with the training needs of the agency as perceived by the team. The results of the
needs assessment show that many staff members are interested in learning more
about infant behavior and development, while others are concerned about the
parent's behavior alone. Presentations on adolescent behavior in general, the primary concern of most of the staff, are also requested. All training sessions are
evaluated by staff members. There is limited time available for training and considerable turnover in case management staff, so the model of a monthly/cluster/
consulting training approach seems to work well within these parameters.

An especially prominent concern of staff members is the physical punishment
of young children by their mothers. Agency rules forbid corporal punishment, yet
it is the disciplinary method of choice for many of the young mothers. This is a
very sensitive issue, and not being able to hit often makes the mothers feel as if the
last bit of control that they had over their child's life has been removed. Therefore
replacing the mothers' hitting with another strategy they can try immediately is
important.

Didactic presentations about effective discipline have been a major topic of
interest in formal monthly training sessions, in training for specific activities such
as Snack Plus, and in an ongoing way on an individual basis with floor staff.
Agency staff, in turn, address alternative methods of discipline with residents
through parent education classes that they provide. The team's impression is that a
number of staff members have made considerable progress in feeling comfortable
about intervening when a mother is disciplining her child harshly. These staff
members seem better able to help mothers calm down and try other methods of
discipline.

The team has developed certain principles regarding training that seem to be
most successful in meeting the needs of the shelter. Training is not "theory bound"
but is practical information tailored to the daily experiences of the case managers
and clients. Team members also use actual episodes, as they occur, to teach on an
individual basis.

DIRECT SERVICES

In many respects the most exciting and challenging part of the project is providing treatment in a community setting, with the potential to use the milieu with a
variety of therapeutic approaches. The direct services offered are crisis intervention, assessment, short- and long-term parent/child therapy, and FOGIN groups.[7]

Crisis intervention plays a continuous role in the provision of services throughout both residential and community services. Many of the young mothers entering

the shelter program are in crisis due to their new homeless state, while long-term residents and community clients may suffer personal attack, the death of a person close to them, or other traumatic events that leave them numb and unable to function completely at that point in time. Crisis events are used as an opportunity for supported personal growth. Interestingly enough, many clients finding themselves homeless or victimized by personal assault or another such highly upsetting situation can be rather blunted in response because of the frequency with which they have found themselves in similar situations.

Certain assessments are built into the therapeutic process for treatment and research purposes. A mother entering into treatment is given the Working Model Interview,[8] designed to provide the clinician with a sense of the parent's representation of the child and her relationship with the child. This is followed by a structured play assessment[9] designed to look at various dimensions of the parent–child relationship through parent–child interaction. Both of these assessments are videotaped and are parent friendly in that the mothers usually find the videotaping interesting. Many of the mothers the team has seen have not had many opportunities to talk about themselves, their feelings, and their relationships with their infants in the context of a supportive therapeutic relationship. Although it can be quite painful for some clients, these assessment procedures seem to clarify and focus the therapeutic goals and to legitimize both the mothers' and children's needs and pain.

One young mother found it difficult to be too close to her 2-year-old. She would shift away from her baby, clearly anxious. She interacted little with her child, who appeared bright but showed delays in expressive language. Through assessment, the team found that issues with her own mother and painful childhood were intruding into her thoughts when interacting with her child. With therapeutic intervention, the mother became able to separate her own childhood feelings from those of her daughter. Her interactions with her child increased, and the child's language skills and behavior improved.

Psychiatric evaluation, another aspect of treatment, is especially helpful due to the "open intake" policy of the agency. It is not unusual for young people suffering from mental illness to present themselves at the agency. If not in an actively dangerous state to themselves or another, the agency will take them in. In these cases, psychiatric evaluation aids in immediate referral to a more appropriate agency or recommendations for treatment and supervision that benefit both other team members and agency staff.

If the child's developmental status is in question, the Bayley Scales of Infant Development[10] may be administered. For a late 2- or 3-year-old, another comparable assessment may be selected at the discretion of the psychologist. A monthly screening program for language development and hearing has been established. Any child for whom any developmental concerns are indicated is referred to local

Fig 1. FOGIN Art Therapy: "Draw a picture of you when you were little."

early-intervention programs and is provided with consultative services with staff and agency day-care providers.

Therapeutic approaches to the mother–infant dyad are varied. Babies are always seen in session with the parent, and infant–parent psychotherapy, as described by Fraiberg,[11] may be employed. Speaking for the Baby,[12] a technique developed to help parents successfully read their babies' cues with the use of videotaped play sessions, is also used in the program. Interaction Guidance,[13] a treatment approach for parent–child relationship disturbances, also uses videotaping as part of the process and is useful with this population. Adolescent mothers seem to enjoy seeing themselves on tape, a fact that makes approaches such as these beneficial.

FOGIN (Family of Origin/Ghosts in the Nursery)[7] therapeutic group meets three times weekly. In FOGIN groups, family-of-origin issues and parenting values and practices are explored to help clients understand how the parenting they received as children influences how they parent their children. FOGIN is an attempt to use a group to integrate patterns of feelings, beliefs, and practices to increase awareness of and choices about learned parenting behaviors and to lead to an improved understanding of the child's needs. The third meeting of the week uses an art therapy format for expressive purposes (Fig 1).

The team learned that a certain perspective is needed before proceeding with treatment of any kind. A willingness to accept and to learn about different styles of culturally validated parenting and a tolerance for a long period of rapport building are essential. Finding a way to keep clients involved is crucial. Team members often see new clients in the residential programs several times a week, especially during times of transition. Often clients leave the agency abruptly and cycle through several times, in which case they are picked up for services again. Adolescent parents can be amazingly resilient in the face of traumatic pasts, and positive attributes need to be gently nurtured and supported. Familiarity with sexual abuse issues, posttraumatic stress disorder, and depression is extremely helpful, in addition to expertise in infant and adolescent mental health and development. Engaging clients in the therapeutic process is challenging, and progress must be viewed in small increments.

PROGRAM EVALUATION/RESEARCH

Program evaluation measures are challenging and broad in focus. Initial attempts to solicit residents' feelings about treatment were complicated by the team's inability to find the resident over the specified periods of time. Follow-up procedures are now being designed that will elicit evaluative feedback from clients who are receiving services currently as well as those we may be able to locate who have received services in the past. Shelter staff members evaluate each training session and complete yearly training needs assessments. Agency administrators meet periodically with the team to report on changing agency needs and give feedback about how they perceive treatment and program recommendations.

Research activities are numerous. Data are collected from the team's standardized assessments, which are videotaped. Data on child and parent exposures to violence and on maternal depression and stress are being collected for later analysis. The team has also obtained permission to abstract health awareness and practice information from shelter medical charts for further analysis.

IMPLICATIONS FOR INFANT MENTAL HEALTH PRACTITIONERS

The experiences of the Infant Mental Health Team arc ongoing at this point, and data for program evaluation and research efforts are yet to be analyzed. Nevertheless, after 2 years of practice, the team has learned that a nontraditional, community-based approach to infant mental health permits a broader range of treatment opportunities and intervention strategies than would be possible in a traditional clinic setting. The team believes that intervention programs may be placed within larger agencies such as schools, homeless shelters, transitional housing facilities, and other treatment programs where other critical services can be provided. Consultative services ought to be integrated within these programs, and all levels of staff should be addressed.

Training activities need to be experience oriented. Staff-requested training topics, using examples from current cases, should be the core of training across levels of service provision. Theory may be used in explanation of actions and in support of recommended intervention approaches, but should not be taught in isolation from actual cases.

Successful intervention relies upon an underpinning of flexible treatment approaches, informal client/clinician relationship opportunities, and sensitivity to and respect for cultural differences. The client's potential for emotional resilience should be a major focus when working with this population. In the team's experience, joint provision of education and psychotherapy regarding parenting is more effective in changing parenting behavior than either alone.

For homeless infants and adolescent parents, stabilization and fulfillment of basic needs must be met before any lasting mental health intervention can occur. Interventions chosen within the larger context of the adolescent's life facilitate optimal service delivery. The team has found that working with this population, while very challenging and at times frustrating, is life affirming and can make a difference.

REFERENCES

1. U.S. Conference of Mayors Survey, Washington, DC; 1990.
2. Osofsky J, Hann D, Peebles C. Adolescent parenthood: risks and opportunities for mothers and infants. In: Zeanah C, ed. *Handbook of Infant Mental Health*. New York, NY: Guilford Press; 1993.
3. Badger C, Elsass S, Sutherland JM. *Mother Training as a Means of Accelerating Childhood Development in a High Risk Population*. Cincinnati, Ohio: University of Cincinnati; 1974.
4. Sameroff AJ, Chandler MJ. Reproductive risk and the continuum of caretaking casualty. In: Hororwitz FD, Hetherington M, Scarr-Salapatek S, et al, eds. *Review of Child Development Research 4*. Chicago, Ill: University of Chicago Press; 1975.
5. Feitel, B, Margetson N, Chamas J, Lipman C. Psychosocial background and behavioral and emotional disorders of homeless and runaway youth. *Hosp Commun Psychiatry*. 1992;43(2):155–159.
6. Shane PG. Changing patterns among homeless and runaway youth. *Am J Orthopsychiatry*. 1989;59(2): 208–214.
7. Fraiberg S, Adelson E, Shapiro V. Ghosts in the Nursery: a psychoanalytic approach to the problems of impaired infant-mother relationships. *J Am Acad Child Psychiatry*. 1975;14:387–421.
8. Zeanah C, Benoit D, Hirshberg L, Barton M, Regan C. Mothers' representations of their infants are concordant with infant attachment classifications. *Dev Issues Psychiatry*. In press.
9. Crowell J, Feldman S. Mothers' internal models of relationships and children's behavioral and developmental status: a study of mother-child interaction. *Child Dev*. 1988;59:1273–1285.
10. Bayley N. *Bayley Scales of Infant Development*. New York, NY: Psychological Corp; 1969.
11. Fraiberg S, ed. *Clinical Infant Studies in the First Year of Life*. New York, NY: Basic Books; 1980.

12. Carter S, Osofsky J, Hann DM. Speaking for the Baby: therapeutic interventions with adolescent mothers and their infants. *Infant Mental Health J*. 1991b;12:291–301.

13. McDonough SC. Interaction guidance: understanding and treating early infant-caregiver relationship disturbances. In: Zeanah C, ed. *Handbook of Infant Mental Health*. New York, NY: Guilford Press; 1993.

Social competence in young children with visual impairments

Elizabeth J. Erwin, EdD
Queens College
City University of New York
School of Education
Flushing, New York

THE LITERATURE in early childhood continues to reflect a strong interest in the social competence of young children. The ability to socialize with others is a fundamental skill that is not only needed in childhood but continues throughout the life cycle. As stated by Odom et al,[1] "social competence is a central organizing theme for development and, essentially, for life."[1(p2)] While there are several dimensions of social competence, this article will specifically examine competence in the context of effective and appropriate interactions with others.

Youngsters who are blind or visually impaired often face challenges regarding social competence due to the nature of their disability. The ability to process visual information plays an important role in the social-communicative process. Not only do the eyes relay messages, but they also serve as a primary tool for retrieving information during social encounters. Without clear access to valuable information, monitoring and maintaining social exchanges become more difficult. The impact and implications of a visual impairment will vary for a child who is blind as compared to a child with low vision.

Given the potential risks, it would seem likely that there would be more literature examining social competence in young children with visual impairments. However, there is a dearth of empirical data regarding peer relationships in youngsters with visual impairments.[2] In fact, most of what is known about social competence and peer relationships is based upon literature of school-aged children with visual impairments.[3] Very little is known regarding specific aspects of socialization in youngsters with visual impairments such as sharing and taking turns, establishing friendships, and resolving conflicts.

The literature regarding social norms in children with visual impairments should be viewed cautiously. Ferrell[4] pointed out concerns about past studies that identified developmental social norms for children who are blind and visually impaired,[5–8] which include: (1) problems regarding technical soundness, (2) measures that are unreliable and invalid, and (3) small sample sizes resulting in generalizability limitations. Thus there is a great need to synthesize the existing literature in early childhood to better understand the implications of visual impairment on social interactions.

This article is supported in part by grant no. H023B10041, awarded by the Office of Special Education Programs, US Department of Education. This material does not necessarily reflect the position or policies of the US Department of Education, and no official endorsement should be inferred.

Inf Young Children, 1994; 6(3): 26–33

SOCIAL INTERACTIONS BETWEEN INFANTS WITH VISUAL IMPAIRMENTS AND THEIR FAMILIES

For the young infant, vision represents security and continuity. But for infants who have a visual impairment, there is a strong need to be frequently held or talked to to be in touch with their caregiver as well as the environment.[5,9]

During a social exchange, if one of the individuals has a vision loss or impairment, establishing a mutual point of reference, interpreting partner's intent, and building upon a particular topic can create obstacles in child/caregiver interactions.[10] It is typically the family who forms the first social attachment with an infant. The members of a family can include mother, father, siblings, grandparent, or other person responsible for the infant's care. However, past studies on early interactions in youngsters with visual impairment have focused on mother and infant dyads.

Empirical evidence on relationships between infants with visual impairments and their mothers reveals that infants' behavior, such as vocalizing and gesturing, did not increase, as would be expected when mothers interacted with them.[11] The five participants in Rowland's study, ranging in age from 11 to 32 months, were all identified as totally blind; some also had additional disabilities. In another study examining social interaction patterns, Rogers and Puchalski[12] discovered that infants who are blind or visually impaired respond to and initiate social exchanges with their mothers less frequently than sighted babies. This study involved 21 infants aged 4 to 25 months with visual impairments and 16 sighted subjects as the control group. Rogers and Puchalski[12] also found that parents of infants who are visually impaired tend to spend less time looking at their baby compared to parents of sighted infants.

There is also evidence to indicate that while infants who are blind and visually impaired exhibit typical behaviors for expressing pleasure and displeasure,[11] they possess a limited range of behaviors for initiating and maintaining social interactions.[5,13] Consequently, the absence of conventional interaction behaviors, such as a smile or eye contact, can often be misinterpreted by the parent as disinterest or lack of affection. This is not meant to suggest that babies who are blind or visually impaired do not smile. Rather, when engaging in interactions, the lack or misinterpretation of communicative signals between an infant with visual impairments and his or her mother can exist.[5,9,13–15] For example, because a baby could not see when her mother smiled at her, the baby did not respond in a way that was reinforcing to the mother. Possibly, then, neither partner receives the benefits of a mutually satisfying interaction.[12] Subsequently a strained relationship can develop in the early months.[5,11]

Parents serve as a critical resource for successfully negotiating the affective turn-taking process,[9,11] and for promoting an understanding of characteristics, functions, and relationships among objects, events, and people in the environment.[10] Acknowledging and translating infant behaviors represent a critical function for parents who have children with visual impairments. However, this is no easy task for family members. In a study that videotaped the natural interactions between six young children with varying degrees of visual impairments and their families, Kekelis and Andersen[10] found that the lack of visual cues frequently made it difficult to understand what the youngster was trying to communicate verbally. Furthermore, Kekelis and Andersen[10] discovered that during conversation, parents of children who are visually impaired presented more child-focused topics rather than environment-focused topics, which may contribute to why youngsters with visual impairments produce mostly self-centered topics during social encounters.

For most infants and toddlers, the immediate family provides the first opportunities for social contact. The communicative competence a young child develops in the early years can be extremely instrumental in establishing a solid foundation for which later learning can be built. Not only does the family's perception of the child's visual impairment have an impact on the quality of social exchanges between that child and family[10] but these early experiences with family members also affect the interactive patterns that children with visual impairments eventually use with social partners outside the home environment.[16]

PEER INTERACTIONS AND YOUNG CHILDREN WITH VISUAL IMPAIRMENTS

The way that others respond to a child's visual impairment can influence the socialization process more than other areas of development.[15] Other people tend to have a powerful effect on this socialization process because the nature of social interactions inherently signifies reciprocity. Scholl[17] maintained that the peer group enhances self-esteem in children who are blind by offering feedback and reinforcement about their actions and behaviors. Scholl[17] further suggested that "the more limited range of peers and peer experiences may have a retarding effect on the development of the self-concept."[17(p79)]

For youngsters with visual impairments, the opportunity to interact, negotiate, and play with peers (some who are sighted and some who are visually impaired) is an essential component in the socialization process. In a study examining age-appropriate social skills, one of the greatest areas for intervention of three kindergarteners who were functionally blind included maintaining peer relationships.[18] Promoting peer networks and friendships is one of the most important challenges faced by practitioners working with youngsters with visual impairments.[2,3,19]

Within the field of vision, the influence of peers during early childhood, particularly in inclusive settings, has not been given much attention. The impact of a vision loss on the development of social competence and friendships has also received little attention.[16] The body of literature that does exist on experiences between sighted and visually impaired young children has either lacked internal and external validity or has been primarily opinion based.[20] Although this type of information does contribute to the bank of knowledge, the lack of scientific evidence compounds the difficulty in producing and implementing effective intervention measures.

One of the most comprehensive investigations on interactions between sighted and visually impaired peers was a year-long qualitative study describing social experiences in kindergarten and first-grade classes.[16] The subjects were six children who were legally blind and did not have any other disabilities. Many themes emerged from this investigation that provide a solid foundation for further inquiry. For example, youngsters with visual impairments tended to use physical contact rather than eye contact during social exchanges with classmates. In some instances this was viewed as inappropriate by the sighted peers, perhaps because in today's society touching others is generally not an acceptable form of behavior.

Another important finding from this study indicates that not only did breakdowns in communication take place between sighted and visually impaired peers, but also the youngsters did not attempt to repair these breakdowns. For example, if during an exchange a child with a visual impairment failed to respond to his or her partner, the interaction just ended. Likewise, peers with visual impairments failed to repair any breakdown with their sighted classmates. Kekelis and Sacks[16] suggested that these communication breakdowns have occurred so often that youngsters with visual impairments took them for granted. At any rate, little effort was initiated to repair these communication breakdowns.

Since not all initiation attempts successfully result in an interaction, understanding the dynamics of how interactions are established, maintained, and terminated can provide some insight into the complexity of social networks in early childhood. Additional research suggested that young children with visual impairments tend to use similar strategies to gain access to and to maintain peer exchanges regardless of the type of setting they attend.[21] This study, which was part of a larger investigation on social participation and peer interactions, examined the social behavior of 30 preschoolers with varying degrees of visual impairments during free play periods and compared behavior across inclusive and specialized settings. Findings indicated that the strategies that study participants in both types of settings use to gain entry to a peer interaction are not necessarily the behaviors that are most successful in maintaining an exchange.

Additional evidence suggested that there are no significant differences between integrated and specialized environments in young children with visual impairment on social participation (ie, unoccupied behavior, solitary play, transition, peer interactions).[2] It is important to note, however, that children in integrated placements attended programs less frequently and were in larger class sizes than youngsters in specialized settings, suggesting that quality may be a better indicator of successful outcomes than quantity. In both types of settings, preschoolers with visual impairments tended to spend the greatest proportion of time engaged in solitary play and the least amount of time transitioning from one activity to another.

While it is important to recognize that children are often quite capable of selecting and establishing their own relationships, teachers can play an important role in broadening the base of peer support. There is a growing body of literature reinforcing the importance of adult involvement in promoting peer relationships between youngsters who are visually impaired and their peers.[18,20,22-24] Since communication breakdown and misinterpretation is at high risk during social encounters with young children with visual impairments, adult intervention can be instrumental in facilitating positive encounters among peers.

In one study that examined teacher involvement and peer interactions, Workman[25] found that teacher verbalizations can facilitate social exchanges between preschoolers who are visually impaired and their typical peers. Workman[25] discovered that specific strategies have a greater impact on promoting interactions between peers. For instance, teacher interventions that were most successful in promoting peer exchanges were descriptions of social environment (ie, "Jose is the doctor") and direct and indirect prompts (ie, "Give the cashier the money"; "Everyone join hands"). Workman[25] suggested that teachers play a fundamental role in mediating the environment. To provide access to social opportunities, educators must skillfully arrange the environment for youngsters who are visually impaired. Workman's[25] study defined the specific behaviors of the teachers; however, it did not identify the type of peer interactions that occurred. Thus additional information about the nature, type, and frequency of social interactions among youngsters with visual impairments is still warranted.

In another study that compared the social competence of both preschoolers who are legally blind and those who are sighted within their natural education environments, Markovits and Strayer[26] found that sighted subjects demonstrated a mean rate of social interactive sequences that was three times higher than youngsters with visual impairments. These data also indicate that exchanges among peers with visual impairments were shorter and fewer than that of typical peers. Subjects with visual impairments also showed a high frequency of ignoring and turning away behaviors. Because social interactions generally depend on effective communication, analyzing language and communication skills in young children with visual impairments can provide a framework for beginning to conceptualize this process.

SOCIAL-COMMUNICATION COMPETENCE IN YOUNG CHILDREN WITH VISUAL IMPAIRMENTS

Although language is not necessary for a social exchange to occur, it serves as a primary source for communicating. The art of communicating tends to be a complex and sophisticated process. Kekelis and Sacks[16] identified the following important dynamics involved during social interactions among peers: (1) eye gaze to regulate reciprocity, (2) eye gaze and gestures to establish topic of conversation, (3) eye gaze and smiles to invite participation from listener, and (4) contextual information to provide information for responses. All of these demand the use of vision in one form or another. Should vision be absent or impaired, barriers to communication may develop.

In studying peer interactions, it can be useful to investigate similarities and differences in language development and competence between children who are sighted and those who are visually impaired. Whereas clinical observations are extremely instrumental for research and intervention purposes in the field of vision, some suggest that this information is also valuable in discovering more about typical development and competence.[27,28] Caution should be taken against the use of sighted developmental norms for acquiring knowledge about youngsters with visual impairments for the following reasons: (1) theories of typical development may be inaccurate, (2) perspectives on the processes followed by children with visual impairments can result in inflexible expectations, and (3) interventions should be based upon empirical data of the population intended to benefit from the results.[13]

Because different learning styles and strategies for sighted and blind children exist, differences regarding language application may also exist. Youngsters who are blind and visually impaired rarely generalized their words to contexts and references beyond the original one,[29–31] possess a limited ability to indicate their interest in a conversational topic or partner,[3] and may encounter difficulty initiating and maintaining social interactions.[5,16,18,21,27] Furthermore, during social exchanges young children who are blind and visually impaired generally produced self-centered topics and referred only to objects and people within their immediate environment.[10,13,29,30–32] These constraints in word usage and application may be directly influenced by the lack of visual input or by the restricted visual input that children who are blind or visually impaired receive when learning about their environment. Urwin[13] suggested that these patterns form during the preverbal stage of development.

Without visual feedback, it is often difficult for children who are blind to determine if and when they are being addressed.[10,16] Research on the social-communicative competence of children with visual impairments leads to a better understanding of the complex dynamic process involved during social interactions.

Although there may be some discrepancies in language acquisition and usage between sighted and blind children, Urwin[13] maintains that when researchers and practitioners assume that children with visual impairments develop in similar ways to sighted children only with something missing, adaptive strategies used by blind children are ignored. The strategies used by children with visual impairments during social encounters may be compensatory rather than deviant. For example, if a youngster who is blind asks an inordinate number of questions during a conversation, he or she may be attempting to elicit information that cannot otherwise be obtained. Wills[33] pointed out that adults tend to correct children with visual impairments based upon the same expectations that are set for sighted children, instead of realizing and supporting their specific learning processes.

Because a vision loss or impairment may exist, children find ways to deal with the demands of the environment that on the surface appear to differ from strategies used by children who develop with their visual modality. For example, Andersen, Dunlea, and Kekelis[29] suggested that youngsters with visual impairments may look competent when engaging in conversational discourse, but that this may represent delayed imitation rather than mastery of communication skills. In fact, because these children may be fully aware of the principles of reciprocity, repeating their partner's verbalization may assist them in sustaining the social exchange.

Other adaptive communicative strategies observed in youngsters who are blind and visually impaired include depending heavily on familiar objects and routines,[13] posing questions to access information,[34] using physical contact to gain partner's attention or in place of eye contact,[16,35] and imitating utterances generally made by familiar people when direct feedback is limited or unavailable.[31] Sighted children may not need to depend on these strategies as extensively because they are able to use visual behaviors such as eye gaze or nodding to initiate and to maintain social exchanges. As evidenced by the limited knowledge base on peer interactions of young children with visual impairments, the sophistication of social-communicative strategies may not have been fully realized.

IMPLICATIONS FOR PRACTICE

Young children with visual impairments tend to encounter difficulties forming and maintaining social interactions. Barriers to successful communication generally exist for both partners during a social exchange when one person is visually impaired. When the nature and scope of these interactions are better understood, service providers and family members can maximize opportunities for friendships and social contacts to develop naturally. The following suggestions may be helpful in addressing the unique social priorities of youngsters with visual impairments.

- *Respond to all of the child's attempts to communicate.* Especially for infants and toddlers, all forms of communication (verbal and nonverbal) should be acknowledged and encouraged. Natural environments and contexts (eg, bathing, family meals, diaper changing) are ideal for promoting communication. Because youngsters with severe visual impairments may not perceive important visual signals during social encounters such as nodding, smiling, or eye gaze, they need alternative signals. These might include a verbal response, soft touch, or imitation of a child's verbalizations. Another strategy is expanding upon a child's utterances. For example, if a child said "ba" while holding her bottle, an expansion might be, "Yes, you are drinking your bottle. You seem hungry today." By responding to the child's attempts at communication, valuable reinforcement is being provided in a very natural and healthy manner.

- *Minimize the child's tolerance for communication breakdown.* Because communication breakdown can occur through a variety of factors (eg, inability to understand message, difficulty interpreting signals, lack of a mutual reference point), reducing this risk can maximize healthier interactions. First, teach children with visual impairments specific strategies that would repair exchanges instead of just accepting breakdown in communication. Such strategies may include verbally asking the partner for clarification (eg, "I'm not sure what you meant") or acknowledgment (eg, calling partner's name) if exchange seems to end abruptly. In addition, teaching children to "officially" withdraw from an exchange (eg, "I'm finished"; "I'm going to play with the cars now"; waving goodbye) will help to bring closure to an interaction.

- *Assist the child in producing varied topics and references during interactions.* Since children with visual impairments may tend to generate more self-centered topics or references within their immediate context, broadening that base of support will promote more flexibility during social encounters. For example, talking about mommy when she is at work, how she got to work, what she might be doing, and when she will be home is one way of expanding content outside of the here and now. Talking about others when they are not present or discussing future and past events may also help in strengthening children's ability to participate in a variety of topical discussions.

- *Encourage the child to use a variety of strategies to initiate a social interaction.* Since the strategies that children with visual impairments use most frequently to initiate an exchange may not necessarily be the most successful, teaching a variety of initiation strategies may increase the probability of maintaining interactions. For instance, a child who physically approaches another peer, verbally greets him, asks what the peer is doing, and suggests reading a story together has used a combination of four different initiation strategies to generate an exchange. Initiation strategies can include soliciting attention, requesting information, collaborating toward a mutual goal, directing a play scheme, or exhibiting affection or praise. Thus teaching a variety of strategies and encouraging young children to use a combination of such strategies may increase the likelihood of generating more successful social exchanges.

•   •   •

In short, young children with visual impairments have unique priorities that must be addressed during social interactions. Providing opportunities for young children that support and encourage a range of social encounters within a variety of natural contexts (ie, home, school, community) is one key to building foundations for early social competence. Further contributions are needed to strengthen the body of knowledge on social competence in young children with visual impairments. Future research efforts might include quantitative and qualitative investigations on friendship patterns, peer networks, adaptive interaction strategies, and the child's self-concept and self-esteem.

REFERENCES

1. Odom SL, McConnell SR, McEvoy MA, eds. *Social Competence of Young Children with Disabilities*. Baltimore, Md: Paul H. Brookes; 1992.
2. Erwin EJ. Social participation of young children with visual impairments in integrated and specialized settings. *J Visual Impair Blindness*. 1993;5:138–142.
3. Skellenger AC, Hill M, Hill E. The social functioning of children with visual impairments. In: Odom SL, McConnell SR, McEvoy MA, eds. *Social Competence of Young Children with Disabilities*. Baltimore, Md: Paul H. Brookes; 1992.
4. Ferrell KA. Infancy and early childhood. In: Scholl GT, ed. *Foundations of Education for Blind and Visually Handicapped Children and Youth: Theory and Practice*. New York, NY: American Foundation for the Blind; 1986.
5. Fraiberg S. *Insights from the Blind*. New York, NY: Basic Books; 1977.
6. Maxfield KE, Bucholz S. *A Social Maturity Scale for Blind Preschool Children: A Guide to Its Use*. New York, NY: American Foundation for the Blind; 1957.
7. Norris M, Spaulding PJ, Brodie FH. *Blindness in Children*. Chicago, Ill: University of Chicago Press; 1957.
8. Reynell J. *Manual for the Reynell Zinkin Scales*. Windsor, Berkshire, England: NFER-NELSON Publishing; 1983.
9. Als H, Tronick E, Brazelton TB. Affective reciprocity and the development of autonomy: the study of a blind infant. *Am Acad Child Psychiatry*. 1980;19:22–40.
10. Kekelis LS, Andersen ES. Family communication styles and language development. *J Visual Impair Blindness*. 1984;78:54–65.
11. Rowland C. Preverbal communication of blind infants and their mothers. *J Visual Impair Blindness*. 1984;78:297–302.

12. Rogers SJ, Puchalski CB. Social characteristics of visually impaired infants' play. *Top Early Childhood Special Educ.* 1984;3:52–56.

13. Urwin C. Language for absent things: learning from visually handicapped children. *Topics Lang Dis.* 1984;4:24–37.

14. Adelson E. Precursors of early language development in children blind from birth. In: Mills AE, ed. *Language Acquisition in the Blind Child.* San Diego, Calif: College-Hill Press; 1983.

15. Warren DH. *Blindness and Early Childhood Development.* 2nd ed. New York, NY: American Foundation for the Blind; 1984.

16. Kekelis LS, Sacks SZ. Mainstreaming visually impaired children into regular education programs: the effects of visual impairment on children's interactions with peers. In: Sacks S, Kekelis L, Gaylord-Ross R, eds. *The Social Development of Visually Impaired Students.* San Francisco, Calif: San Francisco State University; 1988. Unpublished monograph.

17. Scholl GT. Growth and development. In: Scholl GT, ed. *Foundations of Education for Blind and Visually Handicapped Children and Youth.* New York, NY: American Foundation for the Blind; 1986.

18. Read LF. An examination of the social skills of blind kindergarten children. *Educ Visually Handicapped.* 1989;22:142–155.

19. Raver DS, Drash PW. Increasing social skills training for visually impaired children. *Educ Visually Handicapped.* 1988;19(4):147–155.

20. Erwin EJ. Guidelines for integrating young children with visual impairments in general educational settings. *J Visual Impair Blindness.* 1991;85:253–260.

21. Erwin EJ. *The formation and maintenance of peer interactions in young children with visual impairment.* 1993. Submitted for publication.

22. Bishop VE. Identifying the components of success in mainstreaming. *J Visual Impair Blindness.* 1986;80:939–946.

23. Kekelis LS. Peer interactions in childhood: the impact of visual impairment. In: Sacks S, Kekelis L, Gaylord-Ross R, eds. *The Social Development of Visually Impaired Students.* San Francisco, Calif: San Francisco State University; 1988. Unpublished monograph.

24. Taylor-Hershel D, Webster R. Mainstreaming: a case in point. *Childhood Educ.* 1983;59:175–179.

25. Workman SH. Teachers' verbalizations and the social interactions of blind preschoolers. *J Visual Impair Blindness.* 1986;80:532–534.

26. Markovits H, Strayer FF. Toward an applied social ethnology: a case study of social skills among blind children. In: Rubin KH, Ross HS, eds. *Peer Relationships and Social Skills in Childhood.* New York, NY: Springer-Verlag; 1982.

27. Urwin C. Dialogue and cognitive functioning in the early language development of three blind children. In: Mills AE, ed. *Language Acquisition in the Blind Child.* San Diego, Calif: College-Hill Press; 1983.

28. Wode H. Precursors and the study of the impaired language learner. In: Mills AE, ed. *Language Acquisition in the Blind Child.* San Diego, Calif: College-Hill Press; 1983.

29. Andersen ES, Dunlea A, Kekelis LS. Blind children's language: resolving some differences. *Child Lang.* 1984;11:645–664.

30. Bigelow A. Early words of blind children. *Child Lang.* 1987;14:47–56.

31. Dunlea D. *Vision and the Emergence of Meaning: Blind and Sighted Children's Early Language.* Cambridge, England: Cambridge University Press; 1989.

32. Erin JN. Language samples from visually impaired four- and five-year-olds. *J Childhood Commun Dis*. 1990;13:181–191.

33. Wills DM. Early speech development in blind children. *Psychoanalytic Study of the Child*. 1979;34:85–117.

34. Erin JN. Frequencies and types of questions in the language of visually impaired children. *J Visual Impair Blindness*. 1986;80:670–674.

35. Mulford R. Referential development in blind children. In: Mills AE, ed. *Language Acquisition in the Blind Child*. San Diego, Calif: College-Hill Press; 1983.

Parent–child interaction assessment in family-centered intervention

Marilee Comfort, PhD, MPH
Research Coordinator and Assistant
 Professor
Family Center
Department of Pediatrics
Thomas Jefferson University
Philadelphia, Pennsylvania

Dale C. Farran, PhD
Professor and Chair
Department of Human Development
 and Family Studies
University of North Carolina at
 Greensboro
Greensboro, North Carolina

THE FOCUS OF intervention services for young children with special needs broadened from child to family when Public Law 99-457 passed in 1986. This federal law mandated a family-centered approach to assessment and intervention with children with handicapping conditions or significant developmental delays. However, the degree of participation by families in early intervention services is voluntary and varies according to family skills and preferences.[1] For the past two decades parental involvement has been a preferred component of early childhood special education services.[2] A recent review of preschool intervention projects demonstrated that, in contrast to programs for children from low-income families, a relatively small percentage of intervention programs for children with disabilities were conducted with only staff–child intervention.[3] Despite this history, a survey of university preservice training programs in special education conducted by Bailey et al[4] found few hours of instruction devoted to family assessment and intervention. Special education programs that specialized in early childhood and infancy reported more hours of instruction in various facets of family functioning than other programs. Under the guidelines of PL 99-457, more interventionists are expected to work with families than these preservice training programs can produce. To ease this shortage of trained personnel, inservice training is being conducted for practitioners of various disciplines in skills and attitudes fundamental to family-focused assessment and intervention.[5]

As family involvement has become a federal priority, concerns have been raised regarding how well interventionists are prepared to assume this responsibility, how adequate available instruments are for assessing family functioning, and

The authors would like to acknowledge the cooperation of the FAMILIES Project Investigators, Donald B. Bailey and Rune J. Simeonsson, for their generosity in furnishing the illustrative data used in this article. Special thanks to the Early Childhood Intervention Services staff and the North Carolina families who so kindly participated in the project and to William Fullard for comments on the manuscript. Data in this manuscript were obtained with the support of the Special Education Programs, Special Education and Rehabilitative Services, US Department of Education, grants no. G0087C3064 and G008530229. The opinions expressed do not necessarily reflect the position or policy of the US Department of Education, and no official endorsement by the US Department of Education should be inferred.

Inf Young Children, 1994; 6(4): 33–45

how effectively those instruments can be used and integrated with other information to plan intervention with each family and child.[6,7] It is increasingly clear that, for family assessments to be used meaningfully, interventionists need training in administration, as well as interpretation of instruments in the context of other personal and family factors.[8]

One essential area of family assessment is parent–child interaction. This area takes into consideration daily interpersonal behavior and affect beyond the individual levels of the child and family. Early interactions offer a window into the parent–child relationship[9-11] and lay the foundation for subsequent peer and adult relations[12-14] and later social, cognitive, and language development.[10,15,16] Observations of a parent and a child interacting with one another can be useful in monitoring the development of social behavior and affect, as well as in identifying problems that may interfere with daily life and healthy interpersonal relations. These observations also provide information about the caregiver's style and knowledge of child development and management skills and can offer a vehicle for reinforcing sensitive parenting or discussing alternative techniques for handling children. Specific target areas for intervention can be identified as parents help interventionists interpret parent–child observations in the context of other personal and family factors.

This article presents case study profiles based on ratings of play observations of mothers and children scored with the Parent/Caregiver Involvement Scale (P/CIS). Maternal involvement during play is described and interpreted within each family's context. The profiles illustrate the integration of data from a parent–child interaction assessment with personal and family contextual information as staff and families plan intervention goals. The case study profiles are followed by a broader discussion of issues concerning the use of observational scales in intervention settings.

Before presenting the case study profiles, it would be beneficial to clarify the pertinent types of *contextual information.* The extensive research literature on parent–child interaction demonstrates its association with an array of factors, including characteristics of the parent and child, family resources and constraints, and caregiving support. These factors form the framework for interpreting interaction assessments.

Parent and child characteristics

Caregiver characteristics such as gender, age,[17] cultural background,[18] personal beliefs,[19,20] psychological well-being,[21] social skills,[22] perceptions of stress,[23] and parenting knowledge[24,25] have shown associations with the frequency and quality of parent–child behaviors. In addition, research evidence suggests that dyadic exchanges are also associated with child characteristics, including birth status,[26,27] developmental level, handicapping condition,[28] temperament and responsiveness.[29,30]

FAMILY RESOURCES AND CONSTRAINTS

In considering the family context, basic necessities of daily living such as food, clothing, shelter, health, and safety in the home environment may constitute fundamental resources or constraints for family interaction. For example, drug abuse has become a major constraint affecting the lives of countless mothers and children during the past decade.[31] The rapid depletion of health, financial, and material resources associated with maternal cocaine dependency typically results in a decrease in the emotional availability of the mother for her child, unpredictable caregiving, and less maternal sensitivity to the child's needs.[32–35]

CAREGIVING SUPPORT

The various interactive styles of caregivers need to be considered in families in which a child has multiple caregivers. In many African-American and Puerto Rican families, for example, it is common practice for several members of the family or kinship network to share caregiving responsibilities.[36,37] Most published observational studies of alternative caregivers have focused on comparisons of mothers and fathers,[9,38,39] although a few have reported on mothers and grandmothers.[40,41]

Caregiving styles may overlap, complement or conflict with one another. The important clinical concerns are whether the child receives the necessary quantity and quality of interactive behaviors that foster mutually satisfying relationships and the development of the child and are appropriate to the child's needs. For instance, a depressed mother may not alter her facial expression readily, nor respond consistently to her child's eye contact and verbal initiations. These maternal behaviors may be of less concern within a family with a responsive adult who shares the caregiving for the children than in a single-parent family in which no other adult caregivers are available.

Inconsistencies among caregiving styles can be confusing to young children and may elicit excessive limit testing or withdrawal from social interactions. With assessment and discussion of child needs and caregiving behaviors and intervention, discordant caregiving styles can be modified to create a better balance within the caregiving environment. Caregiving by multiple caregivers is an element of the broader area of social support that has been documented consistently as a salient contributor to parent–child interaction. In multivariate studies of parent and child determinants of mother–child interaction, support, in combination with other factors, was significantly associated with positive maternal affect, secure attachment,[42] and mothers' optimal play and teaching behaviors.[20,43,44]

CASE STUDY PROFILES

Participants

The case study profiles presented in this article were drawn from the FAMI-LIES Project,[20,45] a longitudinal study from 1982 to 1986 of families participating in the statewide Early Childhood Intervention Services (ECIS) in North Carolina. ECIS teams worked with families with infants and toddlers at risk or with developmental disabilities using a home-based interdisciplinary service delivery model. Utilizing the ECIS team network, the FAMILIES Project trained early interventionists to collect data on personal and demographic characteristics; developmental and behavioral measures of the child; maternal support; parent–child interactions; and family strengths, needs, and goals.

The case study profiles are based primarily on the maternal and family information gathered at the initial interview and on the parent–child play observation conducted later in the assessment process. These case studies illustrate the bidirectional influences between contextual factors and parent–child interactions. This methodology lends itself particularly well to exploration of complex real-life phenomena that risk oversimplification when assessment instruments focus on single attributes or characteristics of families. Qualitative information enhances the quantitative data drawn from the assessment.[46]

Parent–child interaction assessment

The P/CIS[47] is an example of parent–child observational scales that have been reviewed recently for use by interventionists in assessing families and planning family goals.[48–50] The P/CIS can be used in home visits, in laboratory settings, and in clinics. It requires a 20-minute observation of a caregiver (live or videotaped) in free-play interaction with a child 3 to 60 months of age. The P/CIS has been used with families of various racial and ethnic backgrounds, including African-American, Caucasian, Hispanic, and Hawaiian, and the full range of socioeconomic and educational levels. The children in these families have demonstrated a wide range of developmental abilities and complications, including normal development, prematurity, language and motor delays, cerebral palsy, genetic syndromes (eg, Down syndrome), and severe retardation.

The 11 caregiver behaviors listed in Fig 1 are rated on five-point scales defined by behavioral descriptors in the manual. Each of the behaviors is scored along three dimensions—Amount, Quality, and Appropriateness—that are specifically defined for each caregiver behavior (see example in Fig 2).

Amount scores are neutral frequency ratings that represent how often the caregiver demonstrates each of the 11 P/CIS behaviors, without regard to quality. *Quality* ratings describe aspects of caregiver behaviors that promote optimal de-

Caregiver's name/ID _____ **Date of video**

Child's name/ID _____ **Minutes of video rated** _____ – _____

Child's age (months)_____ **Rater's ID** _____

This scale is designed to assess the behavior of a caregiver during play interaction with his/her child in home or laboratory settings. Play interactions should be observed for 20 minutes before scoring. Each item has behavioral descriptors at odd intervals along the 5-point scale. Please read the descriptors and the conventions in the manual for each item. Next, write the number that best describes the observed caregiver behavior. If a behavioral item is not observed, please score 1 for Amount and NA for Quality and Appropriateness.

	Amount	Quality	Appropriateness
1. Physical Involvement			
2. Verbal Involvement			
3. Responsiveness of Caregiver			
4. Playful Interaction			
5. Teaching Behavior			
6. Control over Child's Activities			
7. Directives			
8. Relationship among Activities			
9. Positive Statements			
10. Negative Statements/Discipline			
11. Goal Setting			

Impression of Caregiver Involvement with Child

Availability	Acceptance	Atmosphere	Enjoyment	Learning Environment

Fig 1. Parent/Caregiver Involvement Scale scoring form.

velopment of the child, such as sensitivity, intensity, consistency, flexibility, and fluidity. *Appropriateness* ratings indicate how closely the caregiver's behaviors are matched to the child's developmental needs and interests during the free play session. Five *Impression* ratings for the overall play session assess the affective climate and the learning environment provided by the caregiver throughout the

***AMOUNT* OF RESPONSIVENESS TO CHILD (to his initiations, verbalizations, demands, distress)**

1	2	3	4	5
Caregiver never responds (If Amount = 1, mark NA {not observed} for Quality and Appropriate- ness)		Caregiver occasionally responds; responds about half of the time		Caregiver almost always responds

***QUALITY* OF CAREGIVER RESPONSIVENESS: INTENSITY**

1	2	3	4	5
Responds abruptly, forcefully, very intensely, or harshly		Neutral; responses not intense at all; OR responses of mixed intensi- ties, sometimes forceful, sometimes gentle		Caregiver responds in a gentle, sensitive, positive way; may respond enthusiastically, with delight; spontaneity is also observed

_____ NA (not observed)

***APPROPRIATENESS* OF CAREGIVER RESPONSIVENESS: TIMING**

1	2	3	4	5
Seldom good synchrony in response to Child's activi- ties; Caregiver overwhelms Child with quickness of response, or is too slow in response		Moderate synchrony of response to Child's needs; about half of the time Caregiver's response is well- timed to Child's needs		Response to Child almost always appropri- ate to Child's needs; good synchrony of response, neither too quick nor too slow

_____ NA (not observed)

Fig 2. Parent/Caregiver Involvement Scale behavioral anchors for responsiveness of caregiver.

session. Global aspects, such as acceptance, enjoyment, and emotional availability, that are not captured elsewhere in the P/CIS behavioral ratings are scored under Impression. Subscale scores for Amount, Quality, Appropriateness and Impression of maternal behavior were derived and plotted for the profiles in this study by calculating the means of the 11 behavioral ratings in each dimension and of the five global ratings for Impression.

P/CIS training usually requires a 4-hour introductory session guided by a training videotape and a workbook of written exercises. The materials define and illustrate the interactive behaviors and offer opportunities to rate mother–child interactions on the videotape with feedback. The P/CIS training is most effective when a consultant is available during the training session to answer specialized questions and to assist in applying the scale to particular characteristics of the program and families. After the introductory session, practice is necessary to gain reliability with expert scoring and with team members. It is not uncommon for P/CIS trainees with backgrounds in child development to gain 85% reliability after the introductory session.

Information on the reliability and validity of the scale has been presented in previous publications.[20,49,51–53]

Contextual factors

Information on personal and family characteristics was collected by means of interviews with the families by the ECIS interventionists. This included discussions of the demographics of family members, parental perceptions of the child's developmental disability and prognosis, family needs and strengths, a description of the sources of and satisfaction with social support, and caregiving responsibilities and current goals for the child and family.

Examples of profiles in context

Individualizing a family service plan requires that differences in personal characteristics and family circumstance be taken into account when interpreting assessments and planning intervention. Eight parent–child interaction profiles derived with the P/CIS are depicted in Fig 3. These are actual ratings from one early interventionist based on live observations of free play sessions between mothers and children in their homes. The variability in parent–child interactions is apparent in the profiles. That variability, however, does not automatically dictate the intervention goals. Each interaction profile must be interpreted in the context of the individual, family, and cultural factors that are related to it.

The following examples illustrate the process of interpreting parent–child assessments and planning interventions. Some of the demographic and contextual

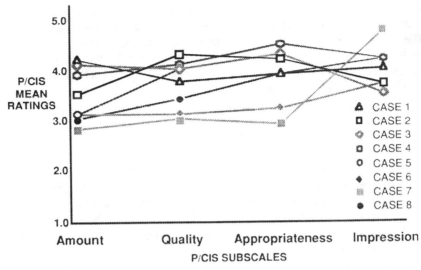

Fig 3. Parent/Caregiver Involvement Scale subscale scores for interventionist caseload.

information has been altered to protect the confidentiality of the families. Fig 4 depicts the P/CIS ratings for a subset of two mothers whose 18-month-old sons had been diagnosed with developmental disabilities of undetermined origin and who demonstrated similar delays in motor and language areas. Both mothers received moderate ratings ($M = 3.1$; 2.8 [M = mean]) on the Amount of their interactions with the child during free play. Otherwise, their ratings diverged dramatically. The Quality ($M = 4.0$; 3.0) and Appropriateness ($M = 4.2$; 2.9) ratings of maternal behaviors with the child indicate more consistent and facilitative caregiving by Mother 5 than Mother 7. The general Impression scores at the right of the profiles diverged in the opposite direction: Mother 7 received more favorable Impression ratings ($M = 4.8$) than Mother 5 ($M = 3.5$). The next step in interpreting these profiles is to place the parent–child interactions within the maternal and family contexts.

Intake information presented distinctly different maternal and family characteristics for the two mother–child dyads. Mother 5 was an American-born citizen of Japanese descent. She and her Caucasian husband worked in professional occupations until the birth of their first child. She chose not to return to work when they learned that their son showed developmental disabilities. The family was economically secure and educationally sophisticated. Mother 5 devoted the majority of her time to caregiving responsibilities and household management and read a great deal about child development and parenting children with special needs. She

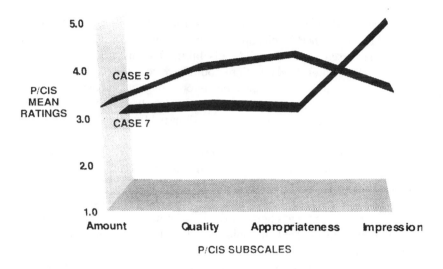

Fig 4. Parent/Caregiver Involvement Scale subscale scores for cases 5 and 7.

was frustrated with her child's delays in development and the unanswered questions about the etiology of them. Mother 5 welcomed support from professionals to address her child's health and developmental problems. The father left childcare matters to his wife because he worked long hours and felt that she managed them better than he could. Both parents viewed themselves as isolated from family and friends since the birth of their son.

During the free play observation with her child, the frequency of Mother 5's involvement was in the moderate range ($M = 3.1$), neither subdued nor highly active. As seen in Fig 3, she was among the bottom four mothers in the ratings of Amount of interaction. Moderately high scores for Quality ($M = 4.0$) and Appropriateness ($M = 4.2$) suggest that she was usually sensitive to her child's cues during the observation and often adapted the developmental level, timing, and intensity of her behavior to her child's needs. Mother 5 appeared to apply much of what she had read to her interactions with her child. These facilitative maternal behaviors during play reinforced her child's exploration of language and the environment, thereby promoting his developmental progress. The Impression score for the overall affective aspects of play and the learning environment provided by Mother 5 was at the moderate level. This was an unusual profile of subscale scores on the P/CIS. Ordinarily, the Impression mean score tends to be in a range similar or a little higher than the more specific Quality and Appropriateness means. The interventionist recorded her impressions of Mother 5's play interactions as moderate acceptance, availability, and atmosphere ratings on the P/CIS. These ratings were then aggregated as part of the Impressions score. This scoring profile might be explained by the mother's indication during the family interview that she continued to be depressed about her child's disabilities and his prospects for future development. These unresolved questions could have been the basis for her infrequent signs of approval and preoccupied behavior throughout the play session. An alternative explanation is that Mother 5's Japanese family background may have proscribed that she diminish praise of her child in public, as is common in that culture.[18]

Very different personal characteristics, family structure, and life circumstances existed for Mother 7. Information from the family interview indicated that she was an African-American adolescent living with her son in a bustling multigenerational household. There was a great deal of traffic and transience of household members, as the grandmother's home was the gathering place for their close-knit family. All of the adults in the household (grandmother, aunts, and uncles) showered attention and affection on the young children. This nurturing envelope of interaction was engrained in the family culture and offered a warm, supportive environment for the children. The grandmother performed the majority of the caregiving responsibilities for Mother 7's son. However, this arrangement recently had become a source of tension between mother and grandmother. As she progressed through adolescence to adulthood, Mother 7 wished to assume more caregiving responsibility. She had gained confidence in her parenting abilities and became better able to shift her focus from herself to her child.

During the free play observation, Mother 7 received moderate ratings for the Amount ($M = 2.8$), Quality ($M = 3.0$), and Appropriateness ($M = 2.9$) of play behaviors with her child. The scores suggest that she played with her infant occasionally during the session (Amount). For approximately half of the session her behaviors were inconsistent or rigid (Quality) and often not attuned to her child's developmental needs (Appropriateness). These maternal behaviors tended to interrupt rather than extend her child's learning through play. Her developmental expectations of her son seemed to be aimed too high for his abilities, and she had difficulty following his lead in selecting toys and creating play activities. In contrast, Mother 7's high score for overall Impression ($M = 4.8$) underscored this inexperienced mother's clear demonstration of acceptance and enjoyment of her child, despite the need to learn more sensitive ways of responding and meeting her child's developmental needs. Her warm affect was congruent with her family's style of behavior with children.

FAMILY-CENTERED INTERVENTION STRATEGIES

Based on the differences in interactive profiles and family contextual information, the intervention strategies designed for these two families differed markedly.

While discussing the P/CIS assessment results, Mother 5 expressed the confidence she felt in interacting with her child. However, she admitted how difficult it was for her to accept her son's disabilities. The father had chosen not to be observed by the interventionist while playing with his son. He stated that he rarely engaged in caregiving and play with his child because he did not know what to do with children too young to talk. To begin learning how to play a larger role in his child's world, the father agreed to participate in some family-centered early intervention activities. The parents and the ECIS team set goals for the family to gather information about others' experiences in parenting children with special needs and to gain support by joining a parent support group. The mother also asked the team for a list of recommended counselors she could contact to explore the conflicted emotions she felt toward her child. In addition, mother and father scheduled weekly evening home visits with the interventionist to work together on developmental activities for their son that could be incorporated into the daily family routine. This strategy would allow Mother 5 to share her strengths in play behavior with her husband and also would encourage them to share the responsibilities and the joys of parenting with one another.

During the review of the P/CIS assessment results with Mother 7, she expressed her appreciation for her supportive family, along with her increasing discomfort with her dependency on them and the limited role she played in caring for her child. She was eager to learn alternative techniques for teaching her child through play and managing his behavior. Mother 7 and the ECIS team developed a plan for her to attend classes toward her GED as an initial step toward personal growth and independence. Concurrently, she agreed to enroll her son in a center-based developmental program that would meet two mornings per week to provide him with a social and learning environment appropriate to his needs. In addition, the center would serve as a respite from caregiving for both grandmother and mother. Mother 7 decided to participate in the classroom bimonthly to learn appropriate developmental tasks for her son and behavior management skills. Instead of attending a parent support group, the mother invited the grandmother to join her at the monthly family activities group sponsored by the developmental program. This intervention plan offered this young mother the type of support she desired to develop autonomy within her family and a closer relationship with her son. Inclusion of the extended family was deemphasized because the mother felt confident in her family's support and preferred to focus on strengthening her interactive skills and her child's developmental progress.

DISCUSSION

These two case study profiles illustrate how parent–child interaction assessment can serve as a focus for discussions between the early intervention team and individual families concerning daily parent–child dynamics, parental and caregiving needs, and support. Parent–child observations helped identify the interactive strengths and needs of the mothers. These assessments were then interpreted within the family context and used by the families and the intervention team to develop collaborative intervention plans tailored to individual family needs, values, and preferences. Before utilizing parent–child interaction observational scales, several issues concerning observations of parents and children require discussion.

Use and misuse of observational scales

Parent–child interaction observational scales are intended to identify specific caregiver and child behaviors that promote or hinder a mutually satisfying relationship within the dyad and the optimal development of the child. Areas of strengths and weaknesses noted in the interactive patterns of the dyad are useful in pinpointing measurable intervention goals.

Parent–child interaction observational scales typically are designed to describe a defined set of behaviors of the dyad observed at a particular point in time as they are engaging in designated activities. Because of the specificity in design, the particular scale to be used for assessment must be selected carefully to match the needs of the families and the goals of the intervention program, as discussed in more detail elsewhere.[54] Training in administration procedures and interpretation of the results must be equally specific. To gain a generalizable picture of the caregiving environment, several observations must be assessed, multiple caregivers must be observed (if applicable), and a variety of activities and settings must be designated for observation. (Unfortunately, the scope of this article does not permit illustration of this point.) *The results of observational scales can be generalized only as far as the definitions of the scale and the observational procedures allow.*

To illustrate, the P/CIS is an observational scale designed to describe parent or caregiver behavior during free play with an infant, toddler, or preschooler. As such, it provides information specific to the parent, not to the child; it assesses behavior during play, not during feeding or bathing. The P/CIS behavioral profiles describe only the 11 behaviors in the scale, as they are defined in the scale. Within these parameters, it can be used in conjunction with other caregiver, child, and family information to plan family intervention goals.

Furthermore, parent–child interaction assessments are not intended for use as the *sole* evaluative criteria of a caregiver or of a home or center caregiving environment. They can be interpreted meaningfully only in the context of other relevant assessment information. The P/CIS was not developed to be used alone as a basis for determining whether a child is at risk of abuse or neglect or whether a family is prepared for reunification. It is not intended to determine parental response to a court-imposed intervention program, nor should it be used to evaluate the competency of a day-care provider. These decisions are too complex to be decided by any single assessment tool.

Judgment

Early interventionists often are concerned about appearing judgmental when observing parent or caregiver behavior. This uneasiness may stem from being placed in the role of parent–child expert without the necessary training. It might also be a function of accusations of cultural insensitivity that are sometimes cast at professionals differing in cultural background from their clients. These are valid concerns, despite the accepted role of clinical judgment in any intervention process. Such concerns can be alleviated somewhat by

- discussing the purpose and procedures of parent–child assessment with the family;
- involving parents in the decision to observe parent–child interactions as part of the assessment process;
- participating in ongoing training regarding cultural diversity and family and child rearing values in various cultures[55];
- carefully selecting an observational scale that has been shown to be unbiased with diverse populations and that identifies behaviorally defined items;
- engaging in systematic training and periodic reliability checks among raters using the scale;
- including reliability checks with raters of the same cultural background as the families assessed[18];
- establishing and maintaining a common understanding among team members regarding the focus of the scale, the purpose of observations, the definitions of items, and the interpretation of the results without cultural bias;
- scheduling multiple observations with a family to gain a representative picture of caregiver–child interactions; and
- communicating sensitively with family members about individual family strengths and needs.

Observational methods and materials that include thorough training and reliability checks, identify strengths as well as needs, and present observational sessions and feedback to parents in a nonthreatening manner can rarely be labeled judgmental.

Briefing and feedback

To include parents as partners in the assessment of interactive strengths and needs, it is essential to involve them in the decision to conduct systematic observations. As with other assessment procedures, a general explanation is needed to acquaint them with the purpose and procedures to be followed and to apprise them of the type of information to expect as results. It is usually advisable to introduce parent–child observational assessments after a comfortable rapport and trust level have been established to ensure that the family will feel free to ask questions and express honest feelings about being observed.

For those families who agreed to the observation, some brief summary comments with those observed immediately after the interaction sessions are helpful to diffuse any suspicions of a judgmental stance on the part of the interventionist.

An appointment with the family should be scheduled soon after each observation to discuss the results of the assessment, as well as other assessment information collected on the family. A general discussion of the major strengths and needs gleaned from family assessments is usually a better strategy for engaging the family in discussion than overwhelming them with the details of scores and itemized lists of competencies and weaknesses. Highlighted areas need to be supported with a few illustrations of behaviors that bring the information to a shared level of understanding between interventionists and family members. Parents, in turn, require the opportunity to clarify assessment information and to add their own observations as part of the preparation for family goal setting. This appointment may be a convenient time to begin working with the family on setting intervention goals.

Goal setting

Thorough discussions of the process of family goal setting are available elsewhere.[56–58] The specific issue of when to include parent–child interaction in the family goal plan is pertinent here. The decision to observe parent–child interactions does not imply that an interactive goal must appear on the Individual Family Service Plan (IFSP). Given the many areas of functioning that are included within the parameters of child and family assessment, it is impossible and unnecessary to address them all simultaneously. The purpose of an IFSP is to target the areas of highest priority for the family at the current time.

The process of deciding whether to include parent–child behavior in the family plan often proceeds as follows. Based on concerns identified by the family, the intervention team initially assesses multiple aspects of the child and family using direct testing, questionnaires, interviews, and observations. Next, the team and family consider the assessment results within the broader family context. Finally, the parents and professionals work collaboratively to prioritize family needs in order to set family and child goals. If parent–child interaction is deemed a high priority for intervention, a goal may be written to work directly on interaction skills, or the staff and family may work to affect changes in parent–child behavior indirectly by targeting a related factor such as parental locus of control or social support. In this manner the family goal plan becomes a collaborative guide for intervention tailored to the strengths and needs of the family.

• • •

PL 99-457 calls for family-centered intervention. Many intervention projects are currently searching for family assessment instruments and procedures. The P/CIS has been used to illustrate the importance of interpreting any parent–child observational scale in the context of information on individual, family, and cultural factors. Assessments agreed on jointly by parents and staff and interpreted in the context of the family's characteristics and life circumstances carry an honest, respectful message of professionals' sensitivity to the heterogeneity of the families and children with developmental delays or disabilities. Parent–child interaction assessment and interpretation can serve as a means of involving parents in the intervention process, from the initial assessment of strengths and needs through family goal setting and review of the IFSP. If handled with care, initial assessments will set the foundation for a collaborative parent–professional partnership throughout family intervention.

REFERENCES

1. Crutcher DM. Family support in the home: home visiting and Public Law 99-457, a parent's perspective. *Am Psychologist.* 1991;46:138–140.

2. Wiegerink R, Comfort M. Parent involvement: support for families of children with special needs. In: Kagan SL, Powell DR, Weissbourd B, Zigler EF, eds. *America's Family Support Programs.* New Haven, Conn: Yale University Press; 1987.

3. Farran DC. Effects of intervention with disadvantaged and disabled children: a decade review. In: Meisels SJ, Shonkoff JP, eds. *Handbook of Early Childhood Intervention.* Cambridge, England: Cambridge University Press; 1990.

4. Bailey DB, Palsha SA, Huntington G. Preservice preparation of special educators to serve infants with handicaps and their families: current status and training needs. *J Early Intervention.* 1990;14:43–54.

5. Bruder MB, Nikitas T. Changing the professional practice of early interventionists: An inservice model to meet the service needs of Public Law 99-457. *J Early Intervention.* 1992;16:173–180.

6. Bailey DB, Blasco PM. Parents' perspectives on a written survey of family needs. *J Early Intervention.* 1990;14:196–203.

7. Healy A, Keesee P, Smith BS. *Early Services for Children With Special Needs: Transactions for Family Support.* 2nd ed. Baltimore, Md: Paul H. Brookes Publishing; 1988.

8. Bailey DB, Simeonsson RJ, eds. *Family Assessment in Early Intervention.* New York, NY: Macmillan; 1988.

9. Lamb ME. *The Role of the Father in Child Development.* New York, NY: John Wiley & Sons; 1981.

10. Maccoby EE, Martin JA. Socialization in the context of the family: parent-child interaction. In: Mussen PH, ed. *Handbook of Child Psychology.* New York, NY: John Wiley & Sons; 1983; 4.

11. *Heart Start: The Emotional Foundations of School Readiness.* Washington, DC: Zero to three/ National Center for Clinical Infant Programs; 1992.

12. Crockenberg SB. How children learn to resolve conflicts in families. *Zero To Three.* 1992;12:11–13.

13. Lewis M. Social development in infancy and early childhood. In: Osofsky JD, ed. *Handbook of Infant Development.* New York, NY: John Wiley & Sons; 1987.

14. Waters E, Wippman J, Sroufe LA. Attachment, positive affect and competence in the peer group: two studies in construct validation. *Child Dev.* 1979;50:821–829.

15. Bee HL, Barnard KE, Eyres SJ, et al. Prediction of IQ and language skill from perinatal status, child performance, family characteristics, and mother-infant interaction. *Child Dev.* 1982;53:1,134–1,156.

16. Ramey CT, Farran DC, Campbell FA. Predicting IQ from mother-infant interactions. *Child Dev.* 1979;50:804–814.

17. Helm JM, Comfort M, Bailey DB, Simeonsson RJ. Adolescent and adult mothers of handicapped children: maternal involvement in play. *Family Relations.* 1990;39:432–437.

18. Fernald A, Morikawa H. Common themes and cultural variations in Japanese and American mothers' speech to infants. *Child Dev.* 1993;64:637–656.

19. Farran DC, Comfort M, Kasari C. Factors affecting parent-child interactions with young handicapped children. Poster presented at the Biennial Meeting of the Society for Research in Child Development; April 1985; Toronto, Canada.

20. Simeonsson RJ, Bailey DB, Huntington G, Comfort M. Testing the concept of goodness of fit in early intervention. *J Infant Mental Health.* 1986;7:81–94.

21. Tronick EZ, Gianino A. Interactive mismatch and repair: challenges to infant coping. *Zero To Three.* 1986;6:1–6.

22. Booth CL, Mitchell SK, Barnard KE, Spieker SJ. Development of maternal social skills in multi-problem families: effects on the mother-child relationship. *Dev Psychol.* 1989;25:403–412.

23. Comfort M. *Parental Involvement in Play Interaction and Caregiving Roles in Families With Young High Risk and Handicapped Children: A Comparison of Father and Mother.* Chapel Hill, NC: University of North Carolina; 1986. Dissertation.

24. King T, Fullard W. Teenage mothers and their infants: new findings on the home environment. *J Adolescence.* 1982;5:333–346.

25. Parks PL, Smeriglio VL. Relationships among parenting knowledge, quality of stimulation in the home and infant development. *Family Relations.* 1986;35:411–416.

26. Cherkes-Julkowski M, Bertrand J, Roth D. Identification of atypical infant development in the care-taking context. 1988. Unpublished manuscript.

27. Goldberg S, Marcovitch S. Temperament and developmentally disabled children. In: Kohnstamm GA, Bates JE, Rothbart MK, eds. *Temperament in Childhood.* New York, NY: John Wiley & Sons; 1989.

28. Marfo K. Interactions between mothers and their mentally retarded children: integration of research findings. *J Appl Dev Psychol.* 1984;5:45–69.

29. Huntington GS, Simeonsson RJ, Bailey DB, Comfort M. Handicapped child characteristics and maternal involvement with young handicapped children. *J Infant Reprod Psychol.* 1987;5:105–118.

30. Lojkasek M, Goldberg S, Marcovitch S, MacGregor D. Influences on maternal responsiveness to developmentally delayed preschoolers. *J Early Intervention.* 1990;14:260–273.

31. United States General Accounting Office. *Report to the Chairman, Committee on Finance, US Senate. Drug-exposed Infants: A Generation at Risk.* Washington, DC: United States General Accounting Office; 1990.

32. Burns K, Chethik L, Burns WJ, Clark R. Dyadic disturbances in cocaine-abusing mothers and their infants. *J Clin Psychol.* 1991;47:316–319.

33. Comfort M. Assessment of parent-child interactions of drug-addicted mothers and their young children. Presented at Drug-Exposed Infants, Children and their Families: A Symposium of Hope; May 1991; Temple University; Philadelphia, Pa.

34. Harvey C, Comfort M. Integrating parent support into residential drug and alcohol treatment programs. *Zero To Three.* 1992;13:11–13.

35. Pawl JH. Interventions to strengthen relationships between infants and drug-abusing or recovering parents. *Zero To Three.* 1992;13:6–10.

36. Crosbie-Burnett M, Lewis EA. Use of African-American family structures and functioning to address the challenge of European-American postdivorce families. *Family Relations.* 1993;42:243–248.

37. Garcia Coll CT. Developmental outcome of minority infants: a process-oriented look into our beginnings. *Child Dev.* 1990;61:270–289.

38. Pedersen FA, ed. *The Father-Infant Relationship: Observational Studies in the Family Setting.* New York, NY: Praeger Publishers; 1980.

39. Stoneman Z, Brody G, Abbott D. In-home observations of young Down syndrome children with their mothers and fathers. *Am J Mental Defic.* 1983;87:591–600.

40. Myers BJ, Jarvis PA, Creasey GL. Infants' behavior with their mothers and grandmothers. *Infant Behav Dev.* 1987;10:245–259.

41. Troll LE. Grandparenting. In: Poon LW, ed. *Aging in the 1980's: Psychological Issues.* New York, NY: American Psychological Association; 1980.

42. Crnic K, Greenberg M, Slough N. Early stress and social support influences on mothers' and high-risk infants' functioning in late infancy. *Infant Mental Health.* 1986;7:34–58.

43. Dunst CJ, Trivette CM. Looking beyond the parent-child dyad for the determinants of maternal styles of interaction. *Infant Mental Health.* 1986;7:69–80.

44. Weinraub M, Wolf BM. Effects of stress and social supports on mother-child interactions in single- and two-parent families. *Child Dev.* 1983;54:1,297–1,311.

45. Bailey DB, Simeonsson RJ, Winton PJ, et al. Family-focused intervention: a functional model for planning, implementing, and evaluating individualized family services in early intervention. *J Division Early Childhood.* 1986;10:156–171.

46. Yin RK. *Case Study Research: Design and Methods.* Newbury Park, Calif: Sage Publications; 1989.

47. Farran DC, Kasari C, Comfort M, Jay S. *Parent/Caregiver Involvement Scale.* Greensboro, NC: Continuing Education, University of North Carolina at Greensboro; 1986.

48. Barnard K, Kelly J. Assessment of parent-child interaction. In: Meisels SJ, Shonkoff JP, eds. *Handbook of Early Childhood Intervention.* Cambridge, England: Cambridge University Press; 1990.

49. Farran DC, Clark K, Ray A. Measures of parent-child interaction. In: Gibbs E, Teti D, eds. *Interdisciplinary Assessment of Infants: A Guide for Early Intervention Professionals.* Baltimore, Md: Paul Brookes Publishing; 1990.

50. Towle P, Farran DC, Comfort M. Parent-handicapped child interaction observational coding systems: a review. In: Marfo K, ed. *Parent-Child Interaction and Developmental Disabilities: Theory, Research and Intervention.* New York, NY: Praeger; 1988.

51. Blasco P, Hrncir E, Blasco PA. The contribution of maternal involvement to mastery performance in infants with cerebral palsy. *J Early Intervention.* 1990;14:161–174.

52. Farran DC, Kasari C, Yoder P, Harber L, Huntington G, Comfort-Smith M. Rating mother-child interactions in handicapped and at-risk infants. In: Tamir D, ed. *Stimulation and Intervention in Infant Development.* London, England: Freund Publishing; 1987.

53. Sparling J, Seeds J, Farran DC. The relationship of obstetrical ultrasound to parent and infant behavior. *Obstet Gynecol.* 1988;72:902–907.

54. Comfort M. Assessing parent-child interaction. In: Bailey DB, Simeonsson RJ, eds. *Family Assessment in Early Intervention.* New York, NY: Macmillan; 1988.

55. Harry B, Torguson C, Katkavich J, Guerrero M. Crossing social class and cultural barriers in working with families. *Teaching Exceptional Children.* 1993;26:48–51.

56. Bailey DB. Collaborative goal-setting with families: resolving differences in values and priorities for services. *Topics in Early Childhood Special Education.* 1987;7:59-71.

57. Bailey DB. Considerations in developing family goals. In: Bailey DB, Simeonsson RJ, eds. *Family Assessment in Early Intervention.* New York, NY: Macmillan; 1988.

58. Winton PJ. The family-focused interview: an assessment measure and goal-setting mechanism. In: Bailey DB, Simeonsson RJ, eds. *Family Assessment in Early Intervention.* New York, NY: Macmillan; 1988.

Poverty and early childhood development: What do we know, and what should we do?

Margot Kaplan-Sanoff, EdD
Associate Clinical Professor of
 Pediatrics (Child Development)
Boston University School of Medicine
Codirector
Child Development Project
Boston City Hospital

Steven Parker, MD
Assistant Professor of Pediatrics
Boston University School of Medicine
Director
Developmental Assessment Clinic
Boston City Hospital

Barry Zuckerman, MD
Professor of Pediatrics
Boston University School of Medicine
Director
Division of Developmental and
 Behavioral Pediatrics
Boston City Hospital
Boston, Massachusetts

IT IS WELL established that poverty places young children at risk for a variety of adverse developmental and behavioral outcomes. The media are replete with stories of school failure, high school drop-out rates, gang violence, unemployment, drug use, adolescent pregnancy, and crime in children living in poverty. This article discusses what we know about the relationship between poverty and early childhood development and offers recommendations for what should be done to ameliorate the deleterious effects of poverty.

DOUBLE JEOPARDY

Children living in poverty experience double jeopardy. First, they are more frequently exposed to risks for achieving optimal development such as medical illnesses, family stress, inadequate social support, and parental depression. Second, they experience more serious consequences from these risks than do children from higher socioeconomic status (SES). It is the synergistic double jeopardy of increased exposure to and greater sequelae from health and environmental risks that predisposes children living in poverty to adverse developmental outcomes.[1]

Biologic vulnerability and the role of the social environment

Early theories of child development implied that negative developmental outcomes were usually the result of a single risk factor, such as a birth injury. This

The work on which this article is based was supported by the Jessie B. Cox Charitable Trust, the Boston Foundation, The Harris Foundation, OSERS Personnel Preparation Training Grant, and the Academic Training Program in Behavioral Pediatrics funded by the Bureau of Health Care Delivery and Assistance, Maternal and Child Health Branch (Grant # MCJ-009094).

Inf Young Children, 1991; 4(1): 68–76
© 1991 Aspen Publishers, Inc.

"main effect" model implied a linear cause-and-effect relationship between risk and outcome and was best represented by the work of Pasaminick and Knobloch,[2] in which they conceptualized a "continuum of reproductive casualty" to explain the relationship between perinatal factors, such as perinatal asphyxia or low birth weight, and outcomes, like cerebral palsy or mental retardation.

However, prospective studies of biologically at-risk newborns during the past 20 years raise important questions about biologic determinism and highlight the importance of the social environment for optimizing development in the face of biologic vulnerabilities. The critical role of the social environment to the long-term outcomes for children is consistent with the transactional model of development.[3] For example, among an extensively studied group of premature infants, IQ scores at 7 years of age were lower among those premature infants who were neurologically less mature at 1 month of age. However, within this group of vulnerable infants, responsive caretaking (measured by direct observation) resulted in an IQ similar to infants who were not neurologically immature.[4] Thus, responsive caretaking appeared to be a protective factor for those premature children with biologic vulnerability.

In another study, children with equivalent levels of perinatal stress had better developmental outcomes at all ages if their families had a high level of stability. It took the combination of high perinatal stress *and* low family stability to impair children's developmental functioning.[5] The importance of the environment has also been shown in studies of drug exposed infants. Lifschitz, Wilson, and colleagues showed that the quality of the postnatal environment, rather than the amount of maternal opiate use, appeared to be a more important determinant of developmental outcomes among opiate exposed infants.[6]

Adverse social factors not only affect developmental outcome, but they also increase exposure to biologic risks. For example, the incidence of low birth weight is 2 to 3 times higher in low SES children and their developmental morbidity is more significant compared to children from high SES.[7] As another example, infants from low SES are more frequently exposed in utero to cytomegalovirus (CMV). Exposure to CMV for low SES children causes 2.7 times more school failure than is experienced by children who were exposed to the same virus but grew up in a more advantaged environment.[8]

Poor children are also far more likely to experience lead poisoning, failure to thrive, chronic ear infections, and asthma. These examples are all illustrative of double jeopardy; children living in poverty experience more health problems and suffer greater consequences from these problems.

Perhaps the best example of the double jeopardy experienced by poor children is lead poisoning. Children living in poor, urban neighborhoods (particularly in the Northeast) are far more likely to be exposed to toxic levels of lead. The risk of lead exposure may come from old lead-based paint used on interior walls and window sills, from airborne lead dust resulting from the demolition and renovation of old buildings, from old leaded water pipes, and from soil that has absorbed lead fumes and lead-based exterior paint. Although these risks apply to all children living in older urban settings, they are much more frequent for poor children who reside in areas that provide greater opportunities for high dose exposure and who grow up in the kind of disorganized family environments that permit such exposures to occur.[9]

Lead exposure has adverse effects on children's learning and behavior. Yet the effects of lead on a child's learning ability are subtle and are not easy to document or assess. Increased lead exposure is associated with slightly worse performance on a variety of outcomes, including visual-motor integration. Exposure may affect attention span and activity levels, which, in turn, may produce delays in speech and language development. Language delays interfere with the child's ability to perform successfully in such school-related activities as reading and listening to the teacher's directions. Even at levels once thought to be safe, lead exposure increases sevenfold a child's risk of dropping out of school and sixfold the risk of reading disabilities.[10] Children from lower SES have more impaired development compared to children with the same lead level from a higher SES. Children exposed to high levels of lead are not automatically doomed to school failure, but the risks of lead exposure, combined with the environmental risks of poverty, predispose them to significant learning problems.[11]

Shonkoff, in reviewing the effects of biologic insults on child development, concludes that children in poverty "carry a disproportionate burden of biologic vulnerability that is largely related to the increased health risks of poverty. Their developmental outcomes will be determined by a highly complex series of transactions among a great number of biological and environmental facilitators and constraints."[12]

Psychosocial constraints to development

A recent study by Sameroff and colleagues[3] demonstrated the cumulative nature of psychosocial risk factors, including maternal mental health problems, maternal anxiety, impaired mother–child interactions, low maternal education, negative parental attitudes and values, unemployment, minority group status, inadequate social support, large family size, and stressful life events. Although these risk factors tended to cluster in families living in poverty, a cumulative deleterious effect was evident regardless of SES. However, the combination of social risk and low SES resulted in much poorer outcomes than did high social risk in more financially advantaged families.

The data strongly support low SES as a marker for potential psychosocial risks that may prevent full recovery from biological insults and, in and of themselves, contribute to developmental problems. These factors, additively or synergistically, interact with the child's inherent strengths and vulnerabilities to shape outcomes. Thus, child outcomes can be understood only by considering the transaction between the content of the child's behaviors and the *context* in which they are manifested. As explained by Sameroff and Chandler, characteristics of the child, like temperament and health, shape responses to the environment which, in turn, transform environmental reactions. Just as the child is shaped by the environment, so is the environment modified by the characteristics and actions of the child.

Stress

People living in poverty experience more frequent and more chronic stress than do middle and upper class families. The incidence of major stressors such as housing problems, financial shortages, death of a relative or friend, or school difficulties, was two to four times greater for mothers with lower incomes than for those with more financial resources.[13] Stress appears to be especially high for poor women with children under 6 years of age.[14]

Increased stress often interferes with a mother's ability to respond appropriately to her infant and has been associated with impaired bonding behaviors between mothers and their premature infants,[15] less positive interactions at 4 months,[16] insecure attachment,[17] lower IQ scores and impaired language development at 4 years,[18] and poorer emotional adjustment and increased school problems at school age.[19] Stress appears to inhibit positive interactions and attachment between parent and child, which contributes to negative outcomes as the children mature.

—this sentence 1st rest after

Maternal depression

Mothers of young children are also at much higher risk for becoming depressed. Clinical depression has been reported in 12% of women[20] while depressive feelings may occur in 30% to 50% of women.[21] Low social class and rearing young children increases the risk of depression among women.[22] Low SES mothers of young children are therefore the most vulnerable for depression and, in combination with increased stress and inadequate social support, may experience the most severe consequences.

Maternal depression has been linked to such adverse health and developmental outcomes for children as lower birth weight, failure to thrive, injuries, attention deficit disorder, and socially isolating behaviors at school age.[22] Although apparently different in their manifestations, each of these child outcomes may share a common mechanism. Depressed mothers often display less spontaneity, more unhappy affect, fewer vocalizations, and less physical contact with their infants. The babies, in turn, respond to their mothers with fewer vocalizations and happy expressions. In this way, the spiraling cycle of psychosocial risk and poverty affects mother–child relationships in negative ways, leading to adverse developmental outcomes.

Maternal drug use

Maternal drug use represents both a health risk to the developing fetus and a social risk to the young child. Maternal use of excessive alcohol, opiates, and/or cocaine during pregnancy is associated with such complications as poor maternal nutrition and weight gain, inadequate prenatal care, an increase in infectious diseases, and preterm labor and delivery, each of which can adversely affect the developing fetus.[23] There is a higher risk of complications in newborns, including intrauterine growth retardation, microcephaly, prematurity, bleeding in the central nervous system, and congenital infections like syphilis and CMV. Cocaine-exposed newborns may be lethargic and poorly responsive, hypertonic when alert, and disorganized in sleeping and eating. When alert, they may be easily overstimulated and become irritable or return to a sleep state.[24] Newborns exposed to excessive alcohol may have various aspects of fetal alcohol syndrome (FAS), including jitteriness, microcephaly, facial abnormalities, and mental retardation.

Drug-exposed newborns can manifest disorganized behaviors that are difficult to understand. Mothering them may be a challenging task, even in the best of circumstances. Often attempts to make eye contact with these babies may result in only fleeting attention before the infant becomes lethargic or irritable. The mother may feel guilty about her behavior during pregnancy and may respond to her infant with rejection or ambivalence. These factors all contribute to negative mother/infant interactions.

Infants and young children living with drug and/or alcohol-using mothers are also at increased risk for developmental and behavioral delays. Their home environments are often chaotic and transient. When women are addicted, their primary focus is on their drug of choice, not on their child, and even when women are in early recovery from drug abuse they are often extremely fatigued, depressed, and preoccupied with themselves. The combination of prenatal cocaine exposure and the environmental risks can lead to a flat affect, poor quality of attachment, and low levels of play skills in the children.[25]

Maternal drug use, like the depression, stress, and inadequate social supports that engender its continuation, places children living in poverty at double jeopardy for poor outcomes. These risk factors are highly intercorrelated and their effects are devastatingly synergistic. Stress is exacerbated by lack of support and the resultant depression inhibits seeking adequate supports. Drugs become the escape valve for a self-perpetuating cycle as stress causes more depression, which elicits less support, which causes more stress. Ultimately, these risks are passed on to the young child through the parent–child relationship and the quality of the caregiving environment.

POVERTY AND CHILD OUTCOMES: A TRANSACTIONAL MODEL

The transactional model explains why many but not all children in poverty experience double jeopardy. It also provides the foundation for developing successful intervention strategies. As the following clinical case demonstrates, the complexity and richness of the interaction between biologic and psychosocial factors on children's development offer multiple avenues for potential developmental delays and for successful intervention strategies.

CASE EXAMPLE

Born at 33 weeks gestation to a poor, adolescent, single mother who received minimal prenatal care and no nutritional supplements through WIC (Women, Infants, and Children), Joey was sent home following a 3-week hospitalization. He was a mildly hypertonic infant who had difficulty maintaining a calm, alert state. The mother felt overwhelmed, depressed, and without support, and Joey's inability to respond to her made her feel inadequate and increasingly depressed. Joey did not look to his environment for stimulation, nor did he vocalize or smile at his mother. This, in turn, further heightened the mother's feelings of inadequacy and depression. She was observed to markedly withdraw from her son, responding only to his whiny, persistent bids for attention. When seen at 2 years of age, Joey was clearly delayed in his language and cognitive development.

What is the etiology of this child's developmental delay? Is it biologically based or related more to maternal depression, inadequate environmental stimulation, or lack of social support? The transactional model provides a framework for considering all of these factors as they affect the child's outcome. Each factor influences and shapes the other; together they create a complex pattern that cannot be understood by examining a single factor in isolation.

By focusing on this dynamic interplay between the physical and maternal environments and the characteristics of the child, the transactional model also offers a rich conceptual framework upon which to build intervention strategies. Changes in any aspect of the equation (eg, more adequate prenatal care and nutrition) can create positive changes in another (eg, full term, more responsive infant) leading to further long-term changes in the system (eg, improved maternal self-esteem and parent–child interaction). Intervention can occur at any time or place within the system, but it must be conceptualized as a factor that will impact on the whole system. Thus, providing therapeutic family support within the context of early intervention can address the immediate needs of the mother for social support, which then has the potential to decrease her feelings of inadequacy and depression. This, in turn, provides a secure emotional base upon which she can draw to establish a positive relationship with her child. Early intervention can also provide direct help to the child's state and motor control, making him more accessible for interaction while also teaching the mother how to relate to his particular needs. By focusing on both maternal and infant needs and how these act upon each other, interventions can implement varying strategies for the changing needs of each family.

INTERVENTION AND POLICY IMPLICATIONS

What does double jeopardy mean for children and their families who are living in poverty? The developmental costs of poverty for children are excessively high; approximately two-thirds of all children who test as mildly retarded have grown up in poverty.[12] The costs to society can be measured in terms of school drop-out, unemployment, delinquency, unwanted pregnancies, and intergenerational cycles of failure. Successful intervention will require changes in strategies to ameliorate the multiple risk factors of poverty.

Health, educational, and social service programs that target only individual problems (such as drug abuse) do not address the complex interaction of multiple biologic and environmental risks. Although we cannot "inoculate" children against the pernicious effects of poverty, we can provide more comprehensive programs to address their needs— programs built on collaboration between medicine and education. At Boston City Hospital, physicians and educators are collaborating on a number of medical/educational projects.

Child Development Project

The Child Development Project (CDP) is a collaboration between early childhood educators and developmental pediatricians designed to conduct developmental assessments, coordinate referrals, and provide intervention services for children from birth through age 5. The CDP operates at Boston City Hospital, an inner-city municipal hospital. After years of unsuccessfully attempting to address developmental problems by traditional physician consultation services, this collaborative approach was implemented. The goals of the Project are: (1) to identify children with developmental delays and disturbances early in life, (2) to ensure treatment for these children by referral to appropriate services, and (3) to serve as a model of medical/education collaboration for other municipal hospitals.[26]

Rather than risk losing patients by establishing a new clinic, with its own procedures and locations, the CDP operates at the site where children already receive their health care. In other words, the CDP has reaggregated resources, placing educators within medical sites, in order to provide "one-stop shopping" for families. All children admitted to the inpatient wards or attending the Lead Poisoning Clinic, Neurology Clinic, Failure to Thrive Clinic, and Adolescent Parent/Child

Clinic are seen by CDP staff, in addition to the regular hospital personnel, because of the assumed high incidence of developmental disturbance among these patients.

A year after the Project's initiation at the hospital, it was expanded to community sites; staff now conduct assessments and case manage children who have been preselected because of concern by staff in neighborhood health centers, Head Start programs, and shelters for the homeless. The assessments are based on developmental tests, clinical health evaluation, history of behavioral and family functioning, and observation of the child's behavior and parent–child interaction.[27] The CDP staff have evaluated over 1,450 children, of whom 28% were referred for services. Another 28% were identified as at risk and were monitored for developmental problems. In making referrals, CDP staff discovered that available community resources were often inadequate or inappropriate. In response, new models of service delivery were developed.

Project Visit

Project Visit, a federally funded training project, was designed to increase the capacity of child-care programs to provide critical intervention services for children at double jeopardy. Increasingly, child-care centers are serving children with lead poisoning, asthma, failure to thrive, and cocaine exposure. Project Visit provides in-depth, on-site inservice training in assessment and therapeutic intervention strategies to the child-care providers, while also providing direct intervention to identified children at their child-care center. Project Visit not only provides direct services but, more importantly, increases the community's ability to provide intervention services for children who are not eligible for early intervention due to age, low severity of developmental problems, or need for full-time child care. Through a weekly call-in hour, child-care providers have direct access to pediatricians who can provide consultation related to the medical and psychosocial risks affecting the children in their programs.

Women and Infants Program

The Women and Infants Program is targeted at cocaine-addicted mothers and their newborns. Past experience demonstrated that the mothers would bring their infants for pediatric care but would not go to drug treatment, even on referral. Apparently drug treatment was both stigmatizing and overwhelming, since it placed an additional demand on mothers trying to care for their infants. Services were again reaggregated; the Women and Infants Program incorporates a drug treatment component with a substance abuse counselor and child development service into the pediatric primary care visit. This represents a "two for one" program, providing care for both mother and infant at one site for relatively low incremental cost.

Key components

Each of these programs shares several key components that have important policy implications. First, professionals provide needed services in places where children and families with problems are already being seen, thus greatly reducing the number of places where families must go for care. Second, the organizational responsibility for directing the program lies with an individual with appropriate authority and resources to help the family develop a flexible service plan, one that might not always correspond to the rigid criteria set by individual program referral systems. For example, when the Women and Infants Program realized that the mothers needed help with time management, flexible operating policies and budget priorities allowed for the immediate purchase of calendars, daily planners and, in some cases, alarm clocks to help the women get their infants to scheduled appointments. A need was identified and a timely solution was implemented. Third, each of these programs is a "two for one" model, serving the health and educational needs of children and the support and training needs of the mothers and child-care providers. Finally, each of these programs seeks to reach the mother or provider through the child, forming a therapeutic alliance that focuses on the whole child within a family context rather than dealing with a single problem.

Need for prevention

The challenge for the future is to eliminate the double jeopardy for young children living in poverty through changes in policy, delivery systems, and intervention strategies. The Comprehensive Child Development Centers Act of 1989 (CCDCA) seeks to demonstrate that educational failure can be prevented by addressing the social, emotional, and health needs of infants, toddlers, and their families. Twenty-two projects have recently been funded to develop models of early (starting with prenatal care), continuous (until children enter kindergarten), and comprehensive (health care, parent support and education, clinical care, early intervention, nutrition, and assistance with parent's formal education, employment, income, and housing) services.

The CCDCA illustrates features that are essential to all prevention programs. Prevention programs should be comprehensive and be delivered in the context of a unified family support model. Individual health, education, and social service programs alone do little to prevent problems that are caused by a complex transactional interaction of biological and environmental stresses. A child receiving nutritional supplements but no educational benefits from Head Start may be better off than one who receives neither, but certainly will not be as well off as a child who receives both. Similarly, a child who has medical care to treat lead poisoning and nutritional supplementation to treat malnutrition will not do as well as a child who receives developmental enrichment in conjunction with these medical benefits. Even comprehensive services cannot be helpful unless their accessibility is ensured. Reaggregation of resources (one-stop shopping) not only improves access, but may even lower administrative costs. Prevention programs must also start early, even before the birth of a child. The prevention of low birth weight through adequate prenatal care and good maternal nutrition improves the mother's health and avoids the biologic vulnerability that can lead to a child's failure in school. Finally, prevention programs must be continuous, meeting the needs of children, from prenatal care until they enter a school-based system of services. Interruption or fragmentation of health, nutrition, preschool, and developmental services impairs their effectiveness and can reduce the ratio of benefit to cost.

•   •   •

We know the biologic and psychosocial risks of poverty that place children at double jeopardy for adverse developmental outcomes and we have sufficient evidence to support policy and programmatic changes needed to ameliorate those effects. Collaboration between health and education is essential to the success of these initiatives; medical/ educational collaboration represents the critical link between childhood poverty and school success.

REFERENCES

1. Parker S, Greer S, Zuckerman B. Double jeopardy: The impact of poverty on early childhood development. *Pediatr Clin North Am.* 1988;35:1227–1239.

2. Pasaminick B, Knobloch H. Retrospective studies on the epidemiology of reproductive casualty: Old and new. *Merrill-Palmer Quarterly*, 1966;12:7–26.

3. Sameroff A, Chandler M. Reproductive risk and the continuum of caretaking casualty. In Horowitz F, Hetherington M, Scarr-Salapatek S, Siegel G. eds. *Review of Child Development Research*, Vol 4. Chicago, Ill: University of Chicago Press; 1975.

4. Beckwith L, Parmelee A. EEG patterns of preterm infants, home environment, and later IQ. *Child Dev.* 1986;57:777–789.

5. Werner E, Smith R. *Kauai's Children Come of Age.* Honolulu, Hawaii: University of Hawaii Press; 1977.

6. Lifschitz M, Wilson G, Smith E, Desmond M. Factors affecting head growth and intellectual function in children of drug addicts. *Pediatrics*, 1985;75:269–274.

7. Egbuonu S, Starheld B. Child health and social status. *Pediatrics.* 1982;9: 550–557.

8. Hanshaw J, Scheiner A, Moxley A, et al. School failure and deafness after silent congenital cytomegalovirus infection. *N Engl J Med*, 1976;295:468–470.

9. Dietrich K, Krafft K, Bornschein R, et al. Effects of low-level fetal lead exposure on neurobehavioral development in early infancy. *Pediatrics* 1987;80: 721–730.

10. Needleman H, Schell A, Bellinger D, Leviton A, Allred, E. The long-term effects of exposure to low doses of lead in childhood: An 11 year follow-up report. *N Engl J Med.* 1990;322:83–88.

11. Bellinger D, Leviton A, Waternaux C, et al. Low-level lead exposure, social class, and infant development. In: *Neurotoxiology Teratology,* 1989.

12. Shonkoff J. Biologic and social factors contributing to mild mental retardation. In: Heller K, Holtzman W, Messiuk, S. eds. *Placing Children in Special Education.* A Strategy for Equity, Washington, DC: National Academy Press; 1982.

13. Roghmann D, Hecht P, Haggerty R. Coping with stress. In: Haggerty R, Roghmann K and Pless I. eds. *Child Health and the Community.* New York, NY: Wiley; 1975.

14. Brown G, Bhrolchain M, Harris T. Social class and psychiatric disturbance among women in an urban population. *Sociol.* 1975;9:225–254.

15. Grossman P. Prematurity, poverty related stress, and the mother infant relationship. *Dissert Abstr Intl.* 1979;40(4a–B): 1954.

16. Crnic K, Greenberg M, Ragozin A, et al. Effects of stress and social support on mothers and premature and full term infants. *Child Dev.* 1983;54:209–219.

17. Thompson R. Stability of infant-mother attachment and its relationship to changing life circumstances in an unselected middle class sample. *Child Dev.* 1982;53: 144–148.

18. Bee H, Hammond M, Etres S, et al. The impact of parental life changes on the early development of children. *Res Nurs Health.* 1986;9:65–74.

19. Sandler W, Block M. Life stresses and maladjustment of poor children. *Am J Commun Psychol.* 1980;8:41–52.

20. Bromet E, Solomon Z, Dunn L, et al. Effective disorders in mothers of young children. *Br J Psychiatry.* 1982;140:30–36.

21. McGee R, Williams S, Kaskani J. Prevalence of self-reported depressive symptoms and associated social factors of mothers in Donedin. *Br J Psychiatry.* 1983;143:473–479.

22. Zuckerman B, Beardslee W. Maternal depression: A concern for pediatricians. *Pedatrics.* 1987:110–117.

23. Zuckerman B, Frank D, Hingson R, Amaro H, Levenson S, Kayne H, et al. Effects of maternal marijuana and cocaine use on fetal growth. *N Engl J Med.* 1989;320:762.

24. Dixon S, Bresnahan K, Zuckerman E. Cocaine babies: Meeting the challenge of management. *Contemp Pediatr.* 1990:70–92.

25. Rodning C, Beckwith L, Howard J. Characteristics of attachment organization and play organization in prenatally drug exposed toddlers. Submitted to *Development and Psychopathology,* 1989.

26. Kaplan-Sanoff M, Parker S, Zuckerman B. Child development project: A model of medical-educational collaboration. *Zero to Three.* 1987;7:18–24.

27. Kaplan-Sanoff M, Nigro J. The educator in a medical setting: Lessons learned from collaboration. *Inf Young Child.* 1988;1(2):1–10.

The diagnosis of attention deficit hyperactivity disorder in young children

W. Douglas Tynan, PhD
Department of Psychiatry and
  Behavioral Sciences
Children's National Medical Center
The George Washington University
  Medical School

Jeannette Nearing, BA
Department of Psychology
The George Washington University
Washington, DC

DIAGNOSING attention deficit hyperactivity disorder (ADHD) in infants and toddlers is a difficult enterprise. It requires identification of developmentally inappropriate inattention, impulsiveness, and hyperactivity. On the one hand, there is abundant evidence that such characteristics appear quite early in childhood. A recently published set of longitudinal data by Barkley et al[1] indicates that the mean age at onset of ADHD is between 3 and 4 years. On the other hand, Crowther et al[2] found that nearly one fourth of 3-year-old boys from preschool and day-care settings were rated clinically overactive, and inattentive using existing criteria (see box, "Diagnostic Criteria for 314.01: Attention Deficit Hyperactivity Disorder"). Furthermore, Campbell[3] reviewed a number of studies and discovered that, on a statistical basis, problems of inattention, overactivity, and difficulty in management are common in 3-year-olds. Such behavior problems, therefore, cannot be taken as definitive evidence of the presence of ADHD. Thus, at issue in the diagnosis of ADHD at such an early age is the ability to distinguish between a curious, active youngster whose parents have difficulty in, coping, and one who truly has a clinical deficit in focused attention, organization, response to reinforcement, and compliance with parental requests and commands.[4,5]

Typically, in the first year of a child's life there are few or no worries about ADHD.[3] Overall, behavioral concerns about infants are somewhat rare. The most common questions concern sleeping, feeding, and crying. From ages 1 to 2, these concerns remain, with additional issues—first about language development and later about bowel and bladder control—arising near the end of the second year. Concerns about behavioral management peak at age 3, which coincides with the common age of first diagnosis.[1] The problem with diagnosis at age 3 is that between the ages of 3 and 6 there can be a significant developmental change in the behaviors that compromise ADHD criteria. Activity level, disobedience, and destructiveness drop sharply between the ages of 3 and 4. Physical aggression and, again, disobedience decrease between the ages of 4 and 6. Admittedly, children with persistent behavior problems did not evidence this natural decline in problematic behavior. However, even in parent-referred, problematic preschoolers, 50% did not exhibit significant behavior problems at age 6.[6] If ADHD is diag-

Inf Young Children, 1994; 6(4): 13–20
© 1994 Aspen Publishers, Inc.

Diagnostic Criteria for 314.01: Attention Deficit Hyperactivity Disorder

A. A disturbance of at least 6 months during which at least eight of the following are present*†:
   (1) often fidgets with hands or feet or squirms in seat (in an adolescent, may be limited to subjective feelings of restlessness)
   (2) has difficulty remaining seated when required to do so
   (3) is easily distracted by extraneous stimuli
   (4) has difficulty awaiting turn in games or group situations
   (5) often blurts out answers to questions before they have been completed
   (6) has difficulty following through on instructions from others (not owing to oppositional behavior or failure of comprehension) (eg, fails to finish chores)
   (7) has difficulty sustaining attention in tasks or play activities
   (8) often shifts from one play activity to another
   (9) has difficulty playing quietly
   (10) often talks excessively
   (11) often interrupts or intrudes on other (eg, butts into other children's games)
   (12) often does not seem to listen to what is being said to him or her
   (13) often loses things necessary for tasks or activities at school or at home (eg, toys, pencils, books, assignments)
   (14) often engages in physically dangerous activities without considering the possible consequences (not for the purpose of thrill seeking) (eg, runs into street without looking)
B. Onset before the age of 7
C. Does not meet the criteria for a pervasive developmental disorder

Criteria for severity of attention deficit hyperactivity disorder

Mild: Few, if any, symptoms in excess of those required to make the diagnosis *and* only minimal or no impairment in school and social functioning

Moderate: Symptoms or functional impairment intermediate between "mild" and "severe"

Severe: Many symptoms in excess of those required to make the diagnosis *and* significant and pervasive impairment in functioning at home and school with peers

*Consider a criterion met only if the behavior is considerably more frequent than that of most people of the same mental age.
†The items in **A** are listed in descending order of discrimination power based on data from a national field trial of the *DSM-III-R.*
Adapted with permission from the American Psychiatric Association. *Diagnostic and Statistical Manual of Mental Disorders.* 3rd ed, rev. Washington, DC: APA; 1987.

nosed in infancy or toddlerhood, particularly if only *DSM-III-R*[7] criteria are used, significantly large numbers of young children could be classified as having ADHD, far exceeding the estimated 5% of children affected by this disorder.[3,5]

Several procedures have been suggested to reduce the uncertainty involved in an ADHD diagnosis in infancy or toddlerhood. Campbell[3] suggests that, except for clear-cut cases, it is preferable to admit that we cannot truly discriminate between a child with ADHD and a parent–child interaction problem. She suggests the use of the *DSM-III-R* coding in the "V" category of a "parent child problem" in the preschool years. Barkley[5] suggests, for children identified in the preschool years, a criterion of persistence of symptoms for 12 months rather than 6 months. (For children who meet that 12-month criterion, he recommends early intervention.) Most major researchers recognize an additional need to monitor recent history in the child's experience. Frequent changes in caregiving arrangements, moving, parental separation or marriage, and parental job loss or gain can contribute to child behavioral difficulties. A preschool-aged child does not have the ability to express a wide range of emotions in subtle ways, and many environmental changes can increase impulsive and inattentive behaviors. Also, conditions of infancy that are associated with ADHD can be identified and treated. Language delay and poor fine motor skills are related to learning disability; these can certainly be a source of frustration for the child and should be evaluated concurrently with the evaluation for ADHD.

Because there is a high rate of continuing problems (nearly 50%),[8,9] as well as a high rate of spontaneous improvement, it is generally not sufficient to wait for children to outgrow their problematic behaviors. As they develop, children who do not spontaneously improve may get lower grades, fail in school more frequently, complete fewer years of education, and be expelled from school more often than normal children of identical academic ability.[10] Such children could benefit from early, direct, and preventive interventions. Such interventions, for practical reasons, often require a diagnosis. So again, the difficult enterprise of diagnosing a young child as having ADHD must be faced.

Accurate assessment and diagnosis of ADHD require a thorough evaluation of several domains. These domains include a comprehensive history, cognitive variables, child temperament, parent–child patterns of interaction, and external stressors. Assessment of these domains requires multiple assessment tools, settings, and sources. Assessment tools include parental questionnaires, laboratory measures, and direct observation. Settings from which behavioral information should be collected include school, home, and other social situations. Sources that should be considered include teachers, both parents, and other significant adults.

TEMPERAMENT

A child's difficult behavior is at least partially a consequence of what the child inherently brings to the situation. In 1968 Thomas et al[11] defined this concept of inherent characteristics as *temperament*. Their New York longitudinal study delineated a constellation of character traits that define a "difficult" temperament. Difficult children have irregular biologic functions such as eating and sleeping.

They usually react negatively (withdraw) from new experiences. They are slow to adapt to changes in their environment and tend to react to changes intensely. Frequent negative moods are common. Of the children defined as "difficult," 70% developed behavior problems.[11] This population, therefore, is obviously at risk for a range of behavioral difficulties. Further studies have substantiated the existence of a constellation of traits that are "difficult" and a high preponderance of ensuing behavior problems.[12] They have also identified further the additional "difficult" characteristic of demandingness in children as they develop.[12]

Of particular relevance to ADHD in the "difficult" child constellation is the slow-to-adapt characteristic. ADHD children are usually thought of as constantly moving and talking, with difficulties in concentration and attention. A second cluster of behaviors, however, is often classified as ADHD; such behaviors are seen in slow-to-adapt children. In the face of new situations these children produce intense, negative reactions. Most recently Barkley[13] has suggested that an inability to inhibit impulsive responses (including difficulty in separating affect from information received), rather than high activity and attentional difficulties, is the hallmark of ADHD. Children can be considered slow to adapt if they persist in maladaptive patterns of responses—that is, they cannot inhibit existing negative emotional responses and learn new more adaptive ways to respond to a situation. These children undoubtedly have difficulty separating affect from information on received signals and respond impulsively. If this lack of inhibition is the primary disorder in ADHD, then certainly a slow-to-adapt child, who by definition lacks inhibitory skills, would certainly tend to have those difficulties.

Despite the correlation between difficult temperament and behavior problems, diagnosing or even predicting ADHD based solely on child temperament lends itself to error. The temperament literature is marked by very mixed results when predicting toddler behavior from infancy, and by even poorer results when predicting school-age temperament from that demonstrated during the toddler period. For example, a recent prospective study by Olson et al[14] found that responsive parent–child interaction and cognitive competence at age 2 predicted impulse control at age 6. The temperament variables simultaneously measured were not predictive of later impulse control in a normal group. In a high-risk sample, on the other hand, the relationship between these variables appears to differ. In particular, response intensity and demandingness do appear to predict the persistence of ADHD symptoms from preschool to school years.[3] Recently, Sanson et al[15] found that difficult temperament *in conjunction with* other risk factors—particularly maternal perception of difficulty and perinatal stress or prematurity—can be very predictive of behavioral maladjustment.

A number of other related factors have been cited that may influence the strength of the prediction of ADHD when combined with a difficult temperament. Barkley[5] has cited delayed motor development, low birth weight, and primary apnea in infancy. Prenatal and maternal environmental factors, including single parent, prenatal substance abuse, low socioeconomic status, parental education, and, most importantly, a family history of ADHD in siblings and other relatives, were also cited as risk factors.

PARENT–CHILD INTERACTION

Incessant behavior problems in an infant or toddler take a toll on parents. Parents may doubt their own parenting skills, become frustrated and angry with their children, and even want to give up the effort of persuading their children to behave.[16] In the face of mounting frustration on both sides, a negative interaction style is often established between parents and children. The cycle often begins when the child appears to ignore a parental request. Parent and child become engaged in a conflict of wills. If the parent gives in, the child learns that failure to comply has no consequence. This is likely to increase episodes of conflict in the future. If the parent forces the child to behave, the child learns that the parent will direct attention and energy when he or she is misbehaving, and the parent is reinforced for using a loud voice and physical control. Again, episodes of conflict are likely to increase rather than decrease. With every conflict the parent–child relationship becomes more negative for both parties. If, by temperament, a child is overactive, distractible, insistent, and not adaptable, the frequency of these conflicts will increase over time.[17–19]

Recent research has identified some parental behaviors that perpetuate such a negative interaction style. Usually the research refers to maternal behaviors because it is the child's mother who participates in the project. From a treatment point of view, perhaps the most significant finding is that mothers of children with behavior problems, particularly aggressive children, use inconsistent patterns of positive praise and reinforcement.[20,21] They reinforce and punish both aversive and compliant child behaviors. In the presence of such inconsistency, children become confused and have great difficulty learning that compliant behavior is favored over aversive behavior. Also, some research suggests that the greater the amount of inconsistency, the greater the amount of family conflict.[21] Mothers caught in this negative interaction style are also less positive, more aversive, and more commanding then mothers of competent children.[20] Such mothers tend to be more impatient and to utilize more powerful assertive and controlling strategies with their children.[9]

Wahler and Sansbury[22] suggest that inconsistent reinforcement is due to monitoring difficulties on the part of the mother. They discovered that professionals and mothers agreed on the definition and presence of positive behaviors in their children. On the definition and presence of negative behaviors, however, there was a significant split. Mothers did not see the same number of negative behaviors as the professionals, and they were inconsistent in the behaviors they identified as negative. It is not too difficult to imagine that a mother faced with a lifetime of negative behaviors eventually fails to notice some of them. On the other hand, the difference between what professionals and mothers perceive and the ensuing inconsistent reinforcement is a primary target for treatment. Although certainly both mother and child contribute to the maladaptive system, clinicians usually target changes in maternal behavior as the first step in helping to change that system.

FAMILY AND COMMUNITY

External social conditions influence a child's behavior directly and indirectly by placing excessive stress on parents. The family structure plays a particularly strong role in that respect. If there is marital distress, if the family structure is unstable, if there is poor family communication, or if there is only one parent, child behavior problems tend to intensify.[9,20] Also, if the mother, or the parents, have poor social support networks, suffer significant financial losses, and experience poor health, or if there is ongoing conflict, their relationship with their child may suffer, and behavior problems may increase.[22,23] In addition, because ADHD has a strong familial component, adults with ADHD do suffer high rates of family and job instability and interpersonal conflict. Such stressors also lend themselves to depression, low self-confidence, and bouts of self-blame. These poor mental states in the parent, again, can have negative repercussions on the relationship with the child and increase behavior problems.[23] Especially the impulsive, noncompliant, and restless activity that appears ADHD-like may be an emotional response to these types of stressors.

TOOLS FOR ASSESSING ADHD IN YOUNG CHILDREN

There are several well-validated questionnaires that are often used to identify behavior problems in children. The Parenting Stress Index (PSI) is a parent-completed questionnaire that evaluates problems typical of preschool and young school-age children.[24] It includes scales of hyperactivity/distractibility, mood and demandingness, and behavior and temperament factors cited earlier as predictive of ADHD. In addition, it includes an acceptability scale and a "reinforces parent" scale. The acceptability scale measures how well the child matches the parent's ideal child. The "reinforces parent" scale indicates how reinforcing or rewarding interactions are in this child. In addition, the PSI measures parental depression, a well-cited risk factor,[5,23] and attachment, another mediating factor of the development of ADHD that has been empirically examined.[14] A life stress measure and other measures of family and stress factors are also included. Of the measures available, it is the only one that attempts to sample child temperament, interactive behavior, parent affect, and external stressors in one instrument.

Achenbach and colleagues[25,26] have empirically derived a very well-respected Child Behavior Checklist (CBCL). This questionnaire consists of 83 items that are descriptions of common childhood behaviors. Parents rate the target child on a 0-to-2 scale for the presence and severity of each behavior. This checklist identifies and differentiates internalizing and externalizing problems. Externalizing behaviors, relevant for most behavior problems identified as ADHD, include two types of behavior: aggressive and destructive. Two additional factors, sleep and somatic problems, appear independently. Thus, temperament items are found in this checklist, but in the context of other factors. Interestingly, although there is clearly an attention factor on the CBCL for ages 4 to 18, this is not found on the CBCL for ages 2 to 3 in its empirical derivation. This suggests that attention difficulties, by adult standards, are so common in this age group as to not be predictive of anything.

For slightly older children (3 to 5 years of age), the Preschool Behavior Questionnaire (PBQ)[6] may be appropriate. Basically it parallels the CBCL in format. Its scales include hostile-aggressive, hyperactive-distractible, and anxious-fearful. This scale is very popular in research but is not as widely available as the PSI or the CBCL 2–3. Recently, the Preschool Socioaffective Profile was published.[27] Based on a large Canadian sample, it yielded three factors: anger-aggression, social competence, and anxiety withdrawal. It appears to complement the PBQ by adding a factor of social competence to the child description.

Occasionally, variations of the Conners 10-Item Scale is recommended for ADHD assessment. The 10-Item Scale consists of two items with the strongest statistical loading from each of five factors determined in a variety of longer scales (the Conners 93-item parent scale and 48-item teacher scale). It is mainly a tool for identifying the presence of psychopathology and for monitoring medication effects. Overall, the data on 3- and 4-year-old subjects are not very extensive on the Conners scales when compared with previously mentioned instruments. A different 10-item Conners scale, distributed by Abbot Laboratories, is not even recommended by Conners.[5]

Laboratory measures have been developed to evaluate impulse control.[28,29] Although these provide somewhat more reliable data for research purposes, most are not practical for clinical settings. The tasks involve rigorous measurement of children's ability to delay a task, pay attention to a stimulus, or follow directions. An example of one instrument that is practical in the clinical setting is the Gordon Diagnostic System,[16] a measure of visual vigilance and impulse control. In addition, a number of studies[20,30] have utilized mutual mother–child problem-solving tasks to evaluate parental responsiveness and interactional style. Although it is difficult to replicate laboratory findings in clinical settings, they can provide insight into specific maternal and child interactive behaviors that the clinician should attempt to observe.

Finally, direct observation should always be included in an ADHD assessment. The simplest place for such observation is the clinic setting. However, in a clinic, while receiving one-on-one attention, an otherwise impulsive, overly active child may be perfectly well behaved. It is most useful, although difficult and time consuming, to observe the child's behavior while he or she is in school, the home, or a public situation (eg, grocery shopping). This is particularly important, as the diagnosis of ADHD demands that the problematic behavior be evident in multiple settings. Although norms do not exist for preschoolers, Barkley[5] does have a Home Situations Questionnaire that asks parents to rate their children's behavior in these different situations, which can be quite useful in targeting behaviors to change.

• • •

This review indicates that the *DSM-III-R* criteria used to diagnose ADHD are difficult to apply to toddlers and infants, and when these or similar criteria are used, they tend to be overly inclusive. Furthermore, research indicates that only about half of impulsive toddlers go on to meet the criteria for ADHD at later ages. Measures predicting impulsive, inattentive, and overly active behaviors are drawn from a wide range of measures that include measures of specific ADHD behaviors, infant and toddler temperament, parent–child interactions, and family risk variables. Although intuitively it would appear that temperamental variables should predict ADHD type symptoms, the research does not support a strong finding there. Instead, parent–child interaction, cognitive development, and adaptation within the family appear to be better predictors of outcome. Accurate diagnosis, intervention, and prediction depend on a thorough evaluation of variables from all of the domains mentioned. For any individual child, problems with impulsivity in the preschool period can certainly be remediated by effective parent–child therapies available, as well as by possible stimulant medication trials. Clinicians and parents should not wait for the child to grow out of these problematic behaviors.

REFERENCES

1. Barkley RA, Fischer M, Edelbrock CS, Smallish L. The adolescent outcome of hyperactive children diagnosed by research criteria: I. An 8 year prospective follow up study. *J Am Acad Child Adolesc Psychiatry.* 1990;29:546–557.

2. Crowther JK, Bond LA, Rolf JE. The incidence, prevalence, and severity of behavior disorders among preschool aged children in day care. *J Abnormal Child Psychol.* 1981;9:23–42.

3. Campbell SB. *Behavior Problems in Preschool Children: Clinical and Developmental Issues.* New York, NY: Guilford Press; 1990.

4. Palfrey JS, Levine MD, Walker DK, Sullivan M. The emergence of attention deficits in early childhood: a prospective study. *Dev Behav Pediatr.* 1985;6:339–348.

5. Barkley RA. *Attention Deficit Hyperactivity Disorder: A Handbook for Diagnosis and Treatment.* New York, NY: Guilford Press; 1990.

6. Campbell S. Parent referred problem three year olds: developmental changes in symptoms. *J Child Psychol Psychiatry.* 1987;28:835–846.

7. American Psychiatric Association. *Diagnostic and Statistical Manual of Mental Disorders. 3rd ed, rev.* Washington, DC: APA; 1987.

8. Campbell S, Ewing L. Follow-up of hard-to-manage preschoolers: adjustment at age 9 and predictors of continuing symptoms. *J Child Psychol Psychiatry.* 1990;31:871–889.

9. Campbell S, March C, Pierce E, Ewing L, Szumowski E. Hard-to-manage preschool boys: family context and the stability of externalizing behavior. *J Abnormal Child Psychol.* 1991;19:301–316.

10. Weiss G, Hechtman L, Perlman T, Hopkin J, Wehar T. Hyperactives as young adults: a controlled prospective 10 year follow up of the psychiatric status of 75 children. *Arch Gen Psychiatry.* 1979;36:675–681.

11. Thomas A, Chess S, Birch H. *Temperament and Behavior Disorders in Children.* New York, NY: New York University Press; 1968.

12. Bates JE. The concept of difficult temperament. *Merrill-Palmer Q.* 1980;20:299–319.

13. Barkley R. A new theory of ADHD. *ADHD Newsletter.* 1993;1(4):1–3.

14. Olson SL, Bates JE, Bayles K. Early antecedents of childhood impulsivity: the role of parent-child interaction, cognitive competence, and temperament. *J Abnormal Child Psychol.* 1990;18:317–334.

15. Sanson A, Oberklaid F, Pedlow R, Prior M. Risk indicators: assessment of infancy predictors of preschool behavioral maladjustment. *J Child Psychol Psychiatry.* 1991;32:609–626.

16. Gordon M. *ADHD/Hyperactivity: A Consumer's Guide.* Dewitt, NY: GSI Publications; 1991.

17. Forehand RL, McMahon RJ. *Helping the Non-Compliant Child: A Clinician's Guide to Parent Training.* New York, NY: The Guilford Press; 1981.

18. Barkley RA. *Defiant Children: A Clinician's Manual for Parent Training.* New York, NY: The Guilford Press; 1987.

19. Webster-Stratton C. *The Parents and Children Series.* Eugene, Ore: Castalia Publishing; 1989.

20. Dumas J, LaFreniere P, Beaudin L, Verlaan P. Mother-child interactions in competent and aggressive dyads: implications of relationship stress for behavior therapy with families. *NZ J Psychol.* 1992;21:3–13.

21. Gardner F. Inconsistent parenting: is there evidence for a link with children's conduct problems? *J Abnormal Child Psychol.* 1989;17:223–233.

22. Wahler R, Sansbury L. The monitoring skills of troubled mothers: their problem in defining child deviance. *J Abnormal Child Psychol.* 1990;18:577–589.

23. Webster-Stratton C. The relationship of marital support, conflict, and divorce to parent perceptions, behaviors, and childhood conduct problems. *J Marriage Family.* 1989;51:417–430.

24. Abidin R. *Parenting Stress Index.* Charlottesville, Va: Pediatric Psychology Press; 1990.

25. Achenbach TM, Edelbrock C, Howell CT. Empirically based assessment of behavioral/emotional problems of 2 and 3 year old children. *J Abnormal Child Psychol.* 1987;15:629–650.

26. Achenbach TM. *Manual for the Child Behavior Checklist/2-3 and 1992 Profile.* Burlington, Vt: University of Vermont Department of Psychiatry; 1992.

27. La Freniere P, Dumas J, Capuano F, Dubeau D. Development and validation of the Preschool Socioaffective Profile. *Psycholog Assessment.* 1992;4:442–450.

28. Arend R, Gove F, Sroufe L. Continuity of individual adaptation from infancy to kindergarten: A predictive study of ego resiliency and curiosity in preschoolers. *Child Dev.* 1979;50:950–959.

29. Murray K, Goldman M, DeVet K. Behavioral battery to assess impulsivity and inhibitory control in toddlers. Presented at the Biennial Meeting of the Society for Research in Child Development; March1993; New Orleans, La.

30. Frankel KA, Bates JE. Mother-toddler problem solving: antecedents in attachment, home behavior and temperament. *Child Dev.* 1990;61:810–819.

Environmental influences on the developmental outcome of children at risk

Glen P. Aylward, PhD
Division of Developmental and
  Behavioral Pediatrics
Departments of Pediatrics and
  Psychiatry
Southern Illinois University School of
  Medicine
Springfield, Illinois

AT-RISK INFANTS are typically the focus of follow-up studies because these infants often display adverse developmental sequelae. Tjossem[1] delineated three categories of risk: established, environmental, and biologic. Established risks are medical disorders of a known etiology whose developmental outcome is well documented (eg, Down syndrome). Environmental risks include the quality of the mother–infant interaction, opportunities for stimulation, and health care. Biologic risks include the exposure to potentially noxious prenatal, perinatal, or postnatal developmental events such as asphyxia, intraventricular hemorrhage, and low birth weight (LBW). Biologic and environmental risks are not mutually exclusive, and children from poor socioeconomic circumstances and poverty also frequently experience medical risk factors, such as poor prenatal care or LBW. This combination of risk is sometimes referred to as double jeopardy.[2]

The outcome of infants with biologic risks (particularly LBW infants) has traditionally been emphasized in developmental follow-up, with prediction being an important issue. However, the prediction of later outcome from early assessment has been problematic. For example, the mean correlation between infant assessments administered at 5 to 7 months of age and intelligence quotients (IQs) obtained at 3 to 5 years is $r = 0.17$.[3] Poor prediction may be due to changes in the developing nervous system, to psychometric issues, or to environmental influences.[4]

Despite mounting evidence that the environment exerts a major effect on outcome,[5] the environmental risk factor unfortunately is often overlooked in developmental follow-up. In fact, a recent metaanalysis of LBW studies published over the last decade revealed that environmental and psychosocial variables were controlled in less than 2% of the investigations.[6]

This article explores the relationship between biologic and environmental risks. Hypothetical models of effect on outcome and major historic and contemporary studies involving evaluation of biologic and environmental risk will be discussed. The identification of specific environmental influences and the implications of these data will be presented .

The author acknowledges Kathy McAnarney for assistance in the preparation of this article.

Inf Young Children, 1990; 2(4): 1–9
© 1990 Aspen Publishers, Inc.

MODELS OF EFFECT ON OUTCOME

An influential, early model of effect is the continuum of reproductive casualty.[7] The basic assumption of this biologic risk-oriented model is that the severity of developmental disabilities (which include cerebral palsy, epilepsy, mental retardation, behavioral disorders, and learning problems) is influenced by the degree of perinatal complications. Specifically, a more serious condition such as cerebral palsy would be associated with more obstetric and perinatal complications than would a milder disorder such as a reading problem; the greater the degree of perinatal complications, the greater the later deviancy. However, studies such as the Kauai Longitudinal Project,[8] reported in the late 1960s and early 1970s, did not support this model.

The interactional model[8] assumes a two-dimensional array of constitution (biologic factors) and environment (ie, good environment + good constitution = good outcome; good constitution + bad environment = medium outcome). This model's lack of insight as to the mechanisms or processes by which biologic and environmental interaction evolves and its assumption that environment and constitution are constant over time are drawbacks.

A more popular model is the transactional approach,[9] in which a degree of plasticity is considered inherent in both the child (biologic component) and the environment. The child is constantly reorganizing and self-righting; a poorly stimulating environment would interfere with this self-righting, and the probability of a disrupted child–environment transaction increases. A more positive environment is assumed to enhance the child's resiliency. This environmental emphasis has led to the concept of a continuum of caretaking casualty.[5] Data from various sources have been supportive of this approach and will be discussed subsequently.

A variation of the transactional model is the risk route concept,[4] which requires the assessment of a child at various times in three areas: the medical/ biologic, environmental/psychosocial, and behavioral/developmental areas. The degree of risk is additive across the three areas at each time of assessment and is cumulative over time (ie, an interaction exists between previous effects and current risk indices). The moving risk model[10] differs slightly from the risk route approach in that the different areas of risk are considered additive or synergistic, but are not cumulative over time. This consideration reportedly allows children to move in and out of risk at different times. Support also exists for these approaches and will be discussed subsequently.

MAJOR HISTORIC STUDIES

One of the earliest investigations that questioned the continuum of reproductive casualty concept was the Kauai Longitudinal Project. Here, 670 children born in

1955 were followed longitudinally to age 18.[8,11] At 20 months of age, children from middle-class homes who had experienced the most severe perinatal complications had mean intelligence scores comparable to those in children having no perinatal stress but living in poor homes.

The most developmentally delayed children experienced the most severe perinatal complications and were also living in the poorest homes. By age 10, children with and without severe perinatal stress who had grown up in middle-class homes achieved IQ scores that were above average; scores were significantly lower in children from low socioeconomic status (SES) households, particularly if they had experienced severe perinatal stress. By age 18, adolescents who lived in poverty were 10 times more likely to have serious learning and behavioral problems than were those who had survived severe perinatal stress. The synergistic effect of combined biologic and environmental stress was apparent in this study, with innate abilities and experiential and environmental influences interacting to affect brain development and outcome.

The relationship between perinatal events such as asphyxia and developmental outcome also has been studied extensively in the National Collaborative Perinatal Project (NCPP).[12] Enrollment lasted from 1959 to 1966,[12] and various measurements were taken at 8 months and at 1, 4, and 7 years. Generally, a weak relationship between perinatal events such as asphyxia and later outcome was found.[13]

When the children were 8 months old, 10 signs of anoxia accounted for 2% to 3% of the variance on developmental indices; birth weight and gestational age were the largest contributors (9%–15%).[14] When the children were 4 years old, neonatal variables accounted for 1% to 2% of the variance on the Stanford-Binet Intelligence Scale,[15] but prenatal variables accounted for 20%.[12] When the children were 7 years old, perinatal asphyxia explained less than 1% of the variance in Wechsler Intelligence Scale for Children (WISC)[16] IQ scores and was not predictive of visual-motor integration as measured by the Bender-Gestalt.[17] Perinatal variables were also not predictive of so-called minimal brain dysfunction (learning difficulties, hyperkinetic-impulsive behavior, neurologic soft signs) at that age.[18] These data do not support the biologic risk model as the sole or primary influence on developmental outcome.

Low birth weight, another biologic risk factor, has been studied extensively by Drillien and coworkers.[19,20] Data from Scottish infants indicated that in the higher socioeconomic classes, deficits in LBW infants (<3.9 lb), declined from a 26 point to a 13 point difference between the ages of 6 months and 4 years; similarly in the lowest socioeconomic class group, the deficits increased from 26 to 32 points. By 5 to 7 years, few children from middle-class homes had mental handicaps unless their birth weight was <3.5 lb; in contrast, there were more children with mental handicaps in poor homes regardless of birth weight. When evaluating children whose IQ was <90, no difference was found in the upper two SES groupings between children who were preterm or fullterm. In the lowest two SES classes, on the other hand, LBW children had a 27% rate of dysfunction, and those born at term had a 14% rate.

REPRESENTATIVE CONTEMPORARY STUDIES

The effects of prematurity have also been studied in the UCLA Longitudinal Project cohort (born from 1972–1974).[21–23] In this sample of 126 children, medical complications again were not related to outcome. By the use of path analysis (a method for relating variables to each other both directly and indirectly), the relationship between perinatal complications and cognitive development at 9 and 24 months was found to be mediated by caregiver–infant interaction; postnatal complications were not related directly to 9- or 24-month outcome, but there was a modest relationship between postnatal complications and caregiver–infant interaction.[22] Postnatal complications were related to 24-month scores only through caregiver–infant interaction. These data suggest that at 9 months, illness deflated developmental progress to some extent, but that by 24 months, pediatric events (illness) had decreasing influence. The environmental path seems to be the most critical in determining outcome, with biologic events having indirect effects.

In the UCLA study,[21] IQ scores of low SES children also began to diverge from normal at 2 years, owing to the increased influence of social factors (years of maternal education and caregiver–infant interaction in the home). By age 5 years, social factors were more important than any other set of variables in relation to cognitive performance; obstetric or neonatal hazardous events were essentially not predictive. In fact, at 5 years of age, three fourths of children with earlier postnatal complications scored within the normal range. However, half of the children who later scored in the borderline to low average range came from the previously average group.

Prenatal and perinatal hazards did not relate to any outcome measure at 8 years of age in English-speaking children; in marked contrast, birth weight, length of hospitalization, and postnatal complications *did* affect 8-year-old IQs in Hispanics.[23] In the English-speaking population, low SES accounted solely for decreased cognitive scores. The Hispanic population generally was socially stressed by poverty and immigration problems, and Hispanic children with the lowest outcome scores also had LBW and more postnatal complications. These findings led the investigators to conclude that neonatal problems are a risk factor but do not necessarily mean that a given child will have trouble later; "social factors appear to swamp biologic factors."[23(p109)]

Escalona[24,25] investigated the interaction of biologic and environmental risks in a cohort of 114 urban, socially disadvantaged children followed from birth to 3.5 years of age. Although the mean developmental quotient at 15 months of age was

99.8, it declined by 28 months to 85.4. A slight improvement was noted at 40 months (89.3). Noteworthy was the finding that there was a slight drop in cognitive scores at 28 months even in the group from the top SES quartile; by 40 months, however, the mean score improved to 102. Unfortunately, children from the lowest SES quartile never recovered: Their mean 40-month cognitive score was 79.9. These data suggest that environmental deficits and stresses impair early cognitive and psychosocial development, with infants who experienced biologic risk (eg, prematurity) being more vulnerable to environmental insufficiencies than their full-term counterparts. Escalona[25] also reported that severe, negative biologic circumstances led to poor outcome, regardless of SES.

In the Louisville Twin Study,[26] mental development scores from 6 months to 3 years for twins born with LBW (<1,750 g) and small for gestational age (SGA) fell into the 89 to 92 range and increased to approximately 100 by age 6 years. The biologic risk indicators of birth weight and gestational age correlated with mental test scores during the first year (0.45–0.55) but declined to 0.15 by age 6. In contrast, correlations between parental education and family status and IQ scores increased as the children got older, ranging from 0.06 at 6 months to 0.45 by 6 years. When these correlations were presented graphically, the slopes of biologic and environmental variables crossed between 18 and 24 months, with maternal education and SES showing dramatic correlational gains by 24 months.

LBW children from high SES families began to improve by 3 years and showed normal scores by age 6; LBW children from low SES families continued to display depressed scores at 6 years. In a rather unique analysis of 12 monozygotic twin pairs in which one twin had been born at <1,750 g and the other was, on average, 815 g heavier, the difference in mean cognitive scores was only 2 points, indicating that differences in IQ scores were not amplified by LBW. Maternal education was again the strongest predictor of subsequent IQ.

The National Heart, Lung, and Blood Institute's Collaborative Antenatal Steroid Study[27] evaluated 619 infants whose mothers were at risk for premature labor. Infants were evaluated at term and at 9, 18, and 36 months. Cognitive, motor, and neurologic assessments were made, and the environment was measured with the SES-Composite Index (SESCOMP),[28] consisting of six marker variables, which accounted for 89% of the common variance of all environmental variables. The six variables were maternal education, paternal education, family occupation,[29] integration of an adult male in the family, the availability of car or telephone, and freedom from public assistance. Scores were divided into the upper, middle two, and lower quartiles.

The evaluation of outcome scores at 9,18, and 36 months revealed a precipitous decline in cognitive function but not motor function in the lowest SES-COMP quartile; there was a markedly lesser decline in cognitive function in the middle SES grouping. No decrease was noted in the upper SES quartile. A similar precipitous decline was noted when subjects were divided by race: Children in the black and "other" (primarily Hispanic and American Indian) racial groups displayed a marked decrease in cognitive scores, whereas white children did not. Most children in the black and other groups were from disadvantaged environments.[28]

Consistency in the diagnosis of cognitive, motor, and neurologic function from 9 to 36 months was also evaluated in this population.[30] Diagnoses of motor functioning were the most stable over time; diagnoses of cognitive functioning were the least stable. There was a one in four chance that a diagnosis of normal cognitive function at 9 months would worsen by 36 months, with the major shift occurring between 18 and 36 months. However, 9 out of 10 infants who had normal motor or neurologic function at 9 months continued to do so. Analysis of the influence of background variables on consistency profiles showed that the clinical center, the child's race, and SES-COMP Index affected cognitive outcome; only the infant's gender influenced later motor function. A linear relationship was found between increased cognitive consistency and higher SES-COMP Index scores. Furthermore, there was a stronger relationship between perinatal factors and 40-week outcome than between these factors and later outcome. Of note was the fact that children diagnosed as normal at 40 weeks conceptional age or at 9 months contributed more to the population of children who were not normal at 36 months than did those who were diagnosed earlier as being abnormal or suspect.

The risk route concept was applied to a subset of this population,[31] in which 14 maternal and prenatal, 24 perinatal, and 12 asphyxia-related variables were correlated with outcome at conceptional age and at 9, 18, and 36 months. Correlations between medical and biologic variables and outcome were weak; the SES-COMP Index and the Early Neuropsychologic Optimality Rating Scale-9 months (ENORS-9)[32] (a behavioral/developmental measure) were better predictors of 36-month outcome. Significant correlations between the SES-COMP Index and cognitive function appeared at 9 months. Again, neurologic function was influenced more by medical/biologic variables, whereas cognitive function was associated with environmental effects. Of children who had optimal SES-COMP Index and ENORS-9 scores (even with nonoptimal prenatal and perinatal variable groups), 94% had normal cognitive function, 98% had normal motor function, and 100% had normal neurologic outcome at 36 months.

ENVIRONMENTAL INFLUENCES

The above discussion indicates that the environment modulates the influences of reproductive and perinatal risk. However, the identification of *how* this occurs and of the specific aspects of the influential environment is still elusive.

Bradley et al[33] evaluated the home environment of 42 children during infancy and middle childhood; the scores were related to achievement and classroom behavior at 10 to 11 years. Three temporal components of environmental action were delineated:

1. the primacy effect of early environment (along the lines of attachment or psychodynamic theory);
2. the predominance of contemporary environment (events contemporary to the time of assessment); and
3. the stability of environment over time (continuation).

The strongest support was found for the contemporary environment model, but all three possibilities received some support. These data suggest a complex interaction that cannot be explained by a single model of environmental action.

SES (when represented by maternal education and occupational status) is not a pure measure and subsumes considerable heterogeneity.[34] Taking a microscopic rather than macroscopic look at environmental risk factors, Sameroff et al[35] used data from the Rochester Longitudinal Study. Environmental variables included maternal mental health, anxiety, parental perspectives on child development, mother–child interaction, education, occupation, minority status, family support, life events, and family size. Multiple regression analyses revealed that SES accounted for 35% of the variance in 4-year verbal IQ; however, a 50% increase in explained variance was achieved with the inclusion of the other 10 environmental variables. As the number of risk factors increased, the verbal IQ decreased (in both high and low SES groups). In children with four or more risk factors, 24% had IQs in the range of 50 to 84; none of the children without or with only one risk factor had IQ scores in this range. These data imply that no single environmental factor uniquely enhances or limits cognitive abilities; rather, it is the accumulation of risk variables that produces developmental morbidity. Unfortunately, most of these factors are not amenable to intervention.

Wallace[36] suggested that the broad concept of environment includes physical properties (crowding, personal space, excessive noise), organization (regularity of experience, physical organization, predictability, structure), and appropriate play materials. Caregiver–child interaction, didactic activities (particularly those that encourage the mastery of language skills), disciplinary techniques, the family social climate (birth order, spacing, size), and the family's values, beliefs, and attitudes (values given to education, intellectual endeavors) are also critical. There clearly are many potential aspects of a nonoptimal environment.

As part of a broader conceptualization of environment, genetics studies have highlighted an intriguing aspect of the constitutional and environmental interaction. Using data from the Texas Adoption Project, Loehlin et al[37] suggested the popular view that genetic effects are fixed at birth and that environmental effects change, may not be accurate. Using path analyses, these authors reported that environmental effects have a *decreasing* influence on IQ as children grow older; in contrast, changes in genetic expression continue into late adolescence or early adulthood. In this study, heritability values between parent and offspring were in the 40% to 50% range, although figures of 60% to 80% have been reported in studies of twins.[38] Therefore, the decline in IQ scores seen over time in children from at-risk environments could be interpreted to reflect the emergence of previously latent constitutional factors, rather than the cumulative, negative effect of environment. These data indicate that heritability should be a consideration in the overall conceptualization of environmental and constitutional influences. The possibility also exists that both the cumulative negative effects of a nonoptimal environment and the emergence of heritability factors influence the child's outcome concurrently or in some other temporal fashion. Obviously, this area needs increased research emphasis.

IMPLICATIONS

From this discussion, it becomes obvious that the effects of environmental risk must be considered in any developmental follow-up study. Although biologic risk factors are strongly implicated in severe mental retardation or multiple handicaps environmental variables influence mild mental retardation.[39] In fact, two thirds of all children with mild mental handicaps have grown up in poverty.[40] It appears that if an adverse biologic influence is so profound so as to irreversibly impair development, compensatory processes are nullified, regardless of environmental influences.[34] For example, the rates of delay in infancy and preschool years are reported to be similar or consistent in established risk (Down syndrome) and children with multiple handicaps (severe biologic risk), whereas consistency rates in children with developmental delays (with no known organic problem) are much lower.[41] These data again suggest that plasticity in cognitive function, which appears to be influenced by the environment, is much less in the former two groups.

The negative components of environmental risk seem to have a synergistic effect on infants who are biologically vulnerable, a finding that supports the use of transactional or risk route interactional approaches. Moreover, environmental effects more strongly influence cognitive function than motor or neurologic functioning,[30] and there is some evidence that the environmental effect is stronger in females than in males.[23] To use the analogy of the signal-to-noise ratio, it can be said that the "signal" of early medical and biologic influences on outcome is gradually obscured or overshadowed by the "noise" generated by the environment[31] and/or heritability.[37]

Negative environmental effects on cognitive abilities become more apparent between 18 and 24 months and are reflected by a decline in function. That age is a critical transition period in cognitive development, during which skills in symbolic function, language development, and early concept formation should be developed. Environmental influences can affect scores as early as 9 to 12 months,[31] although the impact is less on sensorimotor development than on later verbal skills.

It is apparent that cognitive function, the area most influenced by environment, is emphasized in the majority of outcome studies. A recent review of follow-up studies published over the last decade[6] revealed that 68% of the investigations involved measurement of cognitive outcome, 35% measured motor function, 42% measured neurologic function, and 36% measured some combination. Although cognitive function is crucial for later academic and vocational success, it describes only one component of a child's overall outcome. Little emphasis was found in regard to adaptive functioning (how the child functions in society), which is potentially problematic. Moreover, confusion was found regarding impairment, disability, and handicap. Therefore, better measurement of outcome per se is necessary before the influences of environmental and biologic risk on outcome can be distinguished.

It also appears that no single environmental factor is responsible for compromised cognitive outcome; the accumulation of risk factors, rather than specific variables, has a negative impact.[35] Measurements such as SES, maternal education, or the SES-COMP Index[30] are simply marker variables that most likely reflect an array of risk factors. Furthermore, early and concurrent risk factors, as well as their continuity or pattern, are influential, which suggests variability in regard to temporal action. Unfortunately, these risk variables tend to conglomerate and persist over time in children living in abject poverty. Therefore, the attempt to identify specific environmental factors actually may be moot, because single events are minimally influential, and, in most cases, environmental risk factors do not occur in isolation. Moreover, it is feasible that biologic and environmental risk as well as heritability affect outcome in a cumulative, possibly sequential fashion.

Intervention geared toward situations in which development may have been disrupted but not altered conclusively by biologic, environmental, or combined risk may allow for some compensation or "catch-up." Nonetheless, despite the statement of the House Select Committee on Children, Youth, and Families[42] that every $1.00 spent on preschool intervention saves $4.75 in later educational and social costs, the influences of environmental risk on cognitive outcome and their interactions are complex and not easily changed.[35]

REFERENCES

1. Tjossem T. *Intervention Strategies for High Risk Infants and Young Children.* Baltimore: University Park Press; 1976.
2. Parker S, Greer S, Zuckerman B. Double jeopardy: the impact of poverty on early child development. *Pediatr Clin North Am.* 1988;35:1227–1240.

3. Fagan J, Singer LT. Infant recognition memory as a measure of intelligence. In: Lipsitt LP, ed. *Advances in Infant Research*, vol 2. New York: Ablex; 198.

4. Aylward GP, Kenny TJ. Developmental follow-up: inherent problems and a conceptual model. *J Pediatr Psychol.* 1979;4:331–343.

5. Sameroff AK, Chandler MJ. Reproductive risk and the continuum of caretaking casualty. In: Horowitz FD, ed. *Review of Child Development Research*, vol 4. Chicago: University of Chicago Press; 1975.

6. Aylward GP, Pfeiffer SI, Wright A, et al. Outcome studies of low birth weight infants published over the last decade: a meta-analysis. *J Pediatr.* 1989;109:515–520.

7. Pasamanick B, Knobloch H. Epidemiologic studies on the complications of pregnancy and the birth process. In: Caplan G, ed. *Prevention of Mental Disorders in Children.* New York: Basic Books; 1961.

8. Werner E, Simonian BS, Bierman JM, et al. Cumulative effect of perinatal complications and deprived environment on physical, intellectual, and social development of preschool children. *Pediatrics.* 1967;39:490–505.

9. Sameroff AJ. Early influences on development: fact or fancy? *Merrill Palmer Q.* 1975;21:267–294.

10. Gordon BN, Jens KG. A conceptual model for tracking high-risk infants and making early service decisions. *J Dev Behav Pediatr.* 1988;9:279–286.

11. Werner EE. A longitudinal study of perinatal risk. In: Farran DC, McKenney JD, eds. *Risk in Intellectual and Psychosocial Development.* New York: Academic Press; 1986.

12. Broman SH, Nichols PL, Kennedy WA. *Preschool IQ: Prenatal and Early Developmental Correlates.* Hillsdale, NJ: Erlbaum; 1975.

13. Nelson KS, Ellenberg JH. Antecedents of cerebral palsy: multivariate analysis of risk. *New Engl J Med.* 1986;31 5:81–86.

14. Broman SH. Prenatal anoxia and cognitive development in early childhood. In: Field TM, Goldberg S, Shuman HH, eds. *Infants Born at Risk.* New York: Spectrum Publications; 1979.

15. Terman L, Merrill M. *Stanford-Binet Intelligence Scale.* Boston: Houghton-Mifflin; 1972.

16. Wechsler D. *Wechsler Intelligence Scale for Children—Revised.* [Manual]. New York: The Psychological Corporation; 1974.

17. Bender L. A visual motor Gestalt test and its clinical use. *Am Orthopsych Assoc Res Monog.* 1938;3.

18. Nichols PL, Chen T. *Minimal Brain Dysfunction: A Prospective Study.* Hillsdale, NJ: Erlbaum; 1981.

19. Drillien CM. *The Growth and Development of the Prematurely Born Infant.* Baltimore: Williams & Wilkins; 1964.

20. Drillien CM, Thompson AJM, Burgoyne K. Low birthweight children at early school age: a longitudinal study. *Dev Med Child Neurol.* 1980;22:26–47.

21. Cohen SE, Parmelee AH. Prediction of five-year Stanford-Binet scores in preterm infants. *Child Dev.* 1983;54:1242–1253.

22. Sigman M, Cohen SE, Forsythe AB. The relation of early infant measures to later development. In: Friedman SL, Sigman M, eds. *Preterm Birth and Psychological Development.* New York: Academic Press; 1981.

23. Cohen SE, Parmelee AH, Beckwith L, et al. Cognitive development in preterm infants: birth to 8 years. *J Dev Behav Pediatr.* 1986;7:102–110.

24. Escalona SK. Babies at double hazard: early development of infants at biologic and social risk. *Pediatrics.* 1982;70:670–676.

25. Escalona SK. Social and other environmental influences on the cognitive and personality development of low birthweight infants. *Am J Ment Defic.* 1984;5: 508–512.

26. Wilson RS. Risk and resilience in early mental development. *Dev Psychol.* 1985;21:795–805.

27. Collaborative Group on Antenatal Steroid Therapy. Effect of antenatal dexamethasone administration on the infant: long-term follow-up. *J Pediatr.* 1984;104: 259–267.

28. Aylward GP, Dunteman G, Hatcher RP, et al. The SES-Composite Index: a tool for developmental outcome studies. *Psychol Doc.* 1985;15 (MS 2683).

29. Hollingshead AB. Four-factor index of social status. [Working paper]. New Haven, Conn: Yale University; 1975.

30. Aylward GP, Gustafson N, Verhulst SJ, et al. Consistency in diagnosis of cognitive, motor and neurologic function over the first three years. *J Pediatr Psychol.* 1987;12:77–98.

31. Aylward GP, Verhulst SJ, Bell S. Correlation of asphyxia and other risk factors with outcome: a contemporary view. *Dev Med Child Neurol.* 1989;31:329–340.

32. Aylward GP, Verhulst SJ, Bell S. The Early Neuropsychologic Optimality Rating Scale (ENORS-9): a new developmental follow-up technique. *J Dev Behav Pediatr.* 1988;9:140–146.

33. Bradley RH, Caldwell BM, Rock SL. Home environment and school performance: a ten year follow-up and examination of three models of environmental action. *Child Dev.* 1988;59:852–867.

34. Kopp CB, Kaler SR. Risk in infancy. *Am Psychol.* 1989;44:224–230.

35. Sameroff AJ, Seifer R, Barocas R, et al. Intelligence quotient scores of 4-year-old children: social environmental risk factors. *Pediatrics.* 1987;79:343–349.

36. Wallace IF. Socioenvironmental issues in longitudinal research of high-risk infants. In: Vietz PM, Vaughan HG, eds. *Early Identification of Infants with Developmental Disabilities.* Philadelphia: Grune & Stratton; 1988.

37. Loehlin JC, Horn JM, Willerman L. Modeling IQ change: evidence from the Texas Adoption Project. *Child Dev.* 1989;60:993–1004.

38. Horn JM, Loehlin JC, Willerman L. Aspects of inheritance of intellectual abilities. *Behav Genet.* 1982;12:479–516.

39. Zigler E. Familial mental retardation: a continuing dilemma. *Science.* 1972;155:292–298.

40. Shonkoff JP. Biological and social factors contributing to mild mental retardation. In: Heller KA, Holtzman WH, Messick S, eds. *Placing Children in Special Education: A Strategy for Equity.* Washington, DC: National Academic Press; 1982.

41. Brooks-Gunn J, Lewis M. The prediction of mental functioning in young handicapped children. In: Vietz PM, Vaughan HG, eds. *Early Identification of Infants with Developmental Disabilities.* Philadelphia: Grune & Stratton; 1988.

42. *Yearly Report, 1986.* House Select Committee on Children, Youth, and Families.

Pervasive developmental disorders: Dilemmas in diagnosing very young children

Ann E. Wagner, PhD
Associate Director
Center for Child Development
Department of General Pediatrics

Sharon L. Lockwood, PhD
Director
Speech-Language Pathology
Department of Hearing and Speech
Children's National Medical Center
Washington, DC

THIS ARTICLE addresses issues related to developmental evaluation and differential diagnosis of children with atypical development, specifically those who are ultimately assigned diagnoses in the category of the Pervasive Developmental Disorders (PDDs): Autistic Disorder (AD) or Pervasive Developmental Disorder Not Otherwise Specified (PDDNOS). A recent article by Freeman[1] summarizes current knowledge and guidelines for diagnosis of AD in young children. It is our intent to provide further information regarding differential diagnosis within the PDD category and the types of assessment tools that are useful in conducting a thorough evaluation.

Language delay and difficult behavior are often the presenting concerns when parents or pediatricians refer a young child for a developmental evaluation. In some instances, a specific language disorder is the primary deficit, as behavior disorders and language disorders often occur concomitantly.[2,3] On the other hand, language disorders and behavior problems are frequently "red flags" indicating general developmental delay or atypical developmental disorders. Unfortunately, differential diagnosis of developmental disorders in very young children can be difficult. The younger the child is, the more overlap there is in presentation of mental retardation, developmental language disorders, and PDDs (often called *autism spectrum disorders*).[4]

Autism and other disorders that fall in the PDD category are characterized by inconsistency and variability in development.[1] Children within this diagnostic category form a related but heterogeneous group,[1] and much confusion exists regarding the inclusionary and exclusionary characteristics of the disorder. People from different professions may disagree about the diagnosis or may use different terms to label the same syndrome. Parents may seek the assistance of many professionals, each of whom has a different theoretical and experiential background. It is not unusual, therefore, for a child to have a series of diagnoses over the course of his or her early years. There is often an extended period of uncertainty regarding the diagnosis. This uncertainty is confusing and painful for parents and can delay the initiation of appropriate interventions.

Inf Young Children, 1994; 6(4): 21–32
© 1994 Aspen Publishers, Inc.

The following section presents an overview of the PDD diagnostic category. This is followed by a case example of a diagnosis of PDDNOS to illustrate the multidisciplinary evaluation process.

OVERVIEW OF PDDs

The *Diagnostic and Statistical Manual of Mental Disorders, Third Edition, Revised (DSM-III-R)*[5] distinguishes PDD from other developmental disabilities on the basis of three basic deficits: qualitative impairment in reciprocal social interaction; qualitative impairment in verbal and nonverbal communication and in imaginative activity; and a markedly restricted repertoire of activities and interests. Onset must be during infancy or childhood.

According to the *DSM-III-R* diagnostic criteria, the PDDs are further classified into AD and PDDNOS. Under this classification system, AD is the "prototypic" PDD. PDDNOS is basically a "subthreshold" diagnosis[6] that is applied when full criteria for a diagnosis of AD are not met. Specific *DSM-III-R* diagnostic criteria for AD and PDDNOS are listed in the box, "*DSM-III-R* Criteria for PDD."

It is important to bear in mind that PDD is a *behavioral* classification system—that is, it is a description of a particular set of developmental deficits defined by behavior that is unusual or developmentally inappropriate. There is not an assumption of cause inherent in the diagnosis. There are probably many causes for the types of social and communication deficits common to children with PDDs. For the majority of the children, there is no identifiable etiology. Each child is unique, and there are as many differences as similarities among them. The diagnosis provides a framework for communication among people involved in the child's care. It is a guide for planning more comprehensive assessment of the individual child's skills and for designing appropriate intervention strategies.

The clinician begins by attempting to diagnose AD according to *DSM-III-R* criteria.[5] If the child does not meet the criteria for AD but does display the pattern of developmental disparity described previously, a diagnosis of PDDNOS is assigned. Toddlers and young preschoolers may fail to meet AD criteria because there is questionable or mild deviation in the key domains (ie, communication, play, and social reciprocity).

At first glance, this is a straightforward classification system. However, when clinicians are faced with differential diagnosis of an atypical child who does not readily demonstrate all of his or her skills and is not particularly cooperative with testing or interviewing, making this diagnosis is not easy. When the child is younger than 4 years and the parents may be hearing for the first time that the child has a serious developmental disorder, the clinician is compelled to give this diagnosis very careful consideration.

DSM-III-R Criteria for PDD

299.0 Autistic Disorder
At least eight of the following 16 items are present, these to include at least two items from A, one from B, and one from C. *Note:* Consider criterion to be met *only* if the behavior is abnormal for the person's developmental level.

A. Qualitative impairment in reciprocal social interaction as manifested by the following: (The examples within parentheses are arranged so that those first mentioned are most likely to apply to younger or more handicapped persons, and the later ones, to older or less handicapped persons with this disorder.)

   (1) Marked lack of awareness of the existence or feelings of others (eg, treats a person as if he or she were a piece of furniture; does not notice another person's distress; apparently has no concept of the needs of others for privacy)

   (2) No or abnormal seeking of comfort at times of distress (eg, does not come for comfort even when ill, hurt, or tired; seeks comfort in a stereotyped way—eg, says "cheese, cheese, cheese" whenever hurt)

   (3) No or impaired imitation (eg, does not wave bye-bye; does not copy mother's domestic activities; mechanically imitates others' actions out of context)

   (4) No or abnormal social play (eg, does not actively participate in social games; prefers solitary play activities; involves other children in play only as "mechanical aids")

   (5) Gross impairment in ability to make peer friendships (eg, no interest in making peer friendships; despite an interest in making friends, demonstrates a lack of understanding of conventions of social interaction—for example, reads phone book to an uninterested peer)

B. Qualitative impairment in verbal and nonverbal communication and in imaginative activity, as manifested by the following: (The numbered items are arranged so that those first listed are more likely to apply to younger or more handicapped persons, and the later ones, to older or less handicapped persons with this disorder.)

   (1) No mode of communication, such as communicative babbling, facial expression, gesture, mime, or spoken language

   (2) Markedly abnormal nonverbal communication, as in the use of eye-to-eye gaze, facial expression, body posture, or gestures to initiate or modulate social interaction (eg, does not anticipate being held, stiffens when held, does not look at the person or smile when making a social approach, does not greet parents or visitors, has a fixed stare in social situations)

   (3) Absence of imaginative activity, such as playacting of adult roles, fantasy characters, or animals; lack of interest in stories about imaginary events

   (4) Marked abnormalities in the production of speech, including volume, pitch, stress, rate, rhythm, and intonation (eg, monotonous tone, question-like melody, or high pitch)

   (5) Marked abnormalities in the form or content of speech, including stereotyped and repetitive use of speech (eg, immediate echolalia or mechanical repetition of television commercial); use of "you" when "I" is meant (eg, using "you want cookie?" to mean "I want a cookie"); idiosyncratic use of words or phrases (eg, "go on green riding" to mean "I want to go on the swing"); or frequent irrelevant remarks (eg, starts talking about train schedules during a conversation about sports)

continues

(6) Marked impairment in the ability to initiate or sustain a conversation with others, despite adequate speech (eg, indulging in lengthy monologues on one subject regardless of interjections from others)

C. Markedly restricted repertoire of activities and interests, as manifested by the following:

(1) Stereotyped body movements (eg, hand-flicking or hand-twisting, spinning, head-banging, or complex whole-body movements)

(2) Persistent preoccupation with parts of objects (eg, sniffing or smelling objects, repetitive feeling of the texture of materials, spinning the wheels of toy cars) or attachment to unusual objects (eg, insists on carrying around a piece of string)

(3) Marked distress over changes in trivial aspects of environment (eg, when a vase is moved from its usual position)

(4) Unreasonable insistence on following routines in precise detail (eg, insisting that exactly the same route always be followed when shopping)

(5) Markedly restricted range of interests and a preoccupation with one narrow interest (eg, interested only in lining up objects, in amassing facts about meteorology, or in pretending to be a fantasy character)

D. Onset during childhood

Specify if childhood onset (after 36 months of age).

299.80   Pervasive Developmental Disorder Not Otherwise Specified

This category should be used when there is a qualitative impairment in the development of reciprocal social interaction and of verbal and nonverbal communication skills, but the criteria are not met for Autistic Disorder, Schizophrenia, or Schizotypal or Schizoid Personality Disorder. Some people with this diagnosis will exhibit a markedly restricted repertoire of activities and interests, but others will not.

Adapted with permission from the American Psychiatric Association. *Diagnostic and Statistical Manual of Mental Disorders.* 3rd ed, rev. Washington, DC: APA; 1987.

Much of the confusion regarding differential diagnosis of developmental disorders in very young children is related to uncertainty regarding the point at which a developmental "lag" or uneven development is outside the range of normal variability in development. A 5-year-old child who does not yet form novel word combinations or engage in representational play is cause for concern by most people. On the other hand, if the child with these characteristics is just turning 3 years old, many professionals are less confident in labeling the child as deviant.

Even less clarity exists when attempting a differential diagnosis within the PDD spectrum. A thorough understanding of the early (prelinguistic) development of social reciprocity and communication is essential, but professional judgment remains the means by which one decides whether the degree of impairment is sufficient to meet the criteria for AD. There are no empirical "cut-off scores" or definitive characteristics that differentiate between AD and PDDNOS, although attempts are under way to develop such guidelines.[6,7] At present, differential diagnosis at this level relies on knowledge of normal development and developmental disabilities, as well as experience and clinical judgment.

CHANGES IN *DSM-IV* DIAGNOSTIC CRITERIA

The fourth edition of the *Diagnostic and Statistical Manual* (*DSM-IV*) will be released in May 1994. A preliminary draft suggests that *DSM-IV* will retain the format of AD as the prototype of PDD and PDDNOS as a subthreshold diagnosis (American Psychiatric Association, *DSM-IV* field trials for pervasive developmental disorders, unpublished data). Asperger Syndrome[8] will be added as a third category under the global PDD diagnostic category. Asperger Syndrome involves significant social impairment and restricted range of interests in the absence of cognitive and language delays. Motor milestones may be delayed.

Some older children who do not meet AD criteria may be diagnosed with Asperger Syndrome. The diagnosis is typically made in children older than 3 years, when the social impairments become obvious, and will rarely be a consideration in very young children. It may be speculated that some toddlers diagnosed with PDDNOS will later meet Asperger Syndrome criteria, but to date there is no research addressing this question.

A diagnosis of AD per *DSM-IV* criteria will continue to require qualitative impairment in three major areas: social interaction, communication, and interests/activities. The criteria within each area will be consolidated so that there are fewer total options (12 as opposed to 16), but only six will be required for a diagnosis of AD. For a diagnosis of AD in an older child, there must be a history of impairment in at least one of the above areas before age 3. The consolidated *DSM-IV* criteria may help in the diagnosis of PDDs in older children, but does not clear up the ambiguity in diagnosing atypical development in very young children.

A MULTIDISCIPLINARY DIAGNOSTIC PROCESS

Differential diagnosis of PDDs is a three-step process. First, sensory impairments must be ruled out, and an evaluation for identifiable neurologic/genetic syndromes must be completed. Second, other developmental disorders, such as specific language disorders and mental retardation, must be ruled out. Finally, differentiation between AD and PDDNOS is attempted. Each of these steps is considered below in the context of a case example.

Case example: Background and presenting problem

Sandy is a petite, attractive girl, 3 years and 2 months of age, who was referred to the Developmental Clinic at Children's National Medical Center by her community pediatrician for clarification of her diagnosis. Sandy's mother reported a history of language delay, self-stimulation, extreme irritability, and hyperactivity. She reported that Sandy engaged in social contact during familiar routines but rarely initiated social interaction. Sandy did seek comfort from her mother when hurt or upset. She occasionally initiated a hug, but often resisted physical affection.

At age 2, Sandy's mother and pediatrician were concerned about her language delay and hyperactivity. Sensory impairments had been ruled out, as had genetic disorders. A neurologic evaluation that included neuroimaging failed to identify etiologic factors and resulted in a diagnosis of "atypical developmental disorder." Sandy's mother reported that irritability improved and self-stimulating behaviors ceased after Sandy started talking at 24 months of age. However, Sandy continued to be hyperactive and noncompliant, developed echolalia, and remained socially aloof. Sandy was reportedly overreactive to some sounds and underreactive to pain. Play was largely mechanical and repetitive; she liked to arrange objects into symmetric patterns. Sandy had been taught to feed, bathe, and put her dolls to bed, but did not engage in novel imaginative play. Sandy's mother had been reading about developmental disorders and wondered if Sandy might be autistic.

Medical evaluation

Diagnosis of PDD should always include comprehensive physical and neurologic evaluations.[9,10] The presence of a developmental delay warrants the use of evoked response tests, if necessary, to evaluate vision and hearing.

AD is assumed to be a result of dysfunction of the central nervous system (CNS).[10] Whether all disorders classified as PDDNOS are organic in nature is an unresolved issue. However, a number of developmental disorders of known causes have been associated with AD or "autistic-like" behavior. These include disturbance of metabolism (phenylketonuria), progressive neurologic dysfunction (Rett syndrome, Lesch-Nyhan syndrome), and genetic disorders (tuberous sclerosis, fragile X syndrome). It is estimated that CNS dysfunction with known etiology is responsible for 15% to 20% of the population diagnosed as AD.[9] Each of these syndromes has implications for prognosis, intervention, medical care, and genetic counseling of parents regarding future children. The manifestation of each of these disorders is age specific, so the evaluation must be made by someone with knowledge of the developmental course of these syndromes. Careful diagnosis by a developmental pediatrician, a pediatric neurologist, or a geneticist is crucial. In Sandy's case, this had been done prior to our contact with her.

The developmental profile: Evaluating developmental disparity

The key to deciding whether a child meets criteria for PDD as opposed to other categories of developmental disorders lies in the child's developmental profile. Skills typically and reliably measured in young children are "global" developmental level, language abilities (receptive/auditory processing and expressive/pragmatic abilities), spatial skills (perceptual organization and visual-motor integration), motor skills (fine and gross motor), and social/adaptive behaviors (including reciprocal social interaction and play behaviors). Children with PDD have specific deficits in language, reciprocal social interactions, and play behaviors. Nonverbal problem-solving skills and motor skills are more likely to be consistent with overall global developmental level. Nonsocial adaptive behaviors such as dressing, feeding, and other self-help skills are often also consistent with global developmental level.

Administering standardized developmental tests to very young children is often a challenge. The task is even more difficult when the child has developmental delays, behavior problems, or both. Characteristics specific to PDDs, such as poor imitation skills, poor receptive language, and inability to engage in reciprocal social interaction, make the demands of standardized testing stressful and frustrating for the child, the examiner, and the parents. Thus, parents' reports of their child's abilities and typical behaviors are crucial. Behavioral observations, particularly if they can be done in a setting familiar to the child, yield important information as well.

Assessing global developmental level

Standardized developmental instruments are invaluable in assessing general developmental level, but choosing appropriate instruments for children age 3 or younger with developmental delays is always a dilemma. Furthermore, the language/communication disorder that is an integral characteristic of PDDs makes the more verbally mediated tests particularly problematic. Administration can be a challenge, and creativity and flexibility on the part of the examiner are necessary.

Often, instruments designed for testing infants[11] yield approximations of "developmental level" in children who are outside the standardization range. The Bayley Scales of Infant Development, Second Edition (BSID-II)[12] are helpful for evaluating global functioning. These are activity oriented and standardized for children to the age of 3½ years. At Children's National Medical Center (CNMC), we supplement the BSID-II with nonverbal items from other standardized tests, including the Stanford-Binet Intelligence Scale–Fourth Edition,[13] Stanford-Binet Form L-M,[14] McCarthy Scales of Children's Abilities,[15] and Leiter International Performance Scale.[16]

The Psychoeducational Profile–Revised (PEP-R)[17] was developed by the Division for the Treatment and Education of Autistic and Communication Handicapped Children (Division TEACCH) at University of North Carolina, Chapel Hill, to evaluate children with AD and other developmental disorders whose functioning is as low as 6 months. The battery includes assessment of imitation, eye-hand integration, perception, motor skills, language, and cognition. The resulting profile facilitates assessment of disparity among skills. The results of the PEP-R can also be easily converted into an individualized education program.

Using standardized instruments, the clinician can derive age equivalents for nonverbal (perceptual-organization) skills and language abilities. If language abilities are significantly lower than perceptual-organization and visual-motor skills, the clinician should use the nonverbal age equivalent as an estimate of global developmental level.[7] This global developmental level is the baseline with which one then compares communication, social/adaptive, and play skills to determine whether the child's functioning is consistent with a diagnosis of AD or PDDNOS.

It is important to emphasize that a global developmental delay or mental retardation does not preclude a diagnosis of AD or PDDNOS. In fact, 70% to 80% of children with the diagnosis of AD are also mentally retarded.[18] If there are deficits in communication, reciprocal interpersonal relationships, and play behavior *relative to* the child's global developmental level, the diagnosis still applies.

Case example: Results of cognitive testing

The Stanford-Binet Intelligence Scale–Fourth Edition[13] was administered in one session. Sandy was generally cooperative with the evaluation and usually appeared to be trying. She quietly refused to respond to requests to repeat phrases. Her verbal responses were in the form of short phrases, and at times the information she gave was tangential to the question. When pressured to make a verbal response to a difficult question, Sandy made verbalizations that had speech inflection but were not intelligible words. When confronted with a difficult puzzle task, Sandy made symmetric configurations with the pieces while ignoring the form board. Sandy achieved an Intelligence Quotient (IQ) score in the low average range (12th percentile). Factor analysis of her subtest scores revealed that verbal reasoning skills (16th percentile) were significantly stronger than her abstract/nonverbal reasoning skills (2nd percentile).[13,19]

Further evaluation of language

In the case of PDD, there is often a significant difference between the child's acquisition of form (structure/grammar) and the content (semantics) of language.[20] This is most evident in the rote-learned utterances that are grammatically correct but are used as one whole word rather than a flexible combination of words. Consequently, content is restricted. For example, a 3-year-old looks in the mirror at herself and says "Hi, Mary . . . that's Mary!", using her mother's phrase to identify herself. Table 1 illustrates this difference in contrast to patterns more typical in children diagnosed with language impairment or mental retardation, and depicts the manner in which clinicians take into account the profile of language impairment when considering a diagnosis of AD or PDDNOS.

Table 1. Language behaviors related to diagnostic categories

	Language impairment	Mental retardation	AD	PDDNOS
Receptive language/auditory processing	Delayed	Delayed	Severely restricted; little to no attention to language	Severely restricted to familiar routines
Expressive language form	Delayed	Delayed	Absent to advanced form, usually evident in echoed utterances	Limited to advanced form, usually evident in rote utterances used as single words
Content/semantics	Delayed	Delayed to appropriate for developmental age	Restricted	Restricted
Use/pragmatics	Mild to moderate delays; limited vocabulary	Appropriate for developmental age	Severely restricted	Responsive to known persons in familiar routines; limited intents
Speech articulation	Usually delayed	Developmentally appropriate	Normal to advanced	Normal
Intonation/voice	Normal	Normal	Poorly modulated volume, pitch, and intonation	Often poorly modulated intonation; rote-learned patterns
Fluency	Often mild to moderate problems	Normal	Normal	Normal
Play	Frequent lag in symbolic play	Appropriate for developmental age	Nonfunctional, with limited schemes	May be functional, but limited schemes
Social/affective	Interactive/engaging and responsive; often prefers younger children	Interactive/engaging and responsive, appropriate for developmental age	Absent or severely restricted	Limited to familiar routines and people

Scores from standard measures of language are not particularly helpful in the differential diagnosis of children without functional language. Standard instruments usually provide a "language age" that is an average of the child's abilities and may not reflect the disparity between the different domains of language. For example, a 24-month-old child who can follow simple familiar routines in his own environment and can produce intelligible sentences will receive an age-appropriate score. However, this same child may not understand simple directions or questions outside of his routine and may show very little attention to language. His use of the word-sentences in his repertoire may be severely restricted.

The examiner's knowledge of normal development for the domains of language is most important. These domains include form (structure/grammar), content (semantics—ie, vocabulary/word meanings), use (pragmatics—ie, the social, interactional use of language), and speech (phonology/articulation/voicing/fluency). Most language scales do not separate the domains but include questions that allow the examiner to interpret a child's performance accordingly. For example, the Receptive-Expressive Emergent Language Scale–2 (REEL)[21] contains questions such as: "Generally shows intense attention and response to speech over prolonged periods of time" (expected at 11 to 12 months) and "Generally able to listen to speech without being distracted by other competing sounds" (at 9 to 10 months). The Preschool Language Scale–3[22] contains items in the first year of life such as "looks intently at a speaker" (0 to 5 months) and "follows line of regard" and "understands a specific word or phrase (other than 'no')" (6 to 11 months).

Typically, information about communication is best achieved with a thorough history regarding speech-language development, communicative interaction at home and school, and observation in as normal an environment as possible (if not in the home). Prizant and Wetherby[20] suggest that observation of the child's communicative behavior should include answers to the following questions:

- What does the child use/say/do to communicate?
- If the child uses words, do they have referential meaning?
- How many different words and combinations of words does the child use?
- If the child uses multiword utterances, does the child recombine words for different meaning or are the utterances used only as single word entities (eg, "stop doing that" as the only means to protest).[20]

The Communication and Symbolic Behavior Scales (CSBS) by Wetherby and Prizant[23] is specifically designed for the child with PDD. It is particularly useful for establishing baseline behaviors that address each of the preceding four questions. This information leads nicely to intervention strategies such as the most successful method for eliciting a child's interaction and the child's best means for signaling intent (eg, gestures, word, or sign).

Because development of a functional communication system is a first priority for children with PDD, a careful and thorough evaluation of verbal and nonverbal means of communicating, leading to recommendations for teaching strategies, is a crucial component of the diagnostic battery.

Case example: Sandy's language evaluation

Receptive language was estimated to be in the 18- to 30-month range. This range of performance was dependent on her familiarity with the content or routine. Expressive language was estimated to be at the 24- to 30-month level. Sandy demonstrated expressive language that was restricted to familiar phrases, routines, and a rote "repertoire" of verbal responses. This resulted in significant restrictions in content (semantics) and use (pragmatics) of language. Sandy's articulation and fluency were normal, but she often spoke in a barely audible whisper. Intonation of a particular phrase never varied in relation to context. Sandy did not use pointing or gestures to request objects, but did follow the examiner's pointing and line of regard.

Evaluation of social/adaptive behavior

Standard measures of adaptive behavior are important tools for categorizing developmental disorders. The Vineland Adaptive Behavior Scales[24] is administered by interview to the child's parents and has been shown to be useful in assessment of autistic children.[25,26] The Vineland instrument derives standard scores and age equivalents in four adaptive behavior domains: communication, socialization, daily living skills, and motor skills. We have found that discrepancies may not show up in the standard scores, but when raw scores are converted to age equivalents, children with PDD will have relatively lower age equivalents in the communication and socialization domains, reflecting their deficits in verbal and nonverbal communication, interpersonal responsivity, and imaginative play.

Structured behavioral interviews and observations

Traditionally, diagnosis of AD has not been attempted before the age of 2½.[27] This view is changing, and there have been greater attempts to identify behaviors indicative of the communication, play, and social deficits in children at early developmental levels.[6,7,10] Diagnosis is complicated by the fact that many of the behaviors or characteristics that accompany PDD (eg, stereotypic motor movements and preoccupation with sensory aspects of objects) are also apparent in very young children with severe mental retardation or sensory deficits. Most often cited as specific to PDD or AD as opposed to other developmental disorders are deficits in reciprocal interaction and abnormal development of verbal and nonverbal communication. The characteristics associated with AD/PDDNOS that appear to be specific to these disorders are given in the box, "Characteristics of Young Children With PDD."

Characteristics of Young Children With PDD*

Deficits of reciprocal social interaction

Lack of joint attention (ie, pointing, showing objects)[28–31]

Emotionally "distant"[32]

Abnormal use of eye contact[37]

Lack of interest in other children[33]

Lack of motor imitation[33]

Deficits in communication/language (relative to nonverbal skills)

Lack of nonverbal communication[28,30,34]

Delayed speech[32,35]

Poor speech comprehension[18,32]

*These characteristics have been shown to differentiate children with PDD from mental age–matched mentally retarded children.

Structured parent interviews and behavioral observations have been developed to quantify and assist with diagnosis. The Autism Diagnostic Interview (ADI)[36] is a semistructured interview for parents or other primary caregivers that has been shown to discriminate between autistic and mentally retarded children and adolescents. The Childhood Autism Rating Scale (CARS)[37] was originally designed to measure clinicians' ratings of observed behavior, but has also been shown to be useful as a parent/caretaker interview.[36] Parent interviews provide information that cannot be gathered with diagnostic testing or time-limited observations. Information about low-frequency behaviors such as tantrums, reactions to novel events or changes in routine, and upper limits on adaptive behavior can only be obtained by interview.

Parents are often not confident about their assessment of the child's behavior and may not have an accurate developmental framework within which to evaluate their child's abilities. Behavioral observations are therefore crucial to the diagnostic process. The CARS[37] is used by clinicians to rate the child's behavior during a testing session or other observed situation. The Autism Diagnostic Observation Schedule (ADOS)[38] is a structured observation of specific interactional tasks that the clinician engages in with the child. Because these instruments rely on some judgment about the severity of a symptom, training is necessary for accurate use of the instruments. Lord and her colleagues are developing a play observational system for use with prelinguistic young children.[39] When this is complete, it should prove useful in diagnosing very young children and for research regarding early prognostic indicators.

Case example: Adaptive functioning and observation of behavior

The Vineland Adaptive Behavior Scales were completed by interview with Sandy's mother. Results suggested communication skills at the 22-month level, socialization skills at the 26-month level, daily living skills at the 34-month level, and motor skills at the 33-month level. Behavioral rating by the examiner using CARS placed Sandy in the "nonautistic" range.

Assessment of family functioning and social situation

Because the PDD diagnostic category is behavioral, an evaluation of family functioning or of the larger social context is not necessary to form a diagnosis. Nonetheless, assessment of financial and social resources, parent–child interactions, relationships between family members, informal social networks, and integration of the family within the community are crucial components of treatment planning. Research has demonstrated that families with autistic children, as a group, are similar to families without developmentally delayed children.[40] However, there are unique stresses associated with raising a child with developmental disabilities. A thorough discussion of evaluating the family and social context is beyond the scope of this article, but the reader is referred to Angell,[41] Greenspan,[42] Morgan,[40] Powell et al,[43] and Powers[44] for more information.

Case example: Summary of diagnosis

Sandy was given a diagnosis of PDDNOS based on qualitative impairments in social, communication, and play behaviors. Mental retardation was ruled out based on her IQ test scores. Specific language disorder was ruled out based on additional abnormalities in social and play behaviors. A diagnosis of AD was not assigned because Sandy's profile on standardized testing was not consistent with the typical pattern in which verbal skills are more delayed than perceptual-organization abilities, and because of her CARS rating, which was in the "nonautistic" range. However, results of the Vineland and maternal report instruments indicated qualitative impairment in communication, play, and reciprocal social interaction relative to her mental age. Sandy's mother understood that her daughter's development would be monitored and that diagnosis and intervention services would be reviewed and possibly revised based on subsequent development.

Assessment of the social situation revealed that Sandy's intervention services were supplied by private providers in addition to a public school program. Procedures were initiated to integrate all services within the school program to increase consistency and familiarity. Marital strain and financial strain were also identified and targeted for intervention.

●　　●　　●

This article has attempted to clarify the issues related to diagnosis of PDDs in children ages 3 years and younger. There may well be an age at which there has not been sufficient development in the critical domains to assess a disparity in social, communicative, and play abilities. Alternatively, we may not yet have adequate instruments for precise measurement of salient skills in very young children. Further development of assessment batteries for use in young children is clearly needed, as is prospective follow-up of children with AD and PDDNOS diagnoses to determine whether these diagnoses are valid in terms of prognosis and intervention.

In the meantime, clinicians making these diagnoses must rely on multidisciplinary evaluation, experience, and clinical judgment. The goal is to make an accurate diagnosis as early as possible, but there are times when it will be appropriate to defer diagnosis of AD and assign a diagnosis of PDDNOS pending further evaluation or intervention. This uncertainty is difficult for the child's parents. The clinician must always allow time for an open and honest discussion with the parents about the child's current functioning, the source of diagnostic uncertainty, and the steps needed for clarification.

REFERENCES

1. Freeman BJ. The syndrome of autism: Update and guidelines for diagnosis. *Infants Young Child.* 1993;6:1–11.

2. Caulfield MB, Fischel JE, DeBaryshe BD, Whitehurst GJ. Behavioral correlates of developmental expressive language disorder. *Abnormal Child Psychol.* 1989;17:187–201.

3. Jenkins S, Bax M, Hart H. Behavior problems in preschool children. *J Child Psychol Psychiatry.* 1980;21:5–17.

4. Marcus LM, Stone WL. Assessment of the young autistic child. In: Schopler E, Van Bourgondien ME, Bristol MM, eds. *Preschool Issues in Autism.* New York, NY: Plenum; 1993.

5. American Psychiatric Association. *Diagnostic and Statistical Manual of Mental Disorders.* 3rd ed, rev. Washington, DC: APA; 1987.

6. Mayes L, Volkmar F, Hooks M, Cicchetti D. Differentiating pervasive developmental disorder not otherwise specified from autism and language disorders. *J Autism Dev Disord.* 1993;23:79–90.

7. Siegel B. Toward DSM-IV: A developmental approach to autistic disorder. *Psychiatr Clin North Am.* 1991;14:53–68.

8. Wing L. Asperger's syndrome: a clinical account. *Psychol Med.* 1981;11:115–130.

9. Tsai LY. Medical treatment in autism. In: Berkell DE, ed. *Autism, Identification, Education, and Treatment.* Hillsdale, NJ: Lawrence Erlbaum; 1992.

10. Ritvo ER, Freeman BJ. A medical model of autism: etiology, pathology, and treatment. *Pediatr Ann.* 1984;13:293–305.

11. Shelton TL. The assessment of cognition/intelligence in infancy. *Infants Young Child.* 1989;1:10–23.

12. Bayley N. *Manual for the Bayley Scales of Infant Development.* 2nd ed. San Antonio, Tex: Psychological Corp; 1993.

13. Thorndike RL, Hagen EP, Sattler JM. *Stanford-Binet Intelligence Scale.* 4th ed. Chicago, Ill: Riverside Publishing; 1986.

14. Terman LM, Merrill MA. *Stanford-Binet Intelligence Scale (Form L-M)*. Boston, Mass: Houghton Mifflin; 1960.

15. McCarthy DA. *Manual for the McCarthy Scales of Children's Abilities*. San Antonio, Tex: The Psychological Corporation; 1972.

16. Leiter RG. *Leiter International Performance Scale*. Chicago, Ill: Stoelting; 1948.

17. Schopler E, Reichler RJ, Bashford A, Lansing MD, Marcus LM. *Individualized Assessment and Treatment for Autistic and Developmentally Disabled Children: Vol I. Psychoeducational Profile Revised*. Austin, Tex: Pro-Ed; 1990.

18. Wing L, Gould J. Severe impairments of social interaction and associated abnormalities in children: epidemiology and classification. *J Autism Dev Disord.* 1979;9:11–29.

19. Sattler J. *Assessment of Children*. 3rd ed. San Diego, Calif: Author; 1990.

20. Prizant BM, Wetherby AM. Communication in preschool autistic children. In: Schopler E, Van Bourgondien M, Bristol M, eds. *Preschool Issues in Autism*. New York, NY: Plenum Press; 1993.

21. Bzoch KR, League R. *Receptive-Expressive Emergent Language Test*. 2nd ed (REEL-2). Austin, Tex: Pro-Ed; 1991.

22. Zimmerman IL, Steiner VG, Pond RE. *Preschool Language Scale–3*. New York, NY: Harcourt Brace Jovanovich; 1992.

23. Wetherby AM, Prizant BM. *Communication and Symbolic Behavior Scales—Normed Edition*. Chicago, Ill: Riverside Publishing; 1993.

24. Sparrow SS, Balla DA, Cicchetti DV. *Vineland Adaptive Behavior Scales*. Circle Pines, Minn: American Guidance Service; 1984.

25. Volkmar FR, Sparrow SS, Goudreau D, Cicchetti DV, Paul R, Cohen DJ. Social deficits in autism: an operational approach using the Vineland Adaptive Behavior Scales. *J Am Acad Child Adolesc Psychiatry.* 1987;26:156–161.

26. Freeman BJ, Ritvo ER, Yokota A, Childs J, Pollard J. WISC-R and Vineland Adaptive Behavior Scales scores in autistic children. *J Am Acad Child Adolesc Psychiatry.* 1988;27:428–429.

27. Gillberg C, Ehlers S, Schaumann H, et al. Autism under age 3 years: a clinical study of 28 cases referred for autistic symptoms in infancy. *J Child Psychol Psychiatry.* 1990;31:921–934.

28. Mundy P, Sigman M, Ungerer J, Sherman T. Defining the social deficits of autism: the contribution of nonverbal communication measures. *J Child Psychol Psychiatry.* 1986;27:657–669.

29. Sigman M, Mundy P, Sherman T, Ungerer J. Social interactions of autistic, mentally retarded, and normal children and their caregivers. *J Child Psychol Psychiatry.* 1986;27:647–656.

30. Wetherby AM, Yonclas DG, Bryan AA. Communicative profiles of preschool children with handicaps: implications for early identification. *J Speech Hearing Disord.* 1989;54:148–158.

31. Mundy P, Sigman M, Kasari C. A longitudinal study of joint attention and language development in autistic children. *J Autism Dev Disord.* 1990;20:115–128.

32. Volkmar FR, Cohen DJ, Paul R. An evaluation of *DSM-III* criteria for infantile autism. *J Acad Child Psychiatry.* 1986;25:190–197.

33. Stone WL, Lemanek KL, Fishel PT, Fernandez MC, Altemeier WA. Play and imitation skills in the diagnosis of young autistic children. *Pediatrics.* 1990;86:267–272.

34. Sigman M, Ungerer J. Cognitive and language skills in autistic, mentally retarded, and normal children. *Dev Psychol.* 1984;20:293–302.

35. Ohta M, Nagai Y, Hara H, Sasaki M. Parental perception of behavioral symptoms in Japanese autistic children. *J Autism Dev Disord.* 1987;17:549–563.

36. LeCouteur A, Rutter M, Lord C, et al. Autism Diagnostic Interview: a semi-structured interview for parents and caregivers of autistic persons. *J Autism Dev Disord.* 1989;19:363–387.

37. Schopler E, Reichler RJ, Renner BR. *The Childhood Autism Rating Scale (CARS) for Diagnostic Screening and Classification of Autism.* New York, NY: Irving Publishers; 1989.

38. Lord C, Rutter M, Goode S, et al. Autism Diagnostic Observation Schedule: a standardized observation of communicative and social behavior. *J Autism Dev Disord.* 1989;19:185–212.

39. Lord C, DiLavorte PD, Rutter M. Prelinguistic Autism Diagnostic Observation Schedule (PL-ADOS): a semistructured observational schedule for young children with possible autism. Presented at the American Academy of Child and Adolescent Psychiatry; October 1993; San Antonio, Tex.

40. Morgan SB. The autistic child and family functioning: a developmental-family systems perspective. *J Autism Dev Disord.* 1988;18:263–280.

41. Angell R. A parent's perspective on the preschool years. In: Schopler E, Van Bourgondien ME, Bristol MM, eds. *Preschool Issues in Autism.* New York, NY: Plenum; 1993.

42. Greenspan SI. Reconsidering the diagnosis and treatment of very young children with autistic spectrum or pervasive developmental disorder. *Zero to Three.* 1992;13:1–2.

43. Powell TH, Hecimovic A, Christensen L. Meeting the unique needs of families. In: Berkell DE, ed. *Autism: Identification, Education, and Treatment.* Hillside, NJ: Lawrence Erlbaum Associates; 1992.

44. Powers M, ed. *Children With Autism: A Parents' Guide.* Rockville, Md: Woodbine House; 1989.

Neuroplasticity: The basis for brain development, learning, and recovery from injury

Nicholas J. Lenn, MD, PhD
Professor of Neurology
Department of Neurology
SUNY at Stony Brook
Stony Brook, New York
(formerly) Professor of Pediatric
    Neurology
Departments of Neurology and
    Pediatrics
University of Virginia School of
    Medicine
Charlottesville, Virginia

AN UNKNOWING and immobile infant develops into an intelligent and independent person. This observation is so striking that people have historically accepted the idea of plasticity (change) of the mind. Yet until the second half of this century, plasticity of the mind was not thought to involve plasticity of the brain.[1] In this article, current knowledge of neuroplasticity and its clinical implications is summarized. Readers with experience in education and rehabilitation will recognize phenomena from their experiences and will gain understanding of the biological changes in the brain that underlie the observed gains.

WHAT IS NEUROPLASTICITY?

When a songbird begins to sing in the spring, this is the result of a remarkable sequence of structural, chemical, and functional changes that together offer an excellent example of neuroplasticity. Song centers, those parts of the birds' brain which control song, are small in females and in males over the winter.[2] Each spring, the song centers of male birds grow in a manner similar to normal embryonic development in higher animals, including humans. Many new nerve cells are formed that travel to the appropriate site and form connections to and from other nearby and distant brain cells. Their chemical machinery is soon working, and they begin function to allow birdsong. The variety of songs and the ways they are acquired among different types of birds emphasize that learning and experience are important but the neural components must first be formed. The internal trigger for the sequence of events leading to birdsong is a small chemical produced outside the brain, the male sex hormone testosterone. This hormone has the same effect at all ages and, applied experimentally, in both sexes.

The brains of humans and other animals do not appear to have the same capacity for making and integrating new nerve cells naturally, with one exception. The odor-detecting, olfactory nerve cells that extend into the lining of the nose are normally damaged throughout people's lives. Their continuing replacement is like the springtime changes in song centers and like the fetal development of humans' whole brains. Perhaps humans do have the capacity for the replacement of nerve

Inf Young Children, 1991; 3(3): 39–48
© 1991 Aspen Publishers, Inc.

cells, even though it does not occur naturally. It may be a latent capacity that can be stimulated by some treatment. Other forms of neuroplasticity, however, that involve parts of nerve cells, do occur in all parts of the brain, and examples are given in this article. Very likely more vigorous and effective neuroplasticity can be stimulated by treatments waiting to be discovered. Learning how neuroplasticity occurs from studies of birdsong, olfactory nerve cell replacement, and other experimental and clinical situations may provide the keys to unlock potential repair after injury.

In its broad sense, neuroplasticity refers to three processes: normal development, learning, and recovery from injury. Two broad principles apply to neuroplasticity: first, the time and place of events together determine every aspect of brain structure and function. This is true for every step of brain development, for every aspect of normal brain function, and for injury. One liver cell is like another; destroy 30% and a person is okay. But each part of the brain has special functions. Damage has effects that depend on where the insult occurs and at what age. Second, most details of neuroplasticity apply well to the entire animal kingdom[3] and to all parts of the nervous system.[4] For clarity, most of this discussion will be based on the brains of higher animals. It is easier to describe changes in the brain's structure than in its chemistry and function, so this article will emphasize structure. But these three aspects are inseparable so one must always assume that changes in structure are accompanied by changes in chemistry and function. A description of normal brain development involves most types of plasticity and forms a basis for understanding other types of neuroplasticity.

NORMAL BRAIN DEVELOPMENT

Nerve cell formation, migration, and aggregation

The brain begins as a tube whose wall is formed by a single layer of cells, each able to divide into two cells. Usually one of the daughter cells will divide again into two cells, continuing the process. The other cell loses the power to divide while acquiring some fabulous abilities: to follow a chemical "path" into the rapidly thickening and complex brain; to recognize when it has arrived at its final site; and later to form dendrites, axons, and synapses.

Like every aspect of brain development and function, formation of new nerve cells starts and stops at specific times in each part of the brain, stimulated in part by chemicals released by tissues adjoining the brain (they later form muscle, bone and skin of the head). A form of vitamin A is such a signal for formation of arms and legs[5] and probably for parts of the eyes and brain as well. All nerve cells are formed long before birth in most of the brain, and they are not replaced if damaged. The number of nerve cells formed during normal development also is precisely controlled. Up to four times as many nerve cells are formed and migrate than will make up brain parts after birth.[6] Cells for one part of the brain take from a few days to a few months to form.

Later, in a short time period as they contact other nerve cells, a normal process of cell death removes the "excess" nerve cells. Cells die mainly if they fail to make enough contacts to get necessary survival chemicals from their targets. Such chemicals from the target cells enter nerve cell contacts and are carried back to the cell, which needs them to survive. This seems to be a way to eliminate cells that are weak or make inadequate connections and to correct for the formation of fewer than normal nerve cells or damage after formation, errors of migration, mistaken contact patterns, and variations in body size, in each case by affecting which nerve cells and how many survive. Of course, if more is wrong than can be thus corrected, functional deficits such as cerebral palsy or learning problems result.

The migration of the young nerve cells-to-be is also directed by chemical cues, in this case on the surface of cells over which they pass. In much of the brain, they crawl along special cells called "radial glia" because they reach from the inside surface of the tube to its outside like spokes of a wheel.[7] It is like a caterpillar crawling out on a branch. And, as a caterpillar changes to a butterfly, the nerve cell-to-be changes into a complex, often beautifully contoured, mature nerve cell. The place where its migration stops is highly specific,[8] also controlled by the interaction of chemicals on its surface and the surface of like cells. Such groups of similar nerve cells form particular parts of the brain and function cooperatively from then on. The song centers mentioned before and vision centers discussed below are such structurally, chemically, and functionally related brain parts.

Many chemicals influence early brain development. Some are harmful, such as ethanol and medications like isotretinoin and valproate sodium. Other chemicals that regulate development, such as thyroid hormone, corticosteroids, insulin, sex hormones, and other vitamins, had known function in later life before being found to affect development.[9] A new group of compounds, called "growth factors," were found because they affect brain development.[10] Interestingly, some of these compounds are now known to have important functions later in life involving the brain and other organs .

Elaboration of dendrites

As nerve cells mature, the cell body in which the main metabolic machinery is located sends out two types of extensions, axons (discussed below) and dendrites. Dendrites are relatively short and spread out near the cell body, where they receive information from incoming axons. Dendrites appear soon after migration ends. Each type of nerve cell has a distinctive dendritic pattern only partially determined by the nerve cell, since it is only complete if the normal axons contact the dendrite.[11,12] Only if all of the axons it receives are lost is a dendrite completely lost.[13] Dendrites are important throughout life for the formation and function of the contacts between axons and dendrites.[14] General features of nerve cell development—time and place specificity and overproduction followed by elimination—apply to development of dendrite branches and contact sites, as well as to axons.

Axonal elongation and arborization

Axons, the long-distance fibers connecting nerve cells, must elongate, find their target and form contacts with it, continue to elongate as the fetus and infant grow, and perhaps be eliminated. The initial, pioneer axon, like a migrating nerve cell, follows chemical signals that it detects with an amoeba-like motile growth tip which "sniffs around" for the correct path.[4] Later axons of the same type only have to follow the pioneer, whose surface bears a chemical they recognize.[15] While the path of a bundle of axons can be very complex in the adult brain, it may be short and straight at the time of initial growth. Later, as distances in the brain increase and its shape changes, axons have only to maintain their contact, elongating as needed.[16] However, to repair damage, pathfinding would again be needed. The now large and complex brain is a difficult and potentially hostile environment for axon regeneration, constituting a major impediment to recovery after brain and spinal cord injuries. Several chemical and physical treatments help in experimental studies; the most promising involves transplantation of brain parts or peripheral nerve trunks.[17]

Synapse formation

Axons form billions of synapses in the brain. Most of these are contacts with dendrites. These are the "computer chips" with which the brain does its work of solving problems. The brain has more computational power than that contained in many of the largest supercomputers combined. In addition, synapses are far more sophisticated than the simple on-off function of computer elements. Their variable capability and their interaction with many other synapses in determining the output of a nerve cell underlie the power and adaptability of brain function. For some problems, computers perform better when operated in new ways that imitate these features of the brain.

Synapses must be formed correctly in development, with matching chemistry between the axon and dendrite. The major features, such as which axons and dendrites pair to form synapses, the chemistry of synapses, how many synapses an axon forms and a dendrite receives, are probably controlled genetically. Research has brought together the structural, functional, and chemical plasticity of synapses with the plasticity of the mind.

EXPERIMENTAL STUDIES OF SYNAPTIC PLASTICITY

Memory and learning

Brain activity can be considered on two time scales: moment-to-moment and longer term. People must be able to react to moment-to-moment events if necessary without special attention and without forming memory of them. Moment-to-moment changes in the brain are mostly electrical, with associated instantaneous changes in the size and shape of existing synapses and complex chemical events, all lasting no longer than the picture on a television screen. Longer term changes, including normal development, memory, and learning, are different. Progress in understanding how memory and learning occur was stifled until recently by the dogma that the brain's structure was unchanging. It is now evident that a continuous process of synapse formation and elimination throughout life is responsible for longer term functional changes.

How do external events induce synaptic plasticity? As an example, if a cat is paying attention to patterns of light, synapses that are especially sensitive to that pattern are strengthened and retained.[18] If the cat is not attentive, these synapses are not strengthened and may be eliminated, even though the cat sees the pattern carried by axons that contact dendrites in the vision center in both cases. The vision message is the same whether the cat pays attention or not. The difference lies in whether or not synapses coming from the attention center are active while the cat sees the pattern.

The synapses from the attention center are of a special type. Their action increases the response of dendrites in the vision center to visual input, but only if both types of synapse are active at the same time, as occurs when the cat pays attention while seeing the pattern. The stronger the visual signal, the more synaptic "glue" the dendrite makes. The dendrite secretes this glue at the site of active synapses. If enough glue is made because of coordinated activity of the two types of synapse, the synapses are retained. If not, they are eliminated. The chemistry involved in these responses is known.[19] It is impressive that the obvious role of attention in learning has been related to detailed chemical mechanisms.

A snail pulls its snout into the shell when it is touched. But if it is touched repeatedly, it stops reacting; it has learned that the touch on its snout is benign. Learning of this simple type also results from a change in chemical signals at the synapses responsible for the movement. Without conscious thought, the snail responds less to the same touch when it is repeated.[3] A single gene changes a fly's learning of a response to lights.

At the other extreme, rhesus monkeys and human infants can find a toy after it is put under one of two cups while they watch.[20] But they again look under the first cup when the toy is put under the other cup. The correct answer on the second trial depends on a particular part of the cerebrum. The age at which infants find the toy on the second trial, 2 months for monkeys and 9 months for humans, correlates with a change in the structure and chemistry of the brain area involved. Removing this area prenatally in monkeys does not affect later function because neighboring areas take over the structure and function. However, damage to this area, even in infancy, leads to persisting dysfunction.[21] Incomplete damage and vigorous long-term therapy and education should both result in a better outcome. While details of the chemistry of learning are different in the cases of snails touched on the snout, fruit flies responding to light, cats seeing visual patterns, and infants finding toys under cups, all depend on retaining or eliminating synapses.

Synaptic plasticity after injury

Synapses are made and modified during normal development and learning. How do they respond to injury, the third type of neuroplasticity? Synaptic changes after injury are only known from animal experiments, but some features of human disease, described in the next section, follow the same principles. Brain damage removes nerve cells and axons, including all of their synapses. In addition, undamaged nerve cells at a distance that were connected to the damaged nerve cells are affected in two ways, depending on whether the cells sent axons to the damaged area or received synapses from it. Cells that sent axons to the area of damage will survive if they have other connections to undamaged areas. They can form new synapses with any surviving nerve cells within the damaged part of the brain. This may restore function, especially if combined with appropriate training. In the case of nerve cells at a distance that have lost their input from the damaged area, function may be decreased even though the cells are healthy. Later, these cells may attract sprouts from nearby axons and make synapses with these sprouts, again with the possibility of improved function. However, such neuroplasticity as it naturally occurs is variable, as detailed in many experimental studies of different parts of the brain.[22] The synaptic changes vary in extent and function. The changes can be negative, for example, when spastic rigidity adds to the dysfunction caused by weakness and incoordination in children with cerebral palsy.

Much work, including the experiments that started the modern study of neuroplasticity, has been done on vision. It was known that frog optic nerves, which connect the eyeball to the brain, regenerate after being cut. Sperry did this but turned the eyeball upside down.[23] He then tested the frog's vision by holding flies in various positions near the frog. Normally, the frog's tongue strikes at a fly accurately. But with the eye upside down, there were three possibilities. If the eye reconnected to the brain in the same pattern as before, eye rotation would make no difference and the frog would get the fly. If reconnection was haphazard, the frog would strike randomly, possibly getting better with practice. But if each nerve cell in the eye reconnected to the same place in the vision center of the brain that it selected before, the frog would strike at a spot opposite to where the fly was held. In fact, the latter is what happened. The frog acted as though the fly was located where it would have been before the experiment to be seen by the particular spot in the eye. It acted according to what part of the eyeball saw the fly, rather than where the fly was located. Experiments since have revealed effects of such things as age at operation, surgical details, repeated injury, and most recently, drug treatments that can be positive or negative.[22,24]

In mammals, where the vision centers of the cerebrum are more complex, inputs from the two eyes are intermixed at birth. The location of their synapses normally changes, leading to separate, alternating areas for the input from each eye.[25] Perhaps most importantly, the effects on normal development produced by complete darkness, blurring of vision from one eye, and chemically blocking the nerve impulses from the eye to the brain have been recognized as similar. Such experiments show that genetic control alone, such as Sperry[23] seemed to demonstrate, is insufficient to produce normal development and that structure and function at synapses are inseparable in their effects on brain organization.

Related experiments in many parts of the nervous system give similar results while expanding understanding of structure–function relationships in brain development. Similar phenomena also have been found at the level of individual synapses in studies of the interpeduncular nucleus of the rat (elsewhere it has only been possible to study neuroplasticity of regions containing many synapses). These synapses develop from initial intermixing of synapses from right and left sides of the brain to precisely separated patterns normally, and this separation is prevented by mismatching the inputs early in life.[26] Similar injury in the normal adult was followed by less repair.[27]

EVIDENCE OF PLASTICITY IN HUMAN DISEASE

Of course, clinicians' concern for patients demands that they relate experimental results on neuroplasticity in other species to humans. They need to know how differences between people and other animals affect the application of experimental data to patients. Only three major systems are known to exhibit plasticity in response to injury of the human brain: visual, motor, and language.

In the visual system, it has long been known that crossed eyes in infancy lead to decreased vision. Such infants can fix only one eye on objects. The brain seems to ignore what is seen by the other eye, as though its function is suppressed to prevent confusion from two mismatched views of the world through the unaligned eyes. It seemed rather magical that if this condition lasted for several years, the vision in the suppressed eye permanently decreased, often severely. What was not anticipated until experimental work was done was that the organization of synapses in the vision centers of the cerebrum changes when the eyes are crossed. Many synapses from the nonfixated eye are eliminated, producing the deterioration of vision. The synaptic loss will not occur if crossed eyes appear later in life, and the loss cannot be overcome after infancy. Such visual loss from uncorrected crossed eyes is a preventable structural and functional developmental disorder in humans. It has a critical period in the same sense that critical periods in child development are usually understood as optimal times for learning language or other functions. Crossed eyes illustrate both advantageous neuroplasticity, in that double vision is eliminated (especially important before modern medical care), and deleterious plasticity, in that significant recovery does not occur after the critical period even with surgical correction of eye position.

Plasticity in the motor system is evident in several ways. One is the recovery of motor function that, because it occurs over weeks or months after injury, cannot be ascribed to early, reversible disturbances of metabolism. Such recovery occurs at all ages. It obviously depends on the extent of damage, among other factors. Functional motor deficits disappear by 7 years of age in 50% of children who had them at one year of age.[28] However, many adults enjoy similar resolution. Asymmetrical synkinesis (involuntary movement of one hand when the other is moved) is common with early childhood motor dysfunction on one side of the body (hemiparesis),[29] but uncommon after adult injury. Similar animal experiments suggest that synaptic plasticity is involved. Synaptic plasticity in humans is suggested by the absence of facial weakness in hemiparesis of prenatal v later onset.[30] The age effect is absent when hemiparesis is bilateral. These data indicate that there is a critical period that ends at birth during which normal synapse elimination is reduced to compensate for injury, and a period from birth to 1 year of age when partial compensation occurs.

It is generally agreed that damage to the language areas of an infant produces less loss of function than similar damage later in life.[31] Even older children usually recover better than adults. Two types of plasticity may occur after injuries affecting the language system. The first type of plasticity enables recovery due to neighboring areas of the brain taking over language function, especially those areas with related normal functions. The other plasticity brings recovery through the appearance of language function in the opposite side of the brain. The size of the language centers increases on the right side of the brain in non–right handed patients with brain damage.[31] The age range in which such plasticity appears to occur is long but poorly delineated.

MECHANISMS OF DAMAGE AND DYSFUNCTION

Brain damage is often superficially simple; one is hit on the head or has a hemorrhage, a stroke, or an infection. Each directly destroys some portion of the brain.

Lack of oxygen or nutrients kills nerve cells quickly. But it is also possible to injure the brain in a large number of more subtle ways by changing regulation of genes or any of the essential chemicals in the brain. About half of the genes (approximately 50,000 in humans) encode brain-specific proteins. Many proteins are involved in making or eliminating other chemicals. Many of the other genes are also active in the brain, encoding proteins that are essential but not unique to brain.

Place and time again are important. Many genes act only in certain nerve cells, beginning at a specific time after the nerve cell is formed. Some genes and their protein products must only be involved in a transient aspect of development, such as axon pathfinding, since they are active only for a limited time in fetal life. Other proteins must not appear too soon or remain too long because they interfere with the step before or after the one for which they are needed. For example, a protein needed for axon pathfinding may interfere with synapse formation, or vice versa. In normal development, each type of protein appears and disappears at the time required for each step. This is not done by magic, but by chemical messages produced as part of a preceding step or from a more distant tissue. The genes are always present and ready to respond in every cell.

In the example of birdsong, spring light patterns trigger cells to make gonad-stimulating hormones. These travel through the bloodstream to turn on the genes in the testes that cause male hormones to be made and released. The sex hormones travel through the blood to the brain and activate cells that are sensitive to them. In the song centers, male hormones turn on genes in sensitive cells, leading to nerve cell production. A cycle of controls and effects similar to those in normal development then unfolds in sequence. The same process occurs in females if started by injection of male hormone. It is testes and male hormone that are missing in females, not the machinery for neuroplasticity of the song centers. Once triggered, neuroplasticity works as well in females as in males. In the same way, the potential for stimulating genes that are no longer active, but that would be helpful in recovery from brain injury, is real. The keys to stimulate them are hinted at by current knowledge, but they await future discovery.

Brain damage or dysfunction is a potential result of physical or chemical interference not only with every gene, but also with every brain chemical; in aggregate, there are a very large number of potential problems of subtle nature. Even when the injury is not at all subtle, as in a major head injury, much of what ensues is determined by all of the more subtle chemical and metabolic changes. Some of these changes add to the injury, some cause dysfunction, some retard recovery, and some promote recovery in various ways. These complexities presumably explain the variable but often major deficits after head injuries and other forms of brain damage.

Injury also may be caused by normal brain chemicals if present in excess. The most important chemicals, because of the possibility of effective therapy, are the same synaptic chemicals that are necessary for learning, as in the example of the cat seeing patterns. These chemicals normally stimulate nerve cells mildly in a useful way. However, they are released in excess after some injuries, overstimulating nerve cells to exhaustion and killing them. Several drugs that block this overstimulation and prevent such injury have been found in animal experiments. Application to humans can be expected.

Fetuses are especially vulnerable to damage for several reasons. First, there is little or no barrier between blood and brain, so that chemicals that are excluded after birth can enter the brain. Second, because the brain is just forming, a small injury may be magnified by its effect on the entire remaining sequence of development that the injured area had yet to complete after the injury. This phenomenon explains why injuries early in gestation are generally more severe. It is also why recognizable patterns of malformation occur; the parts of the brain that arise from one region of the early brain are malformed after injury of that region. An injury to the germinal cells, which divide to form all the nerve cells, will have a large effect. The fetus relies on the mother to screen out chemicals and promote a constant, safe environment both chemically and physically.

THERAPEUTIC INTERVENTIONS

Up to now, only general medical measures have been applied soon after insult to reduce brain damage in patients, followed by education and training to stimulate recovery and retrain function. Now every possible site and chemical type of injury is recognized to be a site of possible therapy as well. Every chemical change that is harmful can potentially be blocked. Every gene that is no longer functional can potentially be restarted, and each functioning gene can potentially be reset to a different level of function or turned off. Being born with a normal brain, learning to talk as an infant, improving a tennis serve, studying a new language, learning to walk after a stroke, or songbirds' singing in spring are all examples of profound alterations in the brain. These activities involve normal development, facilitation by functional activity, cognitive learning, recovery of function after damage, and the role of a small molecule in triggering complex structural and functional change to produce birdsong. These phenomena were never in doubt; it was accepted that the mind could change. But now that it is understood that the brain also changes in these processes, learning the chemical details may lead to the therapeutic use of those chemicals to initiate, modulate, or augment change.

Goals and expectations for treatment of brain damage are thus much broader and more specifically formulated than in the past: this is the clear message of the body of knowledge about neuroplasticity. Combined therapies, such as medication and physical therapy or augmentative communication devices and speech therapy, are proving to be especially effective. The recovery of cats with acute cerebral palsy was enhanced when physical therapy was combined with a single dose of amphetamine after injury.[32] Recovery was better with physical therapy than with amphetamine alone, but the combination was much better. No one yet knows what amphetamine does or if other drugs may be more effective. But the principle is not surprising. No matter how effective a drug is, training is essential to maximize recovery.

Where damage is too great, or barriers such as distance inhibit regeneration, transplantation of tissue into the brain holds great promise. Immature neurons have been successfully transplanted into almost every brain region in experimental animals. In an increasing number of instances, these grafts survive, grow, and form functional interconnections with the host brain. Even artificial materials that provide a surface for axon elongation might work.

There has been much attention paid to the use of fetal brain tissue to treat Parkinson's disease.[33] But Parkinson's is a very special case. A single cell type that produces a certain chemical ceases functioning in Parkinson's disease. For a long time, the patient is fine simply taking the chemical by mouth. When there are no longer cells to convert the oral medication to its effective form, it may suffice to transplant such cells anywhere in the general region. However, after most brain injuries, the transplant would need to affect more complex processes, such as axon pathfinding and synapse formation. It has generally been thought that fetal cells are required, leading to ethical concerns. However, obtaining cells postnatally from premature infants should be suitable in many cases and avoids the major ethical concerns. Postnatally obtained germinal cells would allow use of more cells and preserve the operation of the normal cycles of control and effect already present in these nerve cells. Furthermore, premature infants are ideal recipients of brain cell transplants, and children should do better with transplants than adults, according to results in other mammals.

·   ·   ·

Considering neuroplasticity as a whole has allowed recognition of the common ground among normal brain development, learning, and recovery from injury. Progress in research is aided by the sharing of concepts among these areas. Deeper insight into current therapies and possible new therapies have been achieved. Increasing knowledge of neuroplasticity and its application to therapy promise fruitful and gratifying future developments, especially in pediatric neuroscience.

REFERENCES

1. Bach-y-Rita P. Brain plasticity as a basis for therapeutic procedures. In: Bach-y-Rita P, ed. Recovery of Function. *Recovery of Function: Theoretical Considerations for Brain Injury Rehabilitation.* Bern, Switzerland: Huber; 1979:1–43.

2. Konishi M. Birdsong for neurobiologists. *Neuron.* 1989;3:541–549.

3. Kandel ER Abrams T, Bernier L, Carew TJ, Hawkins RK, Schwartz JH. Classical conditioning and sensitization share aspects of the same molecular cascade in Aplysia. *Cold Spring Harbor Symp Quant Biol.* 1983;48:821–830.

4. Bastiani MJ, Raper JA, Goodman CS. Pathfinding by neuronal growth cones in grasshopper. *J Neurosci.* 1984;4:2311–2328.

5. Summerbell DJ. The effect of local application of retinoic acid to the anterior margin of the developing chick limb. *J Exp Morphol.* 1983;78:269–289.

6. Oppenheim RW. Muscle activity and motor neuron death in the spinal cord of the chick embryo. *Selective Neuronal Death. Ciba Found Symp.* 1987; 126:96–112.

7. Rakic P. Cell migration and neuronal ectopias. *Birth Defects.* 1975;11:95–129.

8. Rakic P. Neurons in rhesus monkey visual cortex: Systematic relation between time of origin and eventual disposition. *Science.* 1974;183:425–427.

9. Lauder JM, Krebs H. Humoral influences on brain development. *Adv Cell Neurobiol.* 1984;5:3–15.

10. Jacobson M. *Developmental Neurobiology.* New York, NY: Plenum; 1978.

11. Harris RM, Woolsey TA. Dendritic plasticity in mouse barrel cortex following postnatal vibrissa follicle damage. *J Comp Neurol.* 1981; 196:357–376.

12. Sidman RL. Cell–cell recognition in the developing central nervous system. In: Schmitt FL, Worden F, eds. *The Neurosciences: Third Study Program.* Cambridge, Mass: MIT Press; 1974:743–757.

13. Dietch JS, Rubel EW. Afferent influences on brain stem auditory nuclei of the chicken: Time course and specificity of dendritic atrophy following deafferentation. *J Comp Neurol.* 1984;229:66–79.

14. Lenn NJ. Postnatal synaptogenesis in the rat interpeduncular nucleus. *J Comp Neurol.* 1978;81:75–92.

15. Easters SS, Rusoff AC, Kish PE. The growth and organiation of the optic nerve and tract in juvenile and adult goldfish. *J Neurosci.* 1981;1:793–811.

16. Calvert RA, Woodhams PL, Anderson BH. Localiation of an epitope of a microtubule-associated protein MAP l(x) in outgrowing axons of the developing rat central nervous system. *Neuroscience.* 1987;13:233–238.

17. Bjorklund A, Stenevi U, eds. *Neural Grafting in the Mammalian CNS.* Amsterdam, The Netherlands: Elsevier; 1980.

18. Greuel JM, Luhmann HJ, Singer W. Pharmacological induction of use-dependent receptive field modifications in the visual cortex. *Science.* 1988;242: 74–77.

19. Bear M, Cooper LN. Molecular mechanisms for synaptic modification in the visual cortex: Interaction between theory and experiment. In: Gluck M, Rumelhart D, eds. *Neuroscience and Connectionist Theory.* Hillsdale, NJ: Erlbaum; 1989.

20. Diamond A, Goldman-Rakic PS. Comparison of human infanrs and rhesus monkeys on Piaget's AB task: Evidence for dependence on dorsolateral prefrontal cortex. *Exp Brain Res.* 1989;74:24–40.

21. Goldman PS, Galkin TW. Prenatal removal of frontal association cortex in the fetal rhesus monkey: Anatomical and functional consequences in postnatal life. *Brain Res.* 1978;152:451–485.

22. Steward 0. Reorganization of neuronal connections following CNS trauma: Principles and experimental paradigms. *J Neurotrauma.* 1989;6:99–152.

23. Sperry RW. Effect of 180 degree rotation of the retinal field on visuomotor coordination. *J Exp Zool.* 1943;92:263–279.

24. Meyer RP. Tetrodotoxin inhibits the formation of refined retinotopography in goldfish. *Dev Brain Res.* 1983;6:293–298.

25. Ferster D, LeVay S. The axonal arborizations of lateral geniculate neurons in the striate cortex of the cat. *J Comp Neurol.* 1978;182:923–944.

26. Hamill GS, Lenn NJ. Synaptic plasticity within the interpeduncular nucleus after unilateral lesions of the habenula in neonatal rats. *J Neurosci.* 1983;3:2128–2145.

27. Murray M, Zimmer J, Raisman G. Quantitative electron microscopic evidence of reinnervation in adult rat interpeduncular nucleus after lesions of the fasciculus retroflexus. *J Comp Neurol.* 1979;187:447–468.

28. Nelson KB, Ellenberg JH. Children who "outgrew" cerebral palsy. *Pediatrics.* 1982;69:529–536.

29. Nass R. Mirror movement asymmetries in congenital hemiparesis. *Neurology.* 1985;35:1059–1062.

30. Lenn NJ, Freinkel A. Facial sparing in patients with prenatal-onset hemiparesis. *Pediatr Neurol.* 1989;5:291–295.

31. Rapin I. *Children with Brain Dysfunction.* New York, NY: Raven Press; 1975. International Review of Child Neurology Series.

32. Feeney DM, Gonzalez A, Law WA. Amphetamin haloperidol, and experience interact to affect rate of recovery after motor cortex injury. *Science.* 1982;217:855–857.

Developmental issues: Children infected with the human immunodeficiency virus

Caroline B. Johnson, PhD
Chief Psychologist
Child Development Center
Children's Hospital Oakland
Oakland, California

Mardi Gras, a day that so often in previous years included family gatherings and all-night celebrations, brought instead devastation to Annie, a 25-year-old mother of two young children. On this day, in 1986, after numerous hospitalizations for various ailments including respiratory infections, chronic fatigue, and digestive problems, Annie received the diagnosis of acquired immunodeficiency syndrome (AIDS). Her response to the diagnosis was confusion and disbelief. She denied having engaged in any of the risky behaviors commonly associated with the contraction of the human immunodeficiency virus (HIV). Annie soon learned that her partner and the father of her youngest child, unbeknownst to her, had been diagnosed with AIDS and had been receiving treatment for the disease for the past 2 years.

The subsequent months were difficult ones for Annie. Many of her friends disappeared, her health continued to fail, and she had little physical or emotional energy to care for her young daughters. Her mother, her brothers, and her doctor assisted Annie in her final days. Yet many individuals, including some medical professionals, fearful of contracting the virus, deserted her. In May 1987, Annie died in a ward of a local hospital, with no supportive presence except that of her mother. Annie died with the hope that her disease had not been transmitted to her young daughter.

Soon after Annie's death her two young children came under the care of their maternal grandmother. The youngest, Beth, then 5 years old, had been a source of worry for the grandmother since her birth. Beth was described by the grandmother as a sickly infant who had had numerous respiratory infections and a persistent cough. She was thought to have allergies and consequently received numerous medications with little prolonged benefit. Only after Beth began experiencing recurrent fever was she seen by an infectious disease specialist, who tested her for HIV. She was found to be positive.

Although over the years Beth, her grandmother, and her older sister have had to endure ostracism, bouts of depression, and sorrow, the family has managed to cope with Beth's HIV infection and its stigmata. With monthly infusions of immune globulin and the use of medications such as AZT, Beth, now age 10, is presently symptom free and able to attend school.

AIDS IN CHILDREN is a disease of considerable complexity with neurologic, developmental, emotional, and familial implications. In 1983, AIDS was first diagnosed in children. Since that time, the disease has become epidemic in the pediatric population. This article reviews the current knowledge in the field and relates

The author thanks the HIV/AIDS team and families for their contributions to this article and particularly appreciates the comments and suggestions of Ann Petru, MD, Patricia Mittelstadt, PhD, Brad Berman, MD, and Timothy Johnson. Portions of this article were presented at Contemporary Forums, June 1992, San Diego, California.

Inf Young Children, 1993; 6(1): 1–10
© 1993 Aspen Publishers, Inc.

this information to experiences with the population at Children's Hospital Oakland.

The statistics regarding pediatric HIV infection are not heartening. Almost 4,000 HIV-infected children had been reported to the Centers for Disease Control by spring 1992, and half of these children have already died.[1] African-Americans and Hispanics are overrepresented in the AIDS population.[1] New York State reported in 1990 that AIDS was the leading cause of death in African-American and Hispanic children between the ages of 1 and 4 years.[1-3] Anywhere between 12% and 35% of children born to HIV-infected mothers are infected themselves (Petru A. Personal communication. Fall 1992). Vertical transmission, that is infection passed perinatally from mother to child, accounts for the largest number of new cases.[4,5] Intravenous drug use is reported in more than 50% of mothers of congenitally infected children; in another 30% of cases, mothers reported being partners of either intravenous drug users or individuals with HIV infection.[3,5] By 12 months of age, approximately 25% of HIV-infected children will have developed AIDS.[1,4] Survival time after diagnosis appears to depend on a number of factors, including the timing of infection during gestation, premature birth, presence of malnutrition, route of transmission, and type of infections (eg, Epstein-Barr virus or cytomegalovirus) acquired.[4-6]

The HIV/AIDS team at Children's Hospital Oakland had its beginning in the fall of 1987. This pediatric AIDS program provides a multidisciplinary, collaborative model of family-centered care that emphasizes outpatient management and coordination of home-based supportive services. The team presently is composed of three pediatricians with specialization in infectious diseases and particularly HIV infection, three nurses, two social workers, two psychologists, and a nutritionist. At its inception, there was a census of 20 children. Five of these children had transfusion-acquired infections, and the remainder were children younger than 2 years of age thought to have been exposed perinatally. As of October 1992, the census stood at 216 patients, 42 of whom were infants with passively acquired infection and 39 of whom had a diagnosis of full-blown AIDS.

DIAGNOSIS AND CLASSIFICATION OF HIV INFECTION IN CHILDREN

The definition of pediatric AIDS has undergone several revisions.[4,5] The initial definition paralleled that of AIDS in adults. As the population of children with AIDS increased, however, the definition was altered to reflect the differences between pediatric and adult symptomatology. Currently, there are two commonly accepted subdivisions of the definition of HIV/AIDS in children.[4,5]

The first subdivision refers to children at least 15 months of age who either were infected perinatally or acquired the disease through another mode of transmission.

In these children the presence of antibody to HIV is sufficient evidence of infection.

For children younger than 15 months of age with congenitally acquired infection, who fall into the second subdivision, the diagnosis was more complicated until recently. Infants carry passively acquired maternal antibody, which does not prove infection in the infant.[7] Most infants lose maternal antibody by the age of 12 to 15 months, so that antibody positivity only indicates infection beyond 15 months of age.[4,5,7,8] Until fairly recently, this period of approximately 12 to 18 months was one of considerable anxiety for parents as they awaited a determination of their child's infection status. Supplemental testing such as polymerase chain reaction (PCR), culture, and antigen assays now improves the ability to diagnose infection in the infant in the first year of life.[4,5,8]

The classification of HIV-infected children is divided broadly into three groups according to symptoms.[1,4,5] The first group, known as P-0 refers to children younger than 15 months whose HIV status has not been definitively established. Infants born to HIV-infected mothers are classified as P-0 until they are proven infected or until they lose maternal antibody. The second group, P-1, describes infected children who are asymptomatic. The third group, P-2, comprises children who have symptomatic disease that may include certain kinds of lung ailments, progressive neurologic dysfunction, and some types of secondary infections.

Although these categories can reflect apparently mild alterations in clinical signs, they carry significant emotional weight for the families of infected children. For these families, having a diagnosis of HIV infection constitutes an ordeal of waiting for laboratory studies that reflect an ever-weakening immune system or waiting for their child to be catapulted from an asymptomatic status to a diagnosis of full-blown AIDS in a few short hours. Often, parents live with the fear of their child experiencing a rapid deterioration and dying precipitously after an apparently stable neurologic course. Such events have been chronicled in the literature.[4,9]

CLINICAL MANIFESTATIONS OF HIV INFECTION IN CHILDREN

Children infected through vertical transmission have a quite different clinical presentation from that of adults.[4,5] Malignancies such as Kaposi's sarcoma, a common complication in adults, are rare in children.[10] Bacterial infections, on the other hand, until fairly recently were noted in up to 60% of children with AIDS[4,5,11]; recent use of intravenous immune globulin therapy has proved beneficial in the prevention of many of these infections.[1] In addition, children are prone to developing a pulmonary disorder known as lymphocytic interstitial pneumonitis; to contracting opportunistic infections such as *Pneumocystis carinii* pneumonia; and to experiencing failure to thrive, chronic diarrhea; and intractable thrush.[4,5,9,11] In the clinic population at Children's Hospital Oakland, delays in linear growth also are commonly noted.

Neurologic complications are estimated to occur in as much as 78% to 93% of symptomatic children[4,5,12,13] (Table 1). The neurologic presentation in children is variable and may include developmental delay, motor impairment, and encephalopathy. The term *HIV encephalopathy* has come to be used in referring to children with delayed motor and/or mental milestones, abnormal motor signs, weakness, deranged brain stem function, ataxia, blindness, secondary microcephaly, and seizures.[4,7,12,14-16] HIV encephalopathy is reported to occur in approximately 12% of perinatally infected children and is noted in more than half those children with more advanced neurologic disease.[4,7]

Autopsy studies of children with AIDS have revealed the brains of these children to be diminished in weight with dystrophic calcifications of the vascular system in the region of the basal ganglia and deep cerebral white matter.[7,14,17,18] For instance, in 1985 Epstein et al[19] found on radiologic and postmortem studies of

Table 1. Pediatric AIDS research on neurologic manifestations

Author	Year	Age range	Findings
Epstein et al	1985	6–50 months	Basal ganglia calcification, subacute encephalitis
Price et al	1988	14–18 months	Case study showing marked increase in basal ganglia calcification and cerebral atrophy over 4-month period
Belman	1990	3½–4 years	Case study showing progressive atrophy and calcification with signs of spasticity and developmental delay
Ultmann et al	1987	6 months–6 years	Progressive dementia, encephalopathies, acquired microcephaly
Diamond	1989	3–8½ years	Selective spatial and perceptual dysfunction; 75% of cases had positive neurologic findings, including abnormal gait
Dickson et al	1989	4–109 months	Common histopathologic alterations: progressive calcifications of basal ganglia and deep cerebral white matter; subacute encephalitis

congenitally infected children that in 61% of the cases calcification was apparent in the brain, specifically in the basal ganglia. Other studies have further noted a high incidence of subacute encephalitis especially affecting the gray matter of the basal ganglia, thalamus, and brain stem, with the cerebral cortex usually being spared.[13,17] A longitudinal study of a young HIV-infected child conducted by Price et al[20] in 1988 revealed subtle white patches in the area of the basal ganglia on computed tomography (CT) at 14 months of age. A follow-up CT scan only 4 months later showed definite basal ganglia calcification and marked cerebral atrophy.

Similarly, a study by Belman[9] in 1990 of a 3½-year-old child with developmental delay, acquired microcephaly, and mild spasticity revealed signs on CT scan of mild cerebral atrophy and bilateral calcification in the regions of the basal ganglia and frontal white matter. Eight months later, this child displayed progressive atrophy and calcification on CT scan along with the clinical signs of increasing spasticity and developmental arrest.

The neurologic course of the disease in children generally appears to fall into three subtypes.[3–5,7,9,10] For some children, the course is a progressive decline with a relentless loss of developmental milestones, including those involving motor, social, and language skills; increasing spasticity, and acquired microcephaly. In the school-age child, academic and attentional difficulties may be markers of a declining course. Other children experience a more subacute course interrupted by plateaus. These children tend to acquire milestones slowly and then to experience a protracted plateau in which there is no further acquisition of skills. Mild spasticity is commonplace. The plateau period may be followed by either improvement or deterioration in functioning. Still other children follow a somewhat different course. This group of children displays initial delays in motor and language development with gradual gains in milestone acquisition. Cognitive and motor deficits tend to be static. Attentional difficulties are prevalent.

DEVELOPMENTAL SEQUELAE

Developmental delay has been reported in 25% to 90% of children with HIV infection (see the box titled "Developmental Sequelae").[4,5,12,21,22] The developmental course of children with HIV infection, however, is highly variable and difficult to predict.[4,5,23] In general, children with AIDS tend to show more severe cognitive dysfunction.[23] Yet some children may function in the normal range with normal neurologic findings or may exhibit only mild developmental delays.[4,23]

In the young child, motor involvement with corticospinal tract signs frequently is observed to be the most profound delay.[9,15,16,23] Motor delays may initially manifest as hypotonia with increasing spasticity as the child ages. Delays or regression

---

Developmental Sequelae

Young child
- Motor delays or increasing spasticity
- Delays or regression in social smile
- Delays or regression in vocalization/speech
- Generalized developmental delay

Older child
- Psychomotor slowing
- Emotional lability
- Social withdrawal
- Attentional difficulties
- Visual-spatial/visual-perceptual dysfunction

---

in social smile and cooing also has been reported.[9] A mother of a 12-month-old child in the Children's Hospital Oakland clinic recently reported the loss of her child's ability to vocalize to her. This infant over the course of her life exhibited progressive spasticity with a failure in her ability to sit independently and extreme difficulties in fluid reaching. To deflect questions and expressions of concern, this mother began telling strangers that her daughter was 6 months old instead of 12 months.

Older children may exhibit such signs as psychomotor slowing, emotional lability, social withdrawal, and attentional difficulties.[9,14] Persistent fatigue and a general disinterest in academic pursuits also are reported.[9] In addition, a study of 3- to 8½-year-old infected children with relatively stable medical courses found evidence of visual-spatial and visual-perceptual dysfunction.[24] Three quarters of the children studied exhibited positive neurologic findings; poor motor coordination; clumsy, rapid, alternating movements; or abnormal gait.

PSYCHOSOCIAL FACTORS

Krener and Miller state that "pediatric AIDS is increasingly a family disease and that the overwhelming reality is of an entire family dying."[25] Many mothers are identified as carriers only when their child is diagnosed; hence they are confronted with the knowledge of a terminal illness in their child as well as in themselves. These mothers experience agony on many levels. They experience recurring guilt for giving the disease to their offspring and a deep sense of helplessness and anger at their failure to protect their child from harm. In addition, for a number of parents the disclosure of HIV infection implies a connection with unacceptable behavior and attendant feelings of shame and guilt. It may also be the time when

---

Psychosocial Effects

Social stigma
Combined devastation of infected mother and child
Care of infected child by surrogates
Experience of depression, anxiety, and anger
Coping influenced by developmental level, support system, religious and cultural values

---

one partner becomes aware of the hitherto unknown drug or sexual behavior of the other (see the box titled "Psychosocial Effects").

For the infected mother, her child's disease process takes on special meaning. Each piece of news the mother hears from medical personnel on the HIV team about her child directly affects her perception of her own illness. When the child is doing well, the mother has hope and encouragement about herself. However, when the child's immune function deteriorates or a medical complication arises, the mother often despairs both for her child and for herself. Mother and child then are intimately entwined in this process, boundaries between them becoming blurred as the mother struggles to cope with her own as well as her child's demise.

When the natural parent is unable to care for the child, whether as a result of his or her own disease progression or for other reasons (financial or psychosocial), the child with HIV infection comes under the care of a surrogate.[26] The surrogate in some cases is an extended family member, who often is suddenly burdened with an ill child while simultaneously learning of the infection status of the child's parent, who may be the surrogate's child or sibling.[26] In many cases the relative caretaker knows little about HIV infection and is overwhelmed with fears regarding health risks for himself or herself and other family members, concerns about the medical needs of the HIV-infected child, and anxieties related to disclosure of the child's or relative's infection status. Surrogate parents, both relatives and foster parents, also often experience feelings of impotence at their inability to reverse the disease process. When the child continues to deteriorate even after provision of optimal care, feelings of inadequacy, depression, and anger often arise.

Feelings of depression, anxiety, and anger are not limited to the caregivers.[23,25] Children with HIV infection, whether they are aware of their diagnosis or not, often experience a life that is punctuated by anxiety and hurt. Many children with HIV infection enter the hospital on a monthly basis for treatment and other medical interventions. These children frequently must endure painful procedures, including spinal taps and repeated attempts to start an intravenous drip. They often live with a chronic underlying tension that is greatly heightened by visits to the hospital. A number of children relate concerns about their death through expressions of fears about coming to the hospital. For them, the hospital signifies a kind of incarceration that holds the threat that one day they may not be released. Conversely, other children worry about leaving the hospital, perceiving the medical staff and HIV team as their ultimate protectors from harm.

The manner in which children cope with their disease varies widely and depends on a number of factors, including the child's developmental level, the nature of the child's support system, and the child's religious and cultural values.[22] Some children express their anxieties allegorically, describing, for instance, animals or other creatures with tainted blood who become maimed or killed. Others express themselves more directly. One of our patients, for example, attempted to manage her fears through repeatedly watching *The Ryan White Story.* Although this patient disclosed that the movie engendered some "scary feelings," she felt the benefits related to learning about AIDS from a peer.

Among the most difficult aspects of HIV infection are the tremendous sense of isolation and deep-seated fear of ostracism. Parents and children fear not only the disease process itself but also rejection should the diagnosis become known to others. For a number of families, the usual network of support disappears; many worry about negative reactions from others. When, in other circumstances, turning to family and friends would be a natural reaction, they often opt not to disclose information for fear of abandonment. Unfortunately, this fear appears to be well founded because a large portion of society continues to view the patient with HIV infection as a pariah.

FACTORS INFLUENCING DEVELOPMENTAL COURSE

Medical interventions have improved over the course of nearly a decade, enhancing the quality of life and longevity of children with HIV infection. Medications such as AZT are now routinely being used in the pediatric HIV population. Children with prior central nervous system abnormalities have been shown to have improvements in neurodevelopmental functioning after intravenous AZT treatment.[27,28] Unfortunately, AZT carries with its use the major complication of bone marrow suppression and thus must be administered with careful monitoring. Other drugs such as dideoxyinosine (DDI) and dideoxycytidine (DDC) have recently become available for use in some children. Limited data presently exist regarding the effect of these drugs on intellectual and developmental functioning. Studies to date have been mixed regarding positive cognitive outcomes.[29] Although these drugs hold some promise for use in children, they also have potentially toxic effects, DDC tending to cause peripheral neuropathy and DDI pancreatitis.[4,5,28] Intravenous immune globulin prophylaxis has been found to decrease the number of bacterial and viral infections in children with HIV. An improvement in skills, particularly visual-spatial abilities, also has been reported

---

Factors Influencing Developmental Course

Medication interventions
- AZT
- DDC
- DDI
- Intravenous immune globulin

Educational/developmental support
- HIV infection—route of transmission
- Appropriate safety precautions
- Confidentiality of information

---

with immune globulin administration[30] (see the box titled "Factors Influencing Developmental Course").

Although medical science has been successful in prolonging the lives of children with HIV infection, developmental and educational interventions generally have failed to keep pace. Children with HIV infection no longer are dying after a few short months but rather are living and coping with a chronic illness.[31] In fact, some professionals speculate that by 1995 HIV infection will represent the most prevalent etiology of developmental disabilities.[31] Few intervention programs for young children have recognized the likelihood that at least one of their charges is likely to be infected. Early childhood specialists and elementary educators too often are poorly informed about HIV infection, its route of transmission, appropriate precautions for the safety and well-being of the HIV-infected child, and the laws governing confidentiality of information related to HIV infection status.[31] Too frequently, many professionals working with young children fail to develop a policy for their institutions regarding the appropriate handling of bodily fluids and have no universal standard for infection control. In addition, often well-meaning professionals disclose confidential information to staff or others without proper authority and far too frequently without having sufficiently educated themselves or others about HIV infection. As a result, the child with HIV infection becomes a victim of ignorance and fear—rejected, alone, and unable to participate freely in activities of daily life.

•   •   •

No disease in recent history has such devastating physical and emotional consequences and carries such a social stigma. It is our responsibility as professional and compassionate people to educate ourselves and others about HIV infection, so that the patients may no longer be outcasts but may seek information, treatment, and comfort in an atmosphere of acceptance, caring, and support.

REFERENCES

1. Wara D. *Perinatal AIDS and HIV diagnosis and treatment update.* Presented at Advances and Controversies in Clinical Pediatrics; May 14–16, 1992; San Francisco, Calif.

2. Abrams EJ, Nicholas SW. Pediatric HIV infection. *Pediatr Ann.* 1990;19:482–487.

3. Simonds RJ, Rogers M. Epidemiology of HIV in children and other populations. In: Crocker A, Cohen H, Kastner T, eds. *HIV Infection and Developmental Disabilities.* Baltimore, Md: Brookes; 1992:3–13.

4. Calvelli TA, Rubinstein A. Pediatric HIV infection: a review. *Immunodefic Rev.* 1990;2:83–127.

5. Indacochea FJ, Scott GB. HIV infection and the acquired immunodeficiency syndrome in children. *Curr Prob Pediatr.* 1992;22:166–204.

6. Scott G, Hutto C, Makuch R, et al. Survival in children with perinatally acquired HIV type I infection. *N Engl J Med.* 1989;321:1791–1796.

7. Civitello LA. Neurologic complications of HIV infection in children. *Pediatr Neurosurg.* 1991;17:104–112.

8. Centers for Disease Control. Recommendations and reports: interpretation and use of the Western blot assay for serodiagnosis of HIV type I infections. *MMWR.* 1989;38(suppl 7):1–7.

9. Belman AL. AIDS and pediatric neurology. *Neurol Clin.* 1990;8:571–603.

10. Wiznia AA, Nicholas SW. Organic system involvement in HIV-infected children. *Pediatr Ann.* 1990;19:475–481.

11. Wilfert C. HIV infection in maternal and pediatric patients. *Hosp Pract.* 1991;5:55–67.

12. Diamond G, Cohen H. Developmental disabilities in children with HIV infection. In: Crocker A, Cohen H, Kastner T, eds. *HIV Infection and Developmental Disabilities.* Baltimore, Md: Brookes; 1992:33–43.

13. Olson RA, Huszti HC, Mason PJ, Seibert JM. Pediatric AIDS/HIV infection: an emerging challenge to pediatric psychology. *J Pediatr Psychol.* 1989;14:1–21.

14. Iannetti P, Falconieri P, et al. Acquired immune deficiency syndrome in childhood. *Childs Nerv Sys.* 1989;5:281–287.

15. Prose NS. HIV infection in children. *J Am Acad Dermatol.* 1990;22:1223–1231.

16. Fishman MA, Lifschitz MH, Wilson GS. Neurodevelopmental abnormalities. *Semin Pediatr Infect Dis.* 1990;1:107–111.

17. Dickson DW, Belman AL, et al. Central nervous system pathology in pediatric AIDS: an autopsy study. *Apmis Suppl.* 1989;8:40–57.

18. Habibi P, Strobel S, et al. Neurodevelopmental delay and focal seizures as presenting symptoms of human immune deficiency virus infection. *Eur J Pediatr.* 1989;148:315–317.

19. Epstein LG, Sharer LR, Joshi VV, et al. Progressive encephalopathy in children with AIDS. *Ann Neurol.* 1985;17:488–496.

20. Price DB, Inglese CM, Jacobs J, et al. Pediatric AIDS neuroradiologic and neurodevelopmental findings. *Pediatr Radiol.* 1988;18:445–448.

21. Klindworth LM, Dokecki PR, Baumeister AA, Kupstas FD. Pediatric AIDS, developmental disabilities, and education: a review. *AIDS Educ Prev.* 1989;1:291–302.

22. Spiegel L, Mayers A. Psychosocial aspects of AIDS in children and adolescents. *Pediatr Clin North Am.* 1991;38:153–167.

23. Ultmann MH, Diamond GW, Ruff HA. Developmental abnormalities in children with acquired immune deficiency syndrome (AIDS): a follow-up study. *Int J Neurosci.* 1987;32:661–667.

24. Diamond GW. Developmental problems in children with HIV infection. *Ment Retard.* 1989;27:213–217.

25. Krener P, Miller FB. Psychiatric response to HIV spectrum of disease in children and adolescents. *J Am Acad Child Adolescent Psychiatr.* 1989;28:596–605.

26. Grosz J, Hopkins K. Family circumstances affecting caregivers and brothers and sisters. In: Crocker A, Cohen H, Kastner T, eds. *HIV Infection and Developmental Disabilities.* Baltimore, Md: Brookes; 1992:43–51.

27. Pizzo P, Eddy J, Falloon J. Acquired immune deficiency syndrome in children. *Am J Med.* 1988;85(Suppl 2A):295.

28. Brouwers P, Moss H, Wolters P. Effect of continuous-infusion zidovudine therapy on neuropsychologic functioning in children with symptomatic human immunodeficiency virus infection. *J Pediatr.* 1990;117:980–985.

29. Wolters P, Brouwers P, Moss H, El-Amin D. The effect of 2', 3'-dideoxyinosine (DDI) on the cognitive functioning of infants and children with symptomatic HIV infection. Poster session. *Pediatric AIDS 1990;S.* B. 205.

30. Hunziker UA, Nadal D, Jendis JB. Stable human immune deficiency virus encephalopathy in two infants receiving early intravenous gammaglobulin plus antimicrobial prophylaxis. *Eur J Pediatr.* 1989;148:417–422.

31. Rosen S, Granger M. Early interventions and school programs. In: Crocker A, Cohen H, Kastner T, eds. *HIV Infection and Developmental Disabilities.* Baltimore, Md: Brookes; 1992:75–84.

Appendix

Children's Hospital Oakland HIV/AIDS program bibliography of children's books about AIDS and death

Bluebond-Langer M. *The Private Worlds of Dying Children.* Princeton, NJ: Princeton University Press; 1978.

This book is written as a drama based on observations of children with leukemia aged 3 to 9 years in a hospital ward. The book discusses how children come to know they are dying, how and why they attempt to hide this knowledge from their parents and medical staff, and how these adults in turn try to conceal from their children their awareness of the children's impending death.

Boulder J. *Saying Goodbye Activity Book.* Available from the author (PO Box 9358, Santa Rosa, CA 95405).

An imaginative and informative workbook (coloring book) to help children understand and cope with death.

Gravelle K, Haskins C. *Teenagers Face to Face with Bereavement.* Englewood Cliffs, NJ: Simon & Schuster; 1989.

Seventeen young adults discuss the deaths of parents, siblings, and friends in this book. The discussion includes subjects such as personal relationships with the terminally ill; reactions after a death; problems facing classmates and friends; feelings of pain, guilt, and anger; and steps toward renewing family life.

Grollman EA, ed. *Explaining Death to Children.* Boston, Mass: Beacon; 1967.

A book for parents and professionals describing how children perceive death. Suggestions are given for discussing death with children from various religious and cultural perspectives.

Hausherr R. *Children and the AIDS Virus.* New York, NY: Houghton Mifflin; 1989.

A book about AIDS for children, parents, and teachers created especially for young children. The book contains photographs to help young readers deal with their fear of the disease and teaches compassion and concern for those with AIDS.

MacGregor M. *The Sky Goes on Forever.* Cobb, Calif: Dawn Horse; 1989.

A book about death for children told through a story about a bird. It deals with such question as, What are living things? What are dying things? Why does everything die? When you die is that the end? How can we help someone who is dying? What can I do when it is my turn to die?

McQueen K, Fassler D. *What's a Virus Anyway?* Burlington, Vt: Waterfront Books; 1990.

This book explains AIDS from the child's perspective. It introduces children to AIDS information in a guided step-by-step fashion.

Mellonie B, Ingpen R. *Lifetimes.* New York, NY: Bantam; 1983.

A book for children of all ages and parents. It tells about beginnings, endings, and living in between. Large illustrations explain about plants, animals, and people, showing that dying is as much a part of living as being born.

Merrifield M. *Come Sit by Me.* Toronto, Ontario: Women's Press; 1990.

An educational storybook about AIDS and HIV infection for children ages 4 to 8 years and their caregivers.

Paulus T. *Hope for the Flowers.* New York, NY: Paulist Press; 1972.

A tale of a butterfly and hope.

Sanford D. *David has AIDS.* Portland, Ore: Multnomah; 1989.

A boy with AIDS turns to God to help him cope with the pain, fear, and loneliness that surround him.

Schwartz L. *AIDS Questions and Answers for Kids Grades 5–6, AIDS Answers for Teens Grades 7–12.* Santa Barbara, Calif: Learning Work; 1987.

Educational workbook about AIDS for children.

Skeie E. *Summerland: A Story about Death and Hope.* Elgin, Ill: Brethren; 1989.

The experience of death is portrayed through the image of an innocent child walking through a dark valley toward the source of all hope—"The One Who Is Waiting"—the one who bids welcome when all others must say goodbye.

Young children with autism or autistic-like behavior

Mary Coleman, MD
Pediatric Neurologist
Department of Pediatrics
Georgetown University School of
　Medicine
Washington, DC

THE UNDERSTANDING of autism has come a long way since Leo Kanner,[1] a child psychiatrist at Johns Hopkins University, introduced 11 cases of autism in the medical literature in 1943. He chose the word "autistic" because the children had in common an "extreme aloneness from the beginning of life and an anxiously obsessive desire for the preservation of sameness."[1] In the previous decade, theories of mental illness were developed that blamed the illness on the parents who raised the child—for example, Fromm-Reichmann's theory about schizophrenogenic mothers.[2]

Today, two generations later, autism is understood as a neurological syndrome and autistic symptoms are recognized as the common final pathway with which the brain expresses a great variety of lesions and malfunctions of the infant central nervous system (CNS). There are five symptoms that identify a child as autistic:

1. The age of onset is early, almost always before 30 months of age.
2. Social interaction is severely impaired and includes a period in infancy or early childhood of autistic aloneness.
3. There are abnormalities of the development of communication, most prominently expressed by delayed and deviant language development.
4. Abnormal behaviors occur with the substitution of repetitive elaborate routines and inappropriate playing or stereotypes for the usual patterns of play of children.
5. The child has an abnormal response to sensory stimuli, virtually always noted in the auditory system but also seen in the visual system and other sensory systems. The sensory system least impaired is the olfactory system.

All these symptoms are well out of phase with the overall intellectual level of the child for age.[3]

Most autistic patients retain these symptoms throughout their lives, following defined patterns of autistic symptoms in each age group. This is the group most physicians are referring to when they speak about classic infantile autism (IA). In addition, there is a small subgroup of patients who meet classic criteria for IA during one phase of their disease, but move on into a different clinical picture as they grow older. Children with Rett syndrome (limited to girls) are an example of this group of patients.

The author acknowledges the assistance of the John Edward Fowler Memorial Foundation and the members of the Board of the Children's Brain Research Clinic (Bruce Ashkenas, Jeanne Beekhuis, David Carliner, Judith Downey, Margaret Giannini, MD, George Keeler, MD, Irving Levine, Robert Marcus, Eleanor Holmes Norton, Richard Pei, PhD, Blance Prince, Winifred Portenoy, and Curtis Seltzer, PhD). The professional assistance of Corrietta Isreal was especially appreciated.

Many brain-damaged and mentally retarded children have a few autistic symptoms mixed into their clinical picture but do not meet the full criteria of the autistic syndrome. Patients with autistic-like conditions (AC) cover a very wide variety of patient groups. It is important to distinguish between patients with classic IA and patients with AC because the diagnosis, prognosis, and treatment may differ significantly. In patients with AC, the medical approach must be to the underlying main disease entity rather than to the few autistic symptoms. In IA, these symptoms dominate medical diagnostic workup and therapy as well as determine the type of educational approach the child will receive.

EVOLVING MANIFESTATIONS OF AUTISM

The age of onset in autism can begin as early as the first hour of life. In some newborns, autistic symptoms and signs are already noticeable. The first symptom often noted in such infants is a failure to mold in the mother's arms. Signs that can be demonstrated in a significant percentage of autistic patients in the neonatal period include hypertelorism, low seating of the ears, and partial syndactyly of the second and third toes.[4] The hypertelorism, or wide spacing of the eyes, may contribute to the beauty that has been noted in so many young autistic children (Fig 1). Occasionally, a newborn has such severe haptic defensiveness (sensitivity of the tactile system) that the child screams when held; the mother ends up feeding the infant by holding the bottle over the crib without actually touching the infant. Such infants have great difficulty tolerating breast feeding because of the tactile interaction involved.

In a population study of autism that reviewed the medical records from the newborn period, the authors observed that many babies already had aversion of gaze

Fig 1. Autistic children are often very beautiful and their illness is not apparent to a casual observer.

and appeared not to see persons near them. Their gaze might be described as "empty and inwardly focused." It was reported that there was "no response," "no smile."[5] In this study, major sleep problems were found, but they tended to be of opposite types. In some cases, there was a reversed day–night rhythm or a great reduction in the need to sleep, while in other cases the child was described as "too good" and "never seeming to want any attention." Another author describes the two modes of presentation during the first year as "the model baby who appears content just to be left alone" or "the terrible baby who screams 'round the clock, refusing to be fed or held and has trouble sleeping."[6]

The typical autistic child avoids eye contact with other people prior to the end of the first year.[7] The child gazes out of the corner of the eye very briefly and does not show anticipatory movements when about to be picked up. In fact, the child resists being held or touched and also seems to lack initiative or the interested curiosity or exploratory behavior seen in normal infants.

It is often difficult to differentiate between variation and normal patterns of behavior and these early pathologic signs of autism. Many experienced examiners in the field find that the parents are more troubled and more aware of the abnormalities in the child much earlier than the pediatricians, who often hope the child "will grow out of it." In this subspecialty of pediatrics, as in so many others, it is important to listen carefully to what the parents report and to give serious attention to their concerns.

Autistic symptoms can also start later than the first year of life. In fact, they can start at any time up to 30 months of age. In these children there is a previous history of a normal infant with normal social relationships and normal psychomotor milestones. The age of onset can often be pinpointed to a particular month of the child's life.

The disturbance of social relatedness becomes more apparent with age. The young child may use the mother's hand as a depersonalized object to achieve a goal such as feeding. The autistic child may fail to come to his or her parents for comfort or help. As the child grows older, the inability to play reciprocally with age peers becomes more and more apparent. The inability of these children to reciprocate and their failure to treat other humans as anything but objects is often striking. This is a useful way of differentiating them from some of the superficially similar behavior seen in emotionally deprived children.

Often autistic children are not identified as such until it becomes clear that they are not speaking. In fact, they have major problems in the comprehension of human mime and gesture as well as speech. An important and diagnostic sign in the language area is the child's failure to comprehend spoken language. In most mental retardation syndromes, receptive language is far ahead of expressive speech. In contrast, the autistic child's handicap in understanding language is often as severe and lags as far behind as the child's ability to express speech.

Approximately one out of every two autistic children fail to ever develop useful, spoken language. The ones who do develop speech, however often show major abnormalities of development such as pronominal reversal, echolalia (echoing back a word or phrase said to the child), a tendency to use staccato-like or scanning speech, and major problems with pronunciation.

One of the most distinctive symptoms of autistic children is their bizarre behavior problems. Many demand that certain routines be adhered to in a pathologically rigid fashion. They often form odd attachments to particular objects such as stones, pieces of plastic toys, or bottles, rather than to a real toy. The objects are selected because of some peculiar quality of color or texture. They are often carried around by the child, and he or she may become frantic if anyone tries to remove them. These children may line up objects or toys for hours on end. They love to look at spinning objects such as wheels of toy cars. The reaction of the autistic child to interruption of these routines can be severe temper tantrums. When they begin to walk, they may walk on their toes. When they are excited, they may flap their hands or make finger motions in front of the eyes.

Another bizarre behavior of autistic children is their reaction to sensory stimuli. Many autistic children cover their ears to shut out vacuum cleaner sounds, the sounds of crying infants, or sometimes the most ordinary of sounds. Visually, these children may stare into light bulbs or stimulate the retina with waving of fingers. Many of these children have haptic defensiveness, which is particularly marked around the head area. Autistic children may use the olfactory sense in extraordinary ways, such as identifying people and objects by smelling them rather than by looking at them.

There is wide variation in the levels of activity of autistic children. Some are considered quite hyperactive, but some are overly passive.

Many children limit their diet and eat only a few foods. Some have difficulty chewing.

The self-stimulatory behavior of autistic children is often the most disturbing to see. They may bang their heads, bite their wrists, knock their chins, smash their cheeks, and tear their hair out.

ACCOMPANYING HANDICAPS

Mental retardation, epilepsy, blindness, and deafness are major handicaps that are sometimes seen concomitantly in a child with the autistic syndrome. A majority (approximately 67% to 81%) of all autistic children test as mentally retarded.[8,9] It is difficult to interpret why some children with the syndrome appear retarded and others do not. Autopsy studies to date are few in number, but most have shown that large sections of the neocortex are intact. Areas where abnormalities have been reported include the forebrain and the limbic system (particularly nuclei of the amygdala, the entorhinal cortex, the hippocampal complex, the mamillary bodies, and septal nuclei). Cell loss has been described in the neocerebellum.[10]

Another puzzling finding is the fact that electrophysiological data differentiate autistic children with or without mental retardation from children with other types of mental retardation. Using both amplitude and conditioning phenomena, it can be shown that the evoked potentials in autistic children are more similar to normal children than to the other forms of retardation. According to the authors of these electrophysiological studies, "The presence of a conditioning phenomena in the autistic group (although it does not reach a normal level) is in agreement with the finding of a slow but real learning ability in these children."[11(p537)] Some autistic children have savant skills or islets of special intelligence. However, these tend to diminish if the children start to improve.

Epilepsy is another complication sometimes found in autistic children. There appear to be two peaks in the age of onset of seizure disorders, one during infancy and the other at adolescence.[12] In a recent population-based study, 20% of patients with IA and 41% of patients with AC had a seizure disorder.[13] The fact that the infantile spasm syndrome is sometimes followed by an autistic condition has been known for some time. In this recent study, infantile spasms were found in 6% of the cases. However, there were also a number of patients who started seizure disorders before two years of age who had other types of seizures than the classic infantile spasm syndrome. Although a variety of seizure types occurred, psychomotor epilepsy was by far the most frequent of all cases. The majority of these patients had electroencephalogram (EEG) abnormalities that seemed to stem from temporal regions and phylogenetically older parts of the brain in a majority of these cases.[13] In many childhood syndromes, the addition of epilepsy to the syndrome is often associated with mental retardation. This is not necessarily so in autism, since epilepsy can occur in this particular syndrome in the absence of mental retardation.

There is an increased incidence of autism among the blind and the deaf. There are more clinically proven cases of deafness than of blindness in autistic individuals, but both of these major sensory handicaps can be found in a population of autistic persons. The question has been raised as to whether these sensory deprivations may be an etiologic or a contributing factor to the development of autistic symptoms, but this issue is not yet resolved.[14]

In addition to these major groups of symptomatic problems associated with autism, there are also autistic individuals who have two diagnoses: autism and a second medical diagnosis. One such example is Rett syndrome, a syndrome with a distinctive hand-washing or hand-clasping motion. Approximately one half of these young girls go through a phase of autistic symptomology.[15] Their autistic symptoms tend to diminish or disappear around prepuberty. Another syndrome where one half or more of the patients show autistic features is the fragile X syndrome, a chromosome syndrome. In this disease entity, a fragile site has been located on the long arm of the X chromosome at the location of q27. The overwhelming majority of these patients have severe psychiatric symptoms that often include autistic features. Approximately one half of the patients meet the criteria for classic IA.[16]

There are a number of other syndromes where the vast majority of patients have no autistic symptoms but a few case reports have appeared in the literature. These disease entities are tuberous sclerosis, neurofibromatosis Tourette's syndrome, de Lange's syndrome and Möbius' syndrome.[3] Autistic features are also found in about 1% of children with Down syndrome.[17]

ACCOMPANYING MEDICAL CONDITIONS

Possible infectious etiologies

It can be difficult to establish the infectious etiology of a disease, since the mere presence of an infectious agent in an individual does not necessarily mean it has caused the disease (see the box). Thus only when epidemics occur does it become clear that the sequelae of a particular infectious agent can cause autistic symptoms. A clear relationship is also established when there are individual cases of encephalitis with documented rises of titers or brain biopsies. These techniques can establish that the infectious agent is the etiology beyond reasonable doubt that caused the autistic symptoms that follow the illness. In the case of autism, two infectious agents are definitely established to cause autistic symptoms: rubella and herpes simplex.

Rubella is fortunately no longer present in epidemic form in the United States because of rubella inoculations. However, in the last documented epidemic in

---

Infectious Etiologies of Autism

Established
- rubella
- herpes simplex

Possibilities
- cytomegalovirus
- toxoplasmosis
- mumps
- syphilis
- slow viruses

Source: Coleman M, Gillberg C: *The Biology of the Autistic Syndromes.* New York, Praeger Scientific, 1985.

1964,18 patients with full or partial autistic syndrome were identified in a rubella birth defects evaluation follow-up project.[18] This information, combined with other studies, has identified one subgroup of autistic children as those with prenatal infection with the rubella virus.

The herpes simplex virus appears to have caused acute encephalitides associated with rising titer of the herpes simplex and is therefore suspected as a possible etiologic factor. The herpes simplex virus has a predilection for infecting the temporal lobe area of the brain, one of the areas where there is evidence of dysfunction in many autistic patients.[19]

The remaining possible etiologies of autism—cytomegalovirus, toxoplasmosis, mumps, syphilis, and slow viruses—have case material in the literature and immunologic studies that suggest that these agents may be factors. However, the full criteria of linking the specific infectious agent to the autistic symptoms in the patients is not completed in this ongoing research work.[3,20]

Possible metabolic disease entities

In the study of mental retardation, it is customary to check a child for the possibility of amino acidurias, since most errors in amino acid metabolism have been associated with inadequate cognitive functioning of the CNS. However, in the case of autistic patients, although many hundreds have been screened by now, only one amino aciduria has been identified that produces autistic symptoms. In 1969, Friedman[21] wrote a paper pointing out that 50 patients who had been diagnosed as autistic were found to have the amino aciduria called phenylketonuria (PKU) when they were tested. Like rubella, PKU should be a preventable form of autism and should no longer exist in this country. However, in 1980, Lowe et al[22] from the Yale University School of Medicine found three children with PKU. One child, aged two years, had been tested for PKU in the neonatal period and had been reported as negative. The second, aged seven months, had not been screened at all as a newborn, even though he was in a state requiring testing. The third child had been born in a state that did not require testing at that time.[22] (Since then, all 50 states of the United States have a law requiring testing for newborns for PKU.) Thus, because a laboratory can make an error or a specimen can be dropped or a nurse can forget to do a blood test, there is continued need to check a child with autistic symptoms for PKU. Also, because so little is known, it is wise to continue to test all autistic children with an amino acid screen, even though no other amino acidurias have been identified so far.

Investigators have found several errors of purine metabolism in autistic children rather than finding a number of errors of amino acids. Perhaps this is not surprising, since the purine errors documented to date often have had a behavioral or psychiatric component.[3] In some of the earlier purine patients described, autism was merely one feature of a much more complex syndrome (children with AC). But the more recent literature has described purine dysfunction in more classic autistic patients.

In 1974, a large research project (N = 71) studying uric acid excretion in autistic patients and age- and sex-matched controls found that 22% of the autistic patients had hyperuricosuria, or excess excretion of uric acid.[4] A similar study was performed on 21 autistic children in France, and in this case 29% were found to have either hyperuricosuria alone or hyperuricosuria and hyperuricemia.[23]

Two enzyme defects in the purine pathway have been identified in autistic patients with hyperuricosuria. The two enzymes found as abnormal in autistic children are phosphoribosylpyrophosphate (PRPP) synthetase[24] and adenylosuccinate lyase.[25] However, patients with these two enzyme defects account for less than 5% of autistic patients who excrete excessive uric acid in the urine. This raises the question of whether there may be multiple enzyme defects in the purine pathway associated with the autistic condition that have not yet been identified in the cells of autistic patients. Such research is now in progress at the purine laboratory of the University of California at San Diego.

Another possible area of inborn errors of metabolism in autism is the family of disorders of carbohydrate metabolism. Patients have been reported who have pyruvic acidosis and lactic acidosis, the end product of this pathway.[26] In one such patient, preliminary evidence suggests that the child may have a deficiency of pyruvate dehydrogenase complex (PDHC).[3]

There are other nonspecific biochemical errors that have been described in autistic patients, in particular in the neurotransmitters, serotonin, and the catecholamines. In the case of serotonin, the majority of patients appear to have relatively high levels in blood, although a small subgroup has low levels. The specific relationship to any disease entity is unknown. Findings of catecholamine errors (measured by end products in the urine or cerebrospinal fluid [CSF]) are even less impressive and less understood.[3]

In one study,[4] calcium was studied in the serum and urine. No statistically significant difference was found between the patient group and the control group. However, if one took the lowest level of calcium found in any control and compared it to the autistic results, 22% of the autistic patients had hypocalcinuria by these criteria.[4] Because a relationship was observed between extremely low levels of calcium in the urine and myoclonic seizures in some autistic patients, further study is needed. In several such patients, addition of large amounts of calcium in the diet appears to have been helpful in controlling self-abusive behavior; therefore, further investigation in this area is urgently needed.

In the same study,[4] the only statistically significant difference in the serum between the two groups was a lowered level of magnesium. This was the only positive finding in the serum of many variables tested in this large study. Research in calcium and magnesium metabolism in autistic children is a neglected area that needs further evaluation. Since metabolic disease entities such as PKU theoretically have a possibility of specific treatment, the identification of any metabolic errors in autistic patients remains a high priority.

Space-occupying lesions

The search for identifiable lesions such as tumors or cysts in the brain causing autistic symptoms has generally been noninformative. However, in rare cases autistic symptoms are seen in patients with hydrocephalus.[3] Also, six patients with middle fossa subarachnoid cysts near the tip of the temporal lobe have been described.[27]

Instead of space-occupying lesions, developmental hypoplasia of the neocerebellum, particularly vermian lobules VI and VII recently has been described in 14 out of 18 autistic patients.[28]

TREATMENT OF AUTISM

In the years since the handling of autistic patients has been wrestled away from the psychoanalysts into the hands of pediatricians, educators, and neurologists, one major finding regarding treatment has become very clear. Autistic patients need a special kind of education that is specifically geared to their condition and that is different from the type of education offered to most mentally handicapped children. Behavior conditioning programs, occupational and physical therapy programs, and an intensive use of speech and language therapists appear to be essential minimums in these programs. The more teaching a child can have on a one-to-one teacher–pupil basis, the better the results seem to be. (This statement is based on the present author's observations over 20 years as a medical investigator observing the results of educational programs in her patient group.) Without educational intervention specifically geared to their autistic needs, many of these children fare very poorly.

A number of centers specialize in teaching autistic children and training parents and teachers. One outstanding group in the United States is the TEACCH (Treatment and Education of Autistic and Related Communication Handicapped Children) program at the University of North Carolina at Chapel Hill. This center has prepared much reading material and trains people from all over the world. One of the keys to fruitful work with autistic children as originally described by Schopler (Director of the TEACCH program) and Mesibov[29] is involving the family closely in the education of the child. The teacher and parents should work together daily with information passed back and forth so the child has a consistent 24-hour environment. Parents and teachers can be effective cotherapists.

In autism, the disease problem is in the child, not in the parent. These educational programs rescue the parents from the burdens placed on them by some of the psychoanalytic approaches and instead offer them a supportive system of school and home education that is therapeutic for the child and thus helpful to the entire family.

Regarding medical therapy for autistic children, no single drug has been found to be successful. It is unlikely that this will happen in the future, since autism is not a single disease but is a syndrome of many different etiologies.[3] Drugs that have been tried and have been successful in a limited number of children include fenfluramine hydrochloride[30,31] and haloperidol.[32] Pharmacologic doses of vitamin B6 with magnesium also have been reported to help autistic symptoms in some patients in three double blind studies.[3] Many other drugs, such as naltrexone hydrochloride,[33] have been tried and found successful in one or more children, but there are no adequate studies to support a breakthrough in drug therapy in autism at this time.

•   •   •

Ultimately, the most rational therapy for autistic children is specific therapy individually tailored to the particular child. If metabolic errors are present, correction of any biochemical abnormalities found in the individual child is indicated. If infections are present, treatment may be possible in the future. If cysts or tumors are found in the brain, neurosurgical draining or removal should be considered. This individualized approach, however, has not yet reached the published literature and thus remains speculative.

The challenge of diagnosing and working with autistic children has just begun to be realized. These beautiful, enigmatic, fascinating patients need the focus of as many professionals as possible.

REFERENCES

1. Kanner L: Autistic disturbances of affective contact. *Nervous Child.* 1943;2:217–250.

2. Victor G: *The Riddle of Autism.* Lexington, MA, Heath, 1983.

3. Coleman M, Gillberg C: *The Biology of the Autistic Syndromes.* New York, Praeger Scientific, 1985.

4. Coleman M, ed.: *The Autistic Syndromes.* Amsterdam, North Holland Publishing, 1976.

5. Gillberg C, Gillberg I: Infantile autism: A total population study of reduced optimality in the pre-, peri- and neonatal periods. *J Autism Dev Disord.* 1983;13:153–166.

6. Wing L: Infantile autism. Read at a seminar, Gothenburg, Sweden, Nov 1982.

7. Mirenda P, Donnellan A, Yoder D: Gaze behavior: A new look at an old problem. *J Autism Dev Disord.* 1983;13:397–409.

8. Rutter M: Diagnosis and definition of childhood autism. *J Autism Childhood Schizophr.* 1978;8:139–161.

9. Lotter V: Epidemiology of autistic conditions in young children: II. Some characteristics of the parents and children. *Soc Psychiatr.* 1967;1:163–173.

10. Bauman M, Kemper T: Histoanatomic observations of the brain in early infantile autism. *Neurology.* 1985; 35:866–874.

11. Martineau J, Garreau B, Roux S, et al: Auditory evoked responses and their modifications during conditioning paradigm in autistic children. *J Autism Dev Disord.* 1987;17:525–539.

12. Rutter M: Autistic children: Infancy to adulthood. *Semin Psychiatr.* 1970;2:435–450.

13. Olsson I, Steffenburg S, Gillberg C: Epilepsy in autism and autisticlike conditions. *Arch Neurol.* 1988;45:666–68.

14. Rapin I: Effects of early blindness and deafness on cognition, in Katzman R, ed.: *Congenital and Acquired Cognitive Disorders.* New York, Raven Press, 1979.

15. Hagberg B, Aicardi J, Dias K, et al: A progressive syndrome of autism, dementia, ataxia, and loss of purposeful hand use in girls: Rett syndrome: Report of 35 cases. *Ann Neurol.* 1983;14:471–479.

16. Levitas A, Hagerman R, Broden M, et al: Autism and the fragile X syndrome. *J Dev Behav Pediatr.* 1983;4:151–15.

17. Coleman M: Down's syndrome children with autistic features. *Down's Syndrome: Papers and Abstracts for Professionals.* 1986;9:1–2.

18. Chess S, Korn S, Fernandez P: *Psychiatric Disorders of Children with Congenital Rubella.* New York, Brunner/Mazel, 1971.

19. DeLong G, Beau S, Brown F III: Acquired reversible autistic syndrome in acute encephalopathic illness in children. *Arch Neurol.* 1981;38:191–194.

20. Singh V, Fudenberg H, Emerson D, et al: Immunodiagnosis and immunotherapy in autistic children. New York, Academy of Sciences, to be published.

21. Friedman E: The autistic syndrome and phenylketonuria. *Schizophrenia.* 1969;1:249–261.

22. Lowe T, Tanaka K, Seashore M, et al: Detection of phenylketonuria in autistic and psychotic children. *JAMA.* 1980;243:126–128.

23. Rosenberger-Debiesse J, Coleman M: Brief report: Preliminary evidence for multiple etiologies in autism. *J Autism Dev Disord.* 1986;16:385–392.

24. Becker M, Rairo K, Bakoy B, et al: Variant human phosphoribosylpyrophosphate synthetase altered in regulatory and catalytic functions. *J Clin Invest.* 1980;65:107–120.

25. Jaeken J, von den Berghe G: An infantile autistic syndrome characterised by the presence of succinylpurines in body fluid. *Lancet.* 1984;2:1058–1061.

26. Coleman M, Blass J: Autism and lactic acidosis. *J Autism Dev Disord.* 1985;15:1–8.

27. Segawa M, Nomura Y, Nagata E, et al: Autism with middle fossa arachnoid cyst. *J Child Neurol.* 1986;1:276.

28. Courchesne E, Yeung-Courchesne R, Press G, et al: Hypoplasia of cerebellar vermal lobules VI and VII in autism. *N Engl J Med.* 1988;318:1349–1354.

29. Schopler E, Mesibov G, eds.: *Communication Problems in Autism.* New York, Plenum Press, 1985.

30. Ritvo E, Freeman B, Geller E, et al: Effects of fenfluramine on 14 outpatients with the syndrome of autism. *J Am Acad Child Psychiatr.* 1983;22:549–558.

31. Campbell M, Deutsch S, Perry R, et al: Short-term efficacy and safety of fenfluramine in hospitalized preschool-age autistic children: An open study. *Psychopharmacol Bull.* 1986;22:141–147.

32. Campbell M, Anderson L, Meier I, et al: A comparison of haloperidol, behavior therapy and their interaction in autistic children. *J Am Acad Child Psychiatr.* 1978;17:640–655.

33. Campbell M, Sokal S, Small A, et al: Naltrexone in autistic children: An acute open dose study. Read at the Scientific Proceedings for the Annual Meeting, American Academy of Child and Adolescent Psychiatry, Los Angeles, Oct 1986.

Preterm cognitive development: Biologic and environmental influences

Betty R. Vohr, MD
Associate Professor of Pediatrics
Director
Neonatal Follow-up Clinic
Brown University Program in
   Medicine
Providence, Rhode Island

THE 1980s HAVE seen a steady improvement in the survival of very low birth weight infants (<1500 g), with the most dramatic improvement in survival in the weight category of 500 to 1,000 grams.[1-4] At Women and Infants' Hospital in Providence, survival of newborn infants with a birth weight of 1,000 to 1,499 grams rose from 89% in 1981 to 96% in 1988, whereas survival of infants with a birth weight of 500 to 999 grams nearly doubled during the same time period, rising from 32% to 63% (Women and Infants' Hospital of Rhode Island, Providence, Rhode Island. Unpublished data. December 1988). Innovations and modifications in medical management and environment have contributed to changes in both survival and outcome of high-risk premature infants.

The survival and outcome of premature neonates is dependent on multiple factors that interact including the intrauterine climate to which the fetus is exposed, the timing of delivery, the severity of neonatal morbidities, and social and environmental factors. Epidemiologic research has provided greater knowledge of conditions detrimental to the fetus such as cigarette smoking, poor maternal nutrition, maternal infections, and maternal substance abuse. This knowledge has contributed to advances in obstetric and perinatal management including maternal transport, intrauterine monitoring techniques, and intrauterine diagnostic techniques. Simultaneous advances made in the management of high-risk premature infants in neonatal intensive care units such as improved nutritional management, improved ventilatory techniques, and the use of surfactant have likewise contributed to improved long-term survival. These new survivors, however, may suffer serious morbidities in the neonatal period that place them at increased risk of long-term sequelae.

There are three high-risk categories of premature infants: intrauterine growth retardation (IUGR),[5] intraventricular hemorrhage (IVH),[6] and bronchopulmonary dysplasia (BPD),[6] commonly seen in neonatal intensive care units, which are known to place infants at increased biological risk. However, social factors, such as poverty, maternal educational status, and maternal marital status, can also mediate outcome.[8] Data increasingly indicate that a complex interaction of biologic and environmental risk factors determines to a large extent which high-risk infants will have an optimal outcome and which infants will have a less-than optimal outcome.

The author acknowledges the assistance of Achintya Dey in data entry and analysis.

Inf Young Children, 1991; 3(3): 20–29
© 1991 Aspen Publishers, Inc.

INTRAUTERINE GROWTH RETARDATION

The medically accepted definition of IUGR is a neonate whose birth weight falls below the 10th percentile for gestation on a standard intrauterine growth curve such as that developed by Lubchenco and colleagues.[9] IUGR may also be referred to as "intrauterine growth restriction"; this term includes infants with lesser degrees of growth impairment. The timing of the onset of an intrauterine stress or placental deprivation influences the differential growth patterns that result. Fetal head growth velocity increases rapidly between 10 and 20 weeks, peak length velocity increases after about 26 weeks, and weight velocity peaks after 33 weeks.[10] Therefore, onset of impaired nutrient delivery before 20 weeks is more likely to result in restriction of head growth. Early onset produces symmetric IUGR; both head circumference and weight are below the 10th percentile. If onset occurs late, only weight falls below the 10th percentile on the intrauterine growth curve (asymmetric IUGR). Three primary types of growth characteristics are commonly discussed in the literature: (1) appropriate for gestational age (AGA) (birth weight above 10th percentile, birth head circumference above 10th percentile); (2) small for gestational age (SGA), symmetric (birth weight below 10th percentile, birth head circumference below 10th percentile); and (3) small for gestational age asymmetric (birth weight below 10th percentile, birth head circumference above 10th percentile).

These three types may be observed in both premature and full-term infants. Body length may also fall below or above the 10th percentile but does not affect the classic definition of IUGR. Since head growth is often restricted in congenital or genetic abnormalities, its relationship under these circumstances with less optimal neurodevelopmental outcome has been well accepted. The presence of restricted head size in infants without congenital abnormalities, however, has gradually gained in clinical importance as a prognosticator of less-than-optimal outcome.

One of the first studies to evaluate the effect of timing of the onset of head growth failure on outcome was reported by Fancourt et al[11] in 1976. They assessed weekly biparietal (BP) diameters of the fetal head using cranial ultrasound and identified a subgroup of infants with slow head growth prior to 26 weeks gestation in whom the weekly increment in BP diameter fell below the 5th percentile over 2 successive weeks. This study actually identified four separate groups of infants based on differences in head growth, which he followed for 4 years. The group of infants with early onset of head growth failure before 26 weeks was smaller in stature, weight, and head circumference and had a lower intelligence quotient (IQ) at 4 years of age. Infants with an onset of headgrowth slowing at 26 to 34 weeks were smaller in growth parameters but had normal IQ scores, and infants with late onset of slow head growth—that is, infants with slowing after 34 weeks and with no head growth slowing—were normal in growth and IQ scores at 4 years of age. Harvey and coworkers[12] subsequently reported on infants with early onset head growth slowing and confirmed that the negative effects persisted at 5 years of age with evidence of lower cognitive indices, lower perceptual scores, and lower motor scores. Ounsted, Moar, and Scott[13] more recently published data on a cohort of 116 infants with birth weights ranging from 1,070 to 2,010 g followed for 7 years. They identified that SGA infants delivered before 270 days of gestation by elective delivery had a higher IQ than SGA infants allowed to remain in utero past 270 days and for whom there was no obstetrical intervention. This study suggests that the intrauterine environment is not always an optimal environment for the fetus.

There is evidence, however, that there are opportunities for recovery for the compromised SGA infant after delivery. Hack et al[14] identified that SGA infants with a birth weight of less than 1500 g who caught up in extrauterine weight gain between term and 8 months of age had higher Bayley[15] scores, increased head size, and less neurosensory impairment than either SGA infants who did not catch up or AGA infants who fell off the growth curve between term and 8 months. The postnatal deterioration of growth velocity observed in the AGA or SGA infants with less optimal outcome may be referred to as extrauterine growth restriction. Hack et al's study suggests that infants with optimal nutritional intake postnatally will have a more optimal developmental outcome.

A study by Vohr et al[5] of SGA premature infants with a birth weight below 1,500 g compared to weight-matched AGA controls revealed the SGA cohort was lighter and shorter at 2, 3, 4, and 5 years of age. There were, however, no differences in head circumference between the two groups by 1 year of age. Good head growth of the SGA infants during the first year, however, was probably related to their subsequent good cognitive outcome. Although the SGA infants lagged on Bayley[15] and Stanford Binet[16] test scores at 9 months and at 1, 2, and 3 years, there were no differences at 4 and 5 years of age on the Stanford Binet, as shown in Fig 1. These data indicate that there is a gradual developmental catch-up pattern between 9 months and 5 years for both SGA and AGA infants and that even SGA children with significantly more early delay have potential to catch up by 4 to 5 years of age. The study also evaluated the relationship between the Hollinshead[17] four-factor index (maternal education, maternal occupation, paternal education, and paternal occupation) and development during two time periods in the study sample. Fig 2 illustrates the linear relationship between the Hollingshead[17] Social and Environmental Status (SES) score and the Bayley[15] mental developmental index at 8 months to 1 year of age in the upper panel and between SES and Stanford Binet scores at 5 years in the lower panel. At 8 months to 1 year of age, there was no relationship between family SES and developmental quotient; however, at 5 years, the relationship was significant for both SGA and AGA children.

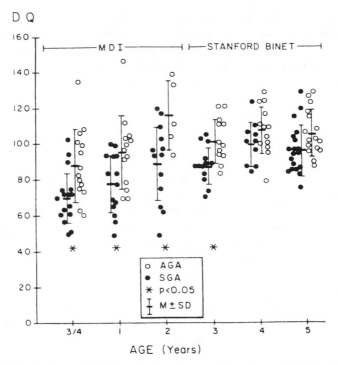

Fig 1. Individual (and mean ± SD) Bayley Developmental Quotients (MDI) for SGA and AGA infants at 9 months and at 1 and 2 years, and Stanford Binet IQ scores at 3, 4, and 5 years. Reprinted with permission from Vohr BR, Oh W. Growth and development of preterm small for gestational age infants. *J Pediatr.* 1983;103:942.

Therefore, by 5 years of age the higher the family Hollingshead SES score, the higher the child's Stanford Binet IQ score. In effect, the low-SES premature children have a disadvantage not only because of their biologic risk but also because of less optimal environmental factors; therefore they do not catch up as well as the high SES children. It is now well accepted that social and environmental factors are important contributors to the outcome of low birth weight infants and can modify the effects of early insults. Escalona[8] followed a cohort of low-SES infants with a birth weight of less than 2,250 g for 3½ years and found that by 28 months of age, a fall in cognitive status was observed associated with lower social class. Therefore, within her study population, low-SES premature infants not only did not catch up cognitively in a pattern similar to the high-SES infant, they actually deteriorated in cognitive function over time.

Studies by Vohr, Garcia Coll, and Oh[18,19] looked further at the interactive effects of SES with other risk variables on language outcome in SGA and AGA

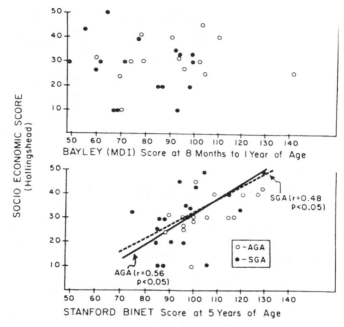

Fig 2. Linear regression analyses done at 8 months to 1 year and at 5 years to demonstrate relationship between DQ (Bayley MDI) and IQ (Stanford Binet) and an SES score for SGA and AGA infants. Reprinted with permission from Vohr BR, Oh W. Growth and development of preterm small for gestational age infants. *J Pediatr.* 1983;103:942.

infants with a birth weight of less than 1,500 g. Multiple regression analysis demonstrated that SES, gestational age at birth, and neurologic status at 8 months all contributed to language scores at 2 and 3 years of age. At 2 years of age, 28% of the low birth weight children had receptive or expressive language delay on the Mullen[20] language subscore (t score > 1.5 SD below the mean), but by 3 years of age none had a t score greater than 1 SD below the mean, indicating a language catch-up pattern between 2 and 3 years. All children with language delay at 2 years were referred to early intervention or speech therapy. These data also demonstrate that many factors, both biological and environmental, actually contribute to outcome and catch-up patterns.

The author and her colleagues[21] recently evaluated the effects of symmetric versus asymmetric intrauterine growth retardation in very low birth weight infants (mean gestation 29 weeks) compared to gestation-matched very low birth weight AGA controls and full-term AGA controls on growth and development during the first 2 years of life. In this study, very low birth weight symmetric SGA infants continued to have a head circumference significantly smaller than all three other study groups at 2 years of age. In addition, they had significantly lower Bayley[15] cognitive scores at 12 months. The authors concluded that symmetric SGA infants delivered as early as 29 (±2) weeks are at increased risk of developmental delay and that this delay is related to their head growth restriction.

Premature infants who suffer from secondary morbidities in the neonatal period associated with prematurity may have less-than-optimal cognitive and developmental catch-up patterns. Two serious secondary morbidities—intraventricular hemorrhage and bronchopulmonary dysplasia—affect the outcomes of preterm infants.

INTRAVENTRICULAR HEMORRHAGE

Very low birth weight infants (less than 1,500 g) are at increased risk for IVH because of the fragile vascular state of the germinal matrix and because of poorly developed cerebral autoregulation.[22,23] IVH is a common morbidity, and incidence rates in neonatal intensive care units vary from 40 to 45 percent.[24–29] Infants with IVH have an increased incidence of major neurologic abnormalities related to the increasing severity of their IVH.[27]

Vohr and colleagues[7] prospectively evaluated the neurologic status and cognitive status of a cohort of premature infants weighing less than 1,750 g who were monitored in the nursery with serial cranial ultrasound assessments. Infants were categorized into groups of no IVH, grades 1 and 2 IVH, and grades 3 and 4 IVH based on Papile's classification.[26] The authors were particularly interested in the sequelae associated with grades 3 and 4 IVH related to the insult imposed on the periventricular white matter by compression secondary to increased intracranial pressure and ventricular dilatation. Two of the authors[30] had previously reported an increased incidence of visual motor integration inefficiencies in premature infants followed to school age. Since in association with ventricular dilatation there is a disproportionate dilatation of the occipital horns, which encroach on the visual radiations, the authors[7] hypothesized that infants with grades 3 and 4 IVH would be at greater risk for vision motor function abnormalities.

A total of 90 premature infants and 22 full-term control infants were enrolled in the study. Neurologic assessments were done at term and at 3, 7, 12, and 24 months corrected age. Results of the neurologic assessments are shown in Fig 3. It is of interest that at term, all three premature groups differed from the full-term control group but did not differ from one another. Repeated measures of analysis of variance, however, revealed that neurologic status of the three premature groups improved significantly over time ($p = < 0.001$), reflecting the plasticity of the central nervous system relative to neurologic abnormality. Whereas at term only 43% of the infants with grades 3 and 4 IVH were scored as neurologically

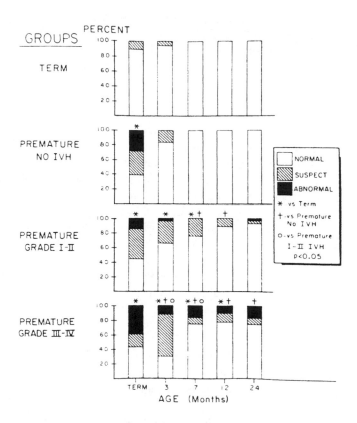

Fig 3. Neurologic status is depicted for the four study groups for the five periods: term, 3 months, 7 months, 12 months, and 24 months of age. Repeated-measures analysis of variance demonstrated that in addition to the group differences at each period, neurologic status within the three premature groups improved significantly over time ($p < 0.001$). Reprinted with permission from Vohr BR, Garcia Coll C, Mayfield S, Braun B, Shaul P, Oh W. Neurologic and developmental status related to the evolution of visual motor abnormalities from birth to 2 years of age in preterm infants with intraventricular hemorrhage (IVH). *J Pediatr.* 1989;114:298.

normal, at 2 years, 75% were scored as neurologically normal. In addition, at 2 years, 93% of infants with grades 1 and 2 IVH were normal, and 100% of premature infants with no IVH were normal. In other words, despite the fact that atypical neurological findings of asymmetry, abnormal tone, and abnormal movement patterns may be present at 37 to 39 weeks in premature infants with and without IVH and with and without ventricular dilatation, the majority of these early abnormalities resolve by 2 years of age. Although infants with grades 3 and 4 IVH still differ significantly from full-term infants at 2 years, these findings support the theory of an inherent plasticity of the central nervous system and the potential ability of the neonate to recover from central nervous system insult.

Developmental status of the study groups at 3, 7, and 12 months was assessed using the Bayley[15] scales. Infants with grades 3 and 4 IVH had scores significantly lower than term infants and infants with no IVH at each age tested. Repeated measures analysis indicated an interesting phenomenon. Whereas full-term infants' cognitive scores improved during the first year, the premature infants with grades 3 and 4 IVH had declining scores during the first year. These data suggest that infants with grades 3 and 4 IVH may have experienced more sustained injuries to pathways associated with integration, fine motor coordination, and auditory and visual processing, and since Bayley test items require more complex responses by 1 year of age, declining performance and test scores result.

Analysis of covariance (ANCOVA) indicated that during the first year there was no effect of SES on the Bayley mental or motor scores. At 2 years of age, the infants with grades 3 and 4 IVH had more visual perceptual abnormalities and visual perceptual motor abnormalities on the Mullen[20] test, confirming the authors'[7] initial hypothesis. In addition, infants with grades 3 and 4 IVH had significantly lower Mullen expressive language scores. Results of ANCOVA covarying for SES indicated that the lower vision receptive and vision expression scores for infants with grades 3 and 4 IVH were due to group differences and not SES. In contrast, consistent with the authors, other longitudinal studies, SES had a significant effect on the receptive and expressive language scores for all four groups of infants.

Early language delay in low birth weight infants at 2 years of age is well documented.[18,19] The importance of this IVH study,[7] however, relates to the identification of visual perceptual problems in a specific cohort of premature infants with grades 3 and 4 IVH as early as 2 years of age. A number of investigators[30,31] have previously reported an increased incidence of visual perceptual motor problems in low birth weight infants at school age. This learning problem can lead to increased difficulty with arithmetic, reading, and writing and increased risk of academic failure. Very early identification of this learning problem in the preschooler will facilitate intervention strategies and subsequent improved academic performance.

Finally, there is evidence for significant motor recovery in premature infants with IVH during the first 2 years of life. Although SES effects on language performance for these infants at 2 years of age were documented, the authors[7] have not been able to demonstrate an SES effect on vision reception and vision motor performance at 2 years of age. These study[7] data will help determine whether these visual perceptual and visual motor developmental delays are permanent or can recover or be overcome with appropriate educational intervention.

BRONCHOPULMONARY DYSPLASIA

Bronchopulmonary dysplasia is a chronic lung disease related to prematurity, positive pressure ventilation, and oxygen administration; BPD was first described by Northway and colleagues[32] in 1967. With the improving survival of very low birth weight infants, BPD has become a common morbidity in the neonatal intensive care unit, ranging in incidence from 5 to 45 percent.[33,34] Early studies[6,35] reported that these infants suffer multiple related morbidities including prolonged hospitalization, increased respiratory infections in the first 2 years of life, increased wheezing, and reactive lung disease. Vohr, Bell, and Oh[6] reported that low birth weight (< 1,500 g) BPD survivors had increased evidence of failure to thrive with poor weight gain during the first year of life. Weinstein and Oh[36] subsequently demonstrated that BPD infants have increased oxygen consumption indicating increased caloric needs during the first 60 days of life compared to non-BPD control infants. This phenomenon contributes to poor weight gain. Vohr et al's[5] initial follow-up study of infants with a birth weight of less than 1,500 g also identified an increased incidence of abnormal and suspect neurological findings in BPD survivors at 2 years and a deterioration in Bayley[15] cognitive scores between 12 and 24 months of age. Meisels and coworkers[37] reported on a cohort of 17 BPD infants with a birth weight of less than 2,501 g followed to 2 years and found evidence of lower Bayley[15] scores, poorer language skills, and poorer sensory motor skills than controls. Because of the prevalence of BPD in low birth weight survivors, many professionals are interested in its long-term consequences, including the growth and neurodevelopmental characteristics of BPD survivors during early school age and adolescence. This author and her colleagues[38] recently reported on a cohort of BPD children and controls evaluated at 11 years of age. In this study, BPD survivors continued to have evidence of growth lag and increased neurologic impairment at 10 to 12 years of age. In 1989, Northway and coworkers[39] reported the follow-up of 22 low birth weight survivors (mean age of 17 years) with a history of stage 4 bronchopulmonary dysplasia compared to controls. BPD survivors had increased evidence of reactive lung disease, abnormal pulmonary function tests, and shorter stature. This information is worrisome, since it again implies that certain subgroups of premature infants have less potential for complete recovery and catch up over time. Also, because smaller infants with more severe lung disease, including prolonged oxygen requirements, have survived since the early 1980s, this study[39] suggests that these new survivors may have even greater long-term sequelae associated with pulmonary disease. Although surfactant can radically alter early pulmonary function, including oxygen requirements, the most current multicenter study by Horbar et al[40] found no change in the incidence of BPD. Prospective longitudinal studies evaluating the new very low birth weight BPD survivors are indicated.

FACTORS CONTRIBUTING TO OUTCOME

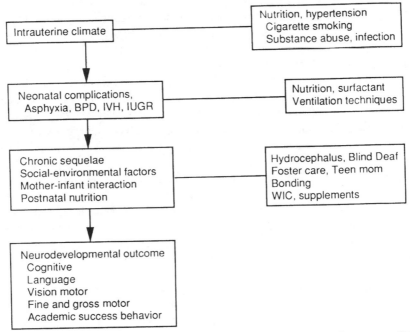

Fig 4. A continuum of events that contributes to the neurodevelopmental outcome of high risk infants.

•   •   •

The outcome of low birth weight infants is based on a continuum of events rather than on any single biologic, social, or environmental factor. The continuum begins at the time of conception and may be modified by the intrauterine climate, the severity of neonatal complications, early childhood events, and SES factors (Fig 4). This process may or may not contribute to recovery and catch up. Premature infants may have a head start on extrauterine experiences, but their immature organ systems make them very vulnerable to insult. Opportunities to recover and catch up must be provided. It is critical for health care professionals who care for the neonatal intensive care patient to be aware of the modifiers of outcome and to initiate medical, social, and academic mechanisms for treatment when appropriate. Parents likewise will benefit from optimistic but realistic guidance and goal setting.

REFERENCES

1. Hack M, Caron B, Rivers A, Fanaroff AA. The very low birth weight infant: The broader spectrum of morbidity during infancy and early childhood. *Pediatrics.* 1983;4:243–249.

2. Saigal S, Saroj, Rosenbaum P, Hattersley B, Milner R. Decreased disability rate among 3-year-old survivors weighing 501 to 1000 grams at birth and born to residents of a geographically defined region from 1981 to 1984 compared with 1977 to 1980. *J Pediatr.* 1989;114:839–846.

3. Buckwald S, Zorn WA, Egan EA. Mortality and follow-up data for neonates weighing 800 g at birth. *Am J Dis Child.* 1984;138:779–782.

4. Bennett FC. Robinson NM, Sells CJ. Growth and development of infants weighing less than 800 grams at birth. *Pediatrics.* 1983;71:319–323.

5. Vohr BR, Oh W, Rosenfeld AG, Cowett RM. The preterm small for gestational age infant: A two year follow-up study. *Am J Obstet Gynecol.* 1979;1.3 425–431.

6. Vohr BR, Bell EF, Oh W: Infants with bronchopulmonary dysplasia: Growth patterns and neurologic and developmental outcome. *Am J Dis Child.* 1982; 136:443–447.

7. Vohr BR, Garcia-Coll C, Mayfield S, Braun B, Shaul P, Oh W. Neurologic and developmental status related to the evolution of visual motor abnormalities from birth to 2 years of age in preterm infants with intraventricular hemorrhage (IVH). *J Pediatr.* 1989;115:296–302.

8. Escalona SK. Babies at double hazard: Early development of infants at biologic and social risk. *Pediatrics.* 1982;70:670–676.

9. Lubchenco LO, Hansman C, Dressler M, Boyd E. Intrauterine growth as estimated from liveborn birth weight data at 24 to 42 weeks of gestation. *Pediatrics.* 1963;32:793–800.

10. Kolb B. Brain development, plasticity and behavior. *Am Psychol.* 1989;44:1203–1212.

11. Fancourt R, Campbell S, Harvey D, Norman AP. Follow-up of small-for-dates babies. *Br Med J.* 1976;1:1435–1437.

12. Harvey D, Prince J, Bunton J, Parkinson C, Campbell S. Abilities of children who were small for gestational age babies. *Pediatrics.* 1982;69:296–300.

13. Ounsted M, Moar VA, Scott A. Small-for-dates babies, gestational age and developmental ability at 7 years. *Early Hum Dev.* 1989;19:77–86.

14. Hack M, Merkatz IR, Gordon D, Jones PK, Fanaroff AA. The prognostic significance of postnatal growth in very low birth weight infants. *Am J Obstet Gynecol.* 1982;143:693–699.

15. Bayley N. *Bayley Scales of Infant Development.* New York, NY: Psychological Corporation; 1969.

16. Terman LM, Merrill MA. *Stanford Binet Intelligence Scale.* Boston, Mass: Houghton Mifflin, 1973.

17. Hollingshead AB. *Four-Factor Index of Social Status: Working Paper.* New Haven, Conn: Yale University; 1975.

18. Vohr BR, Garcia Coll C, Oh W. Language development of low birth weight infants at two years. *Dev Med Child Neuro.* 1988;30:608–615.

19. Vohr BR, Garcia-Coll C, Oh W. Language development of low birth weight infants at two years. *Dev Med Child Neuro.* 1988;30:582–590.

20. Mullen EM. *Mullen Scales of Early Learning.* Providence, RI: Total Child, Inc; 1984.

21. Vohr BR, Garcia Coll C, Oh W. Increased morbidity in very low birth weight (VLBW) small for gestational age (SGA) infants with reduced head circumference (HC) at birth: A 2 year follow-up study. *Pediatr Res.* 1990;27:10A. Abstract.

22. Volpe JJ. Neurology of the newborn. In: Schaffer AJ, ed. *Major Problems in Clinical Pediatrics.* Philadelphia, Penn: WB Saunders; 1981.

23. Takashima S, Tamaka K. Microangiography and vascular permeability of the subependymal matrix in the premature infant. *Can J Neurol Sci.* 1978;5:45–50.

24. Ahmann PA, Lazzara A, Dykes FD, et al. Intraventricular hemorrhage in the high risk preterm infant: Incidence and outcome. *Am Neurol.* 1980;7:118–124.

25. Leech RW, Kohnen P. Subependymal and intraventricular hemorrhage: A study of infants with birth weight less than 1500 grams. *Am J Pathol.* 1974;77: 465–475.

26. Papile LA, Burstein L, Burstein R, Koffler H. Incidence of evolution of subependymal and intraventricular hemorrhage: A study of infants with birth weight less than 1500 grams. *J Pediatr.* 1978;92:529–534.

27. Papile LA, Munsick-Bruno G, Saefer A. Relationship of cerebral intraventricular hemorrhage and early childhood neurologic handicap. *J Pediatr.* 1983;103:273–280.

28. Shinnar S, Molteni RA, Gammon K, D'Souza BJ, Altman J, Freeman JM. Intraventricular hemorrhage in the premature infant: A changing outlook. *N Engl J Med.* 1982;306:1464–1467.

29. Fitzhardinge PM, Flodmark O, Fitz CR, Ashby S. The prognostic value of computed tomography of the brain in asphyxiated preterm infants. *J Pediatr.* 1982;100:476–481.

30. Vohr BR Garcia-Coll CT. Neurodevelopmental and school performance of very-low-birth-weight infants: A seven-year longitudinal study. *Pediatrics.* 1985;76:345–350.

31. Klein N, Hack M, Gallagher J, Fanaroff AA. Preschool performance of children with normal intelligence who were very low birth weight infants. *Pediatrics.* 1985;75:531–537.

32. Northway WH Jr, Rosan RC, Porter DY. Pulmonary disease following respiratory therapy by hyaline membrane disease: Bronchopulmonary dysplasia. *N Engl J Med.* 1967;276:357–368.

33. Saigal S, Rosenbaum P, Stoskopf B, Sinclair JC. Outcome in infants 501–1000 gm birth weight delivered to residents of the McMaster Health Region. *J Pediatr.* 1984;105:969–976.

34. Rhodes PG, Hall RT, Leonidas JC. Chronic pulmonary disease in neonates with assisted ventilation. *Pediatrics.* 1975;55:788–796.

35. Smyth JA, Talachnuk E, Duncan WJ, Reilly BJ, Levison H. Pulmonary function and bronchial hyperactivity in long term survivors of bronchopulmonary dysplasia. *Pediatrics.* 1981;68: 336–340.

36. Weinstein MR, Oh W. Oxygen consumption in infants with bronchopulmonary dysplasia. *J Pediatr.* 1981;99:958–961.

37. Meisels SJ, Plunkett JW, Roloff DW, Pasick PL, Stiefel GS. Growth and development of preterm infants with respiratory distress syndrome and bronchopulmonary dysplasia. *Pediatrics.* 198;77: 345–352.

38. Vohr BR, Garcia-Coll C, Lobato D, et al. Neurodevelopmental and medical status of low birth weight (LBW) survivors with bronchopulmonary dysplasia (BPD) at 10–12 years of age. *Pediatr Res.* 1988;24:458A. Abstract.

39. Northway WH, Moss RB, Carlisle KB, et al. 23 year follow-up of bronchopulmonary dysplasia (BPD). *Pediatr Res.* 1989;25:370A. Abstract.

40. Horbar JD, Soll RF, Sutherland JM, et al. A multicenter randomized placebo-controlled trial of surfactant therapy for respiratory distress syndrome. *N Engl J Med.* 1989;320:959–965.

Development of visual function in preterm infants: Implications for early intervention

Penny Glass, PhD
Associate Professor of Pediatrics
George Washington University
  Medical School
Director
Center for Child Development
Children's National Medical Center
Washington, DC

VISION IS A PRIMARY sensory system that has broad implications for development. It is undergoing extensive maturation and differentiation during the third trimester of the human fetus within the sensory environment of the womb or, as in the case of a preterm infant, within the neonatal intensive care unit (NICU). The visual system can be modified by the biologic consequences of preterm birth as well as by hyperstimulation and deprivation. Visual stimulation is a frequently used intervention in the NICU and beyond, but it may be excessive and misguided. This article considers how vision affects early development, describes how we see, and outlines the early development of the visual system. The association between preterm birth and vulnerability of the visual system is presented. Finally, a theoretical foundation for early developmental intervention is provided.

IMPORTANCE OF THE VISUAL SYSTEM

Vision affects development in a number of ways.[1] The ability to attend to, process, and remember relevant visual information is fundamental to the ability to read and negotiate spatially. In addition, from what we have learned from visually impaired infants, vision affects the development of motor milestones and exploratory behavior. For example, visually impaired infants have delayed head righting in the prone position and do not reach for or manually explore objects until a later age than normal. Adult behavior toward these infants is also affected. Adults speak less to visually impaired infants because of the absence of behavioral cues showing infant attention or interest. Onset of first words occurs later among otherwise normal blind infants. Thus early language development is secondarily affected by visual status. Finally, it is well known that the development of attachment and bonding is mediated by visual regard and is disrupted in visually impaired infants.[2]

The author is most grateful to David Friendly, MD, Chairman of Ophthalmology, Children's National Medical Center and to Richard Walk, PhD, Professor, Department of Psychology, George Washington University as role models of intellectual and academic pursuit.

Inf Young Children, 1993; 6(1): 11–20

HOW DO WE SEE?

Light energy is transmitted through the cornea, pupil, lens, and optic media to the retinal layers. There it bypasses a layer of blood vessels, ganglion cells, and bipolar cells before reaching the outer segments of the photoreceptors (rods and cones). Light is absorbed by the photoreceptors in a photochemical response that converts the radiant energy to an electrical impulse. The amount of light energy necessary to stimulate a single photoreceptor cell is extremely small: 1 quantum.[3] The electrical impulse travels to the ganglion cells, which transmit to the optic nerve. The normal absence of photoreceptors at the site of the optic nerve causes the well-known blind spot we all possess. The impulse then travels from the eye along the visual pathway from the lateral geniculate nucleus to the visual cortex, which is located in the back portion of the brain.

The information from the eye travels to the brain in a special way. Fibers from the nasal half of each retina divide, and half these fibers cross to the other side of the brain. Fibers from the outer half of each retina do not divide. Therefore, visual information from the left (or right) visual field will fall on the opposite portion of each retina and from there will pass on to the same hemisphere of the brain (Fig 1). Representation in the visual cortex is thus topographic, although upside-down and reversed. This anatomic organization means that even with loss of vision in one eye information is transmitted to both hemispheres of the brain. It also means that damage in the region of the left or right occipital cortex can cause a loss of vision in the opposite visual field.

EARLY DEVELOPMENT OF THE VISUAL SYSTEM

The eye is an outgrowth of the brain from the early embryonic period. By gestation week 24, gross anatomic structures are in place, and the visual pathway is complete. Between gestation weeks 24 and 40, the visual system is undergoing extensive maturation, differentiation, and remodeling, most critically in the region of the retina and visual cortex (Table 1).[4] The functional visual responses that correspond to these anatomic changes are described below, followed by the major milestones in visual function that occur after term birth and up to 4 months of age.[5–15]

Gestation weeks 24 to 28

Although differentiation of sleep and wake periods is not readily apparent, either behaviorally or by electroencephalographic (EEG) pattern, immature visual function is present once the anatomic pathway to the visual cortex is complete. A visually evoked response to bright light is obtainable but is quite primitive: a long-latency negative wave that readily fatigues. Behavioral response to bright light

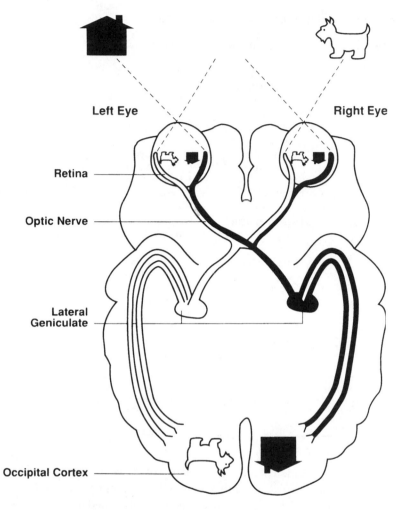

Fig 1. Location of objects in the visual environment and the visual pathway: from the retina along the optic nerve, dividing at the optic chiasm, proceeding along the optic tract to the lateral geniculate nucleus, and finally ending at the visual cortex.

consists of lid tightening, but this response also fatigues quickly. The refractive error is about – 5 diopters, or extreme myopia.

Gestation weeks 30 to 34

Important functional changes occur. Sleep and wake become differentiated electrophysiologically. The structure of the visually evoked response is more

Table 1. Maturation of the fetal eye in the third trimester

Structure	24–28 Weeks	30–34 Weeks	36 Weeks
Eye lid	Fused early in development, now reopens	Less translucent	
Pupil	Tunica vasculosa lentis begins to atrophy	Fully atrophied by end of period	
Lens	Second layer of four-layer nucleus forming	Second layer complete, third begins to form	
Media	Cloudy	Clears	Less dense than in adult
	Hyaloid system begins to regress	Hyaloid has almost disappeared	Some remnants may still be present
Retina	Rod differentiation begins	Complete except for foveal region	Cone number in fovea increases
	Vascularization just beginning	Nasal portion nearly complete	Temporal region nearly fully vascularized
Visual cortex	Rapid growth and differentiation of nerve cells and dendrites	Marked development of dendritic spines and synapses	Structure appears similar to that of full-term

Adapted with permission from Glass P. The vulnerable neonate in the NICU environment. In: Avery G, MacDonald M, Fletcher MA, eds. Neonatology: Pathophysiology and Management. Philadelphia, Pa: Lippincott; 1993.

complex with the addition of a positive wave, and the latency decreases. The pupillary reflex is more efficient. A bright light will cause immediate lid closure, and the response sustains. The eyes may open spontaneously, and the infant may even briefly fixate. This has been described as the beginning of attention (32 to 34 weeks). Attention as such may be elicited with a larger high-contrast form than at term but under similar conditions of low illumination (5 footcandles).

Gestation week 36

Concordance of eye movement, EEG pattern, respiration, and behavioral parameters during sleep is evident early in this stage, reflecting greater maturation of the central nervous system. The visually evoked response now resembles that of a full-term infant, but the latency is still longer for the preterm infant and remains so. The awake state is more sustained, although still shorter than at term. Behaviorally, the preterm infant shows a spontaneous orientation toward a soft light and can track an object horizontally and vertically. The preterm infant prefers a patterned to a nonpatterned surface, like a full-term infant. The myopia is no longer evident, and the refractive error is now nearly zero.

Term to 1 month

The visual system at this age is relatively immature compared to the other sensory systems, with considerable development occurring over the next 6 months. Because the optic media is less dense than that of an adult and the macular region of the retina has less pigmentation, the newborn eye transmits four times more short-wavelength (blue to ultraviolet) light than that of an adult.[15] This is essentially why newborns are photophobic and are therefore more visually responsive under low illumination. The refractive error is slightly hyperopic (+1 diopter) in a full-term infant and more commonly myopic in a preterm infant. Acuity estimates are in the range of 20/200 Snellen equivalents, which has misled many into thinking that newborns are functionally blind. In fact, the normal newborn will attend to form, object, and face.

Under low illumination, the infant can fixate on a high-contrast form only $\frac{1}{16}$-inch wide at a distance of 1 foot and will show preference for patterns along dimensions of brightness and complexity. Color vision, at least for red, is probably present. The infant will track a bright object horizontally across midline and, to a lesser extent, vertically or even in an arc. Attention to the human face by a neonate can be explained as a predisposition to respond to contrast (eyes or open mouth) or to edge (hairline), to slow movement (nodding), and to contingent stimulation (when the adult captures the infant's gaze). Another misconception is that a newborn sees no farther than 8 to 12 inches. Although accommodation by the lens is limited, most infants at this age are actually able to focus on objects at a distance of 2.5 feet.[11] The ability to attend and the ability to see have been confused.

2 months

Whether newborn attention is evidence of cortical visual function is still debated, but significant changes occur by 2 months past term that are more unequivocally cortically mediated. In essence, attention is more selective at this age. The infant can alternate gaze between two objects or two patterns presented simultaneously and will respond preferentially. When fixating centrally, the infant can reliably respond to an object approaching from the periphery, will scan the features on a person's face, and may even smile. The infant demonstrates preference for a face compared to an object. Most infants at this age can now focus at a distance of 5 feet.[11] Parents traditionally report that their infant intently watches someone at a distance and follows a person moving across the room. This capability requires both improvement in lens accommodation as well as cortical control of visual function. Finally, when appropriately positioned supine, the infant will engage in a classic milestone, hand regard. If both the toy and the infant's hand are in the visual field, the infant may even bat or stroke the toy. Thus eye-hand coordination begins to develop. This milestone is not observed in infants exposed to excessive amounts of visual stimulation and is prolonged in infants deprived of normal sources of stimulation.[17]

4 months

By this age vision is clearly available for more conceptual tasks. In addition to selective attention and discrimination of patterns, visual information processing now includes recognition memory. The 4-month-old infant will reliably shift attention from a familiar complex pattern to a novel one. Long-term memory for a visual display can be demonstrated over a period of weeks. In addition, vision is used to engage socially and to solicit from a distance. Competence in object permanence is also demonstrated, with visual regard being sustained after an object or person disappears behind a barrier. Important advances in visual motor integration occur as well. If an object is placed in the infant's hand, the infant will bring the object into view. In addition, the infant's *seeing* an object is sufficient to activate reaching, even if the infant's hands are not simultaneously in view.

VISUAL DEFICITS ASSOCIATED WITH PREMATURITY

The increased vulnerability of the preterm visual system has been widely recognized. The most well-known visual problem of preterm infants is retrolental fibroplasia (RLF), which was first described in the 1940s. In the 1970s, structural differences in the preterm eye that affect vision were described, and subsequently visual perceptual problems among preterm infants and children were reported that may be more centrally mediated.[16,18–25]

RLF is now generally called retinopathy of prematurity (ROP). It is the single most common cause of blindness in infants, affecting up to 4% of infants who weigh less than 1,000 g at birth.[18] ROP is a proliferative vascular disease that is graded according to severity and is defined by the stage of disease progression as well as by extent and location. Normally in the immature eye there is a gradation in the appearance of the posterior retina in the region where the developing blood vessels are advancing compared to the adjacent avascular region. In stage 1 ROP, a thin demarcation line becomes apparent between these two regions. By stage 2 the line has thickened into a ridge. Although nearly 75% of infants weighing less than 1,000 g at birth may develop active ROP, most ROP arrests and regresses at this stage with few sequelae.[26] Progression to more severe disease is largely unpredictable. Stage 3 is characterized by extraretinal fibrovascular proliferation into the vitreous, which produces scarring and at times traction. Stage 4 is partial or complete retinal detachment. The more posterior in the eye the disease occurs, the poorer the prognosis. This is because the damage may occur to the macular region, which is the area of the retina densely populated with cones, the photoreceptors responsible for high acuity. Thus, severe forms of ROP cause significant vision loss or blindness. The term *RLF* is currently reserved for only severe ROP.

The most common predisposing factor for ROP is extreme prematurity. Although previously it was thought that ROP was only associated with exposure of preterm infants to high levels of oxygen, other factors are now recognized as possibly contributing, including hypoxia, hypercarbia, hypocarbia, blood transfusion, sepsis, and even light.[18,26] ROP is thus of multifactorial origin but most strongly associated with the degree of immaturity of the retina. Because vascular development at gestation week 24 is minimal, the short-gestation preterm infant is more likely to develop ROP, and if ROP occurs in these infants it tends to be more severe.

Not all visual impairment in preterm infants is a result of retinopathy. Cortical visual impairment also occurs in preterm infants and is generally associated with severe central nervous system damage such as periventricular leukomalacia.

Visual disorders other than ROP also occur more frequently among preterm children: thicker lenses, poorer visual acuity, astigmatism, high myopia (extreme nearsightedness), strabismus (crossed eyes), amblyopia (lazy eye), and anisometropia.[19] The last is an unequal refraction of the two eyes, one eye being more nearsighted (or farsighted) than the other for structural reasons. Like ROP, these problems are also more common among short-gestation infants. Visual disorders correlate with the presence of significant ROP but occur frequently even among preterm infants who did not have ROP.

In addition to these anatomic effects, it has been recognized for more than a decade that infants and children born preterm also have difficulty processing visual information. Measures of visual attention, pattern discrimination, visual recognition memory, and visual-motor integration repeatedly indicate particular vulnerability of the preterm infant compared to the full-term infant on visually mediated tasks.[16,20-25] For example, visual attention in the preterm infant at gestation week 40 is characterized by prolonged attention to unchanging pattern compared to full-term infants.[25] Prolonged attention to unchanging stimuli is regarded as an immature response. Indeed, Sigman and her associates[27] found that longer attention to a checkerboard at gestation week 40 was associated with a lower IQ in childhood. These concepts are particularly important when one is considering the appropriateness of visual stimulation with the immature infant.

Unlike full-term infants, preterm infants at 4 months (corrected age) fail to demonstrate a response to novel pattern.[16] Likewise, at 6 and 12 months preterm infants show delays on visual as well as visual-haptic tasks.[20] For example, cross-modal tasks require the ability visually to recognize an object that was handled. On visual-motor tasks, preterm infants show a longer latency to reach for a toy, less interest in novel toys, and a lesser degree of exploration of objects.[24] Of course these are group data and do not speak to individual differences, but they do indicate that visual information processing may be compromised among preterm infants.

Studies of older children indicate that the problem may persist, even if the comparison is limited to children with a normal IQ.[21] The studied tasks have included visual discrimination by a match to sample, selection of the one visual pattern that does not belong to the group, and visual-motor integration (reproducing a visual pattern with pencil and paper). These data in infancy and childhood support the vulnerability of the visual system and suggest some framework for intervention.

DEVELOPMENTAL INTERVENTION: LIGHT AND PATTERN

Given the importance of the visual system for development and the specific vulnerability of the preterm, considerable attention has been directed toward early intervention in the NICU. The visual system of the preterm is developing in a unique environment and may be affected by precocious exposure to light and pattern.

Light

The womb is generally dark, but under certain conditions light can transmit to the fetus. A behavioral response by a fetus to light has been described. Transmission through all the tissue is limited to small amounts of red, or long-wavelength, light. Probably only 2% of incident light reaches the uterus (Sliney D. Personal communication, June 1992). Thus it is unlikely that light exposure is a necessary condition for fetal development or that periodic exposure to low levels of long-wavelength light is harmful. After birth, ambient light increases, although typically the infant's room at home is kept dim. Recall that in dim light the newborn is more likely to open his or her eyes.

In stark contrast, modern NICUs are brightly lit with ambient environmental light in excess of standard adult office lighting, or in the general range of 30 to 150 footcandles with peaks over 1,500 footcandles from sunlight.[28] Light exposure is typically 24 hours a day throughout the infant's hospital stay. The length of hospital stay is a function of the degree of immaturity and medical complications. Light exposure is therefore greatest for those most vulnerable to visual problems.

In addition to ambient light, preterm infants are routinely exposed to supplementary sources, such as the Bili-Lite, the heat lamp, and the indirect ophthalmoscope. The standard double-bank phototherapy unit produces 300-400 footcandles of illumination. The Mini Bili-Lite has an intense beam, estimated at more than 10,000 footcandles. Infants' eyes are routinely patched during phototherapy, but eye pads may slip off. A commonly used heat lamp will produce an intensity of more than 300 footcandles at an infant's face. Exposure time varies but is typically longer for younger and sicker infants. The eyes of infants are not typically covered while they are under the heat lamp. Finally, an indirect ophthalmoscope is used for routine eye examinations to rule out ROP. Exposure for 2 minutes (approximate time of a retinal examination) at maximum power has been estimated to be equivalent to exposure at 2,000 footcandles for 3 hours.[29] Extra precautions for protecting the infant's dilated eyes from ambient or supplementary sources of light before and after the eye examination are not routine. For the smallest infants the addition of a heat lamp during the examination is often necessary to maintain the infant's temperature.

Phototoxicity has been reported in animals exposed to similar levels of light.[29] The mechanisms proposed include direct damage to retinal structures, alteration of the retinal metabolism, and generation of oxygen free radicals.[30] All these considerations raise significant concerns regarding the light in the NICU. Initial evidence with preterm infants supports an association between light and ROP.[31,32] There is, however, no evidence that light is a necessary condition for ROP or that maintaining a preterm infant in the dark will completely prevent it. The optimal level of NICU lighting has not been determined, but no study supports the safety of the bright light levels still common in many NICUs.

A prudent approach in the NICU is to limit ambient nursery light to necessary levels and to shield the infant's eyes from ambient as well as supplementary sources.[27] Shielding does not mean occluding the infant's eyes. No evidence supports the usefulness of patching infants' eyes beyond what is necessary for phototherapy. Prolonged patching may be detrimental in terms of both stimulus deprivation and possible effects on corneal growth.

Animals that have sustained photic damage show recovery when returned to normal light-dark environments.[29] The effect on the preterm is not known. It is logistically difficult to cycle light levels when one is caring for critically ill neonates, but it may be feasible when the infants are stable and growing. A day-night regimen in the intermediate care nursery before hospital discharge has shown positive effects on behavior.[33] However, light, noise, and handling were all reduced at night in the experimental unit. That does not negate the effect, but early entrainment of preterm infants to light-dark cycles is not supported by the evidence. Aspects of the day-night regimen that reach the fetus are probably more mediated by maternal sources such as rest-activity cycles and hormones than directly by light. Thus periodicity may be important, although not necessarily mediated through light and dark. Even in the normal newborn at home, sleep periods and feeding occur every 3 to 4 hours. The optimal timing of such events during postnatal development of the preterm infant is not known.

In any event, given that visual attention is facilitated under conditions of low illumination, providing opportunities for spontaneous eye opening under dim or dark conditions would have a physiologic basis, at least after the onset of attention (after conceptional age 32 to 34 weeks).

Pattern

The question then becomes whether to provide patterned stimulation for the preterm infant, and if so, what type. A number of important considerations directly address these issues. First, the sensory systems are organized in an hierarchical manner according to functional maturity: tactile-vestibular, auditory, and then visual.[34] Stimulation of more mature senses (eg, the tactile-vestibular) influences development of later maturing ones (eg, the visual).[20,35] This hierarchical organization and integration of function support the principle that developmental intervention in the NICU should begin with the most mature system (tactile-vestibular). Actual practice is often to the contrary, however.

An infant's ability to respond to a level of stimulation does not necessarily mean that he or she should be stimulated at that level. For that matter, infants will even stare at light bulbs. The fact that infants will attend more readily to high-contrast black-and-white stimuli than to pastel stimuli does not mean that an infant does not see pastel; this mistaken belief has misled most approaches to developmental intervention. As a parallel argument, infants are also more likely to respond to a louder sound, yet we do not recommend their exposure to high-intensity sound just because they hear it better. As stated earlier, prolonged or obligatory visual attention is not a preferred behavior.[25] The appropriate behavioral goal is selective attention and information processing.

The most appropriate visual stimulus in early infancy is probably the human face, which bears no resemblance to strong black-and-white patterns. The face is three dimensional. It contains some contrast at the edge of the hair or at the features; provides slow, contingent movement around the eyes and mouth; and is situated at a variable distance from the infant. The intensity, amplitude, and distance of this stimulus are dependent on whether the intent is to arouse or quiet the infant. Furthermore, it is not always present. There is probably no better substitute. When inanimate visual stimulation is provided, it behooves us to follow the same model: to begin with softer, simpler forms and three-dimensional objects rather than high-contrast designs and to vary the stimuli depending on intent to soothe or arouse. If a mobile is hung over an infant's bed, it should be approximately 2 feet from the infant's face, slightly to one side or the other, and more above the stomach than the face. These considerations allow for selective attention by the infant, a choice to look or not. Opportunities for hand regard should be provided through supportive positioning, with the ultimate goal being visually directed reaching.

Black-and-white pattern should be reserved for infants after term who are visually impaired, who are unable to attend to a face or toy, and who have already received other forms of sensory intervention. As soon as a visual response can be elicited with the high-contrast pattern, the transition should be made to the more normal ones.

• • •

Appropriate developmental intervention contains at least these essential components: a hierarchical rather than a unitary approach to sensory stimulation; a basic principle to facilitate, not accelerate, normal developmental processes; and a behavioral goal of selective attention and information processing.[4] These three principles provide a basic foundation for all intervention with high-risk infants.

REFERENCES

1. Warren D. *Blindness and Early Childhood Development*. New York, NY: American Foundation for the Blind; 1977.

2. Fraiberg S. *Insights from the Blind*. New York, NY: Basic Books; 1977.

3. Gregory RL. *Eye and Brain: The Psychology of Seeing*. 4th ed. New York, NY: McGraw-Hill; 1990.

4. Glass P. The vulnerable neonate in the NICU environment. In: Avery G, MacDonald M, Fletcher MA, eds. *Neonatology: Pathophysiology and Management*. Philadelphia, Pa: Lippincott; 1993.

5. Senecal J, Defawe G, Roussey M, Poullain C. Le comportement visuel du premature. *Arch Fr Pediatr*. 1979;36:454–461.

6. Mann I. *Development of the Human Eye*. New York, NY: Grune & Stratton; 1964.

7. Abramov I, Gordon J, Hendrickson A, et al. The retina of the newborn human infant. *Science*. 1982;217:265–267.

8. Haith MM. *Rules That Babies Look By*. Hillsdale, NJ: Erlbaum; 1980.

9. Hack M, Mostow A, Miranda SB. Development of attention in preterm infants. *Pediatrics*. 1976;58:669–674.

10. Dreyfus-Brisac C. Neurophysiological studies in human premature and fullterm newborns. *Biol Psychiatr*. 1975;10:485–496.

11. Atkinson J, Braddick O. Visual development in the human infant. *Arch Ital Biol*. 1978;116:352–357.

12. Parmelee AH, Sigman M. Development of visual behavior and neurological organization in preterm and fullterm infants. In: *Minnesota Symposium on Child Psychology*. Minneapolis, Minn: University of Minnesota Press; 1976;10.

13. Miranda SB. Visual abilities and pattern preferences of premature infants and full-term neonates. *J Exp Child Psychol*. 1970;10:189.

14. Purpura DP. Morphogenesis of visual cortex in the preterm infant. In: Brazier MAB, ed. *Growth and Development of the Brain: Nutritional, Genetic, and Environmental Factors*. New York, NY: Raven; 1975.

15. Werner JS, Lipsitt LP. The infancy of human sensory systems. In: Gollin ES, ed. *Developmental Plasticity: Behavioral and Biological Aspects of Variations in Development*. New York, NY: Academic Press; 1981.

16. Sigman M, Parmelee A. Visual preferences of four month old premature and fullterm infants. *Child Dev*. 1974;45:959–965.

17. White BL, Castle PW. Visual exploratory behavior following postnatal handling of human infants. *Percept Motor Skills*. 1964;18:497.

18. Phelps D. Retinopathy of prematurity. *Curr Probl Pediatr*. 1992;22:349–371.

19. Fledelius T. Prematurity and the eye. *Acta Ophthalmol*. 1976;128.

20. Rose SA. Enhancing visual recognition memory in preterm infants. *Dev Psychol*. 1980;16:85.

21. Siegel L. The prediction of possible learning disabilities in preterm and fullterm children. In: Field T, Sostek A, eds. *Infants Born at Risk: Physiological, Perceptual, and Cognitive Processes*. New York, NY: Grune & Stratton; 1983.

22. Caron A, Caron R. Processing of relational information as an index of infant risk. In: Friedman S, Sigman M, eds. *Preterm Birth and Psychological Development*. New York, NY: Academic Press; 1981.

23. Dubowitz LM, Dubowitz V, Morante A, Verghote M. Visual function in the preterm and fullterm newborn infant. *Dev Med Child Neurol*. 1980;22:465.

24. Sigman M. Early development of preterm and fullterm infants: Exploratory behavior in eight-month olds. *Child Development*. 1976;47:606.

25. Spungen L, Kurtzberg D, Vaughan H. Patterns of looking behavior in full-term and low birthweight infants at 40 weeks post-conceptual age. *Dev Behav Pediatr*. 1985;6:287–294.

26. Avery GB, Glass P. Retinopathy of prematurity: what causes it? *Clin Perinatol*. 1988;15:917–928.

27. Sigman M, Cohen S, Beckwith L, and Parmelee A. Infant attention in relation to intellectual abilities in childhood. *Developmental Psychology*. 1986;22:788.

28. Landry RJ, Scheidt PC, Hammond RW. Ambient light and phototherapy conditions of eight neonatal care units: a summary report. *Pediatrics*. 1985;75:434.

29. Lanum J. The damaging effects of light on the retina: empirical findings, theoretical and practical implications. *Surv Ophthalmol*. 1978;22:221.

30. Ham WT, Mueller HA, Ruffolo JJ. Mechanisms underlying the production of photochemical lesions in the mammalian retina. *Curr Eye Res*. 1984;3:165.

31. Glass P, Avery GB, Subramanian KN, et al. Effect of bright light in the hospital nursery on the incidence of retinopathy of prematurity. *N Engl J Med*. 1985;313:401–404.

32. Glass P. Light and the developing retina. *Doc Ophthalmol*. 1990;74:195–203.

33. Mann NP, Haddow R, Stokes L, Goodley S, Rutter N. Effect of night and day on preterm infants in a newborn nursery: randomised trial. *Br Med J*. 1986;293:1265–1267.

34. Gottlieb G. The psychobiological approach to developmental issues. In: Mussen PH, ed. *Handbook of Child Psychology*. 4th ed. Toronto, Ontario: Wiley; 1983;2.

35. Turkewitz G, Kenny PA. The role of developmental limitations of sensory input on sensory/perceptual organization. *Dev Behav Pediatr*. 1985;6:302.

Index